Digital Literacies
Research and Resources in Language Teaching

Gavin Dudeney, Nicky Hockly and Mark Pegrum

PEARSON

Harlow, England • London • New York • Boston • San Francisco • Toronto • Sydney • Auckland • Singapore • Hong Kong
Tokyo • Seoul • Taipei • New Delhi • Cape Town • São Paulo • Mexico City • Madrid • Amsterdam • Munich • Paris • Milan

PEARSON EDUCATION LIMITED
Edinburgh Gate
Harlow CM20 2JE
United Kingdom
Tel: +44 (0)1279 623623
Web: www.pearson.com/uk

First published 2013 (print and electronic)

Pearson Education is not responsible for the content of third-party internet sites.

ISBN: 978-1-4082-9689-9 (print)
       978-0-273-78332-9 (PDF)
       978-0-273-78614-6 (eText)

British Library Cataloguing-in-Publication Data
A catalogue record for the print edition is available from the British Library

Library of Congress Cataloging-in-Publication Data
A catalog record for the print edition is available from the Library of Congress

The screenshots in this book are reprinted by permission of Microsoft Corporation. Facebook is a Trademark of Facebook Inc.

10 9 8 7 6 5 4 3 2 1
17 16 15 14 13

Front cover image © Getty Images

Print edition typeset in 10/13pt Scene std by 35
Print edition printed and bound in Malaysia (CTP-PPSB)

NOTE THAT ANY PAGE CROSS REFERENCES REFER TO THE PRINT EDITION

Contents

Preface

About the series

Research and Resources in Language Teaching is a ground-breaking series whose aim is to integrate the latest research in language teaching and learning with innovative classroom practice. The books are written by a partnership of writers, who combine research and materials writing skills and experience. Books in the series offer accessible accounts of current research on a particular topic, linked to a wide range of practical and imme-diately useable classroom activities. Using the series, language educators will be able both to connect research findings directly to their everyday practice through imaginative and practical communicative tasks and to real-ise the research potential of such tasks in the classroom. We believe the series represents a new departure in language education publishing, bring-ing together the twin perspectives of research and materials writing, illus-trating how research and practice can be combined to provide practical and useable activities for classroom teachers and at the same time encouraging researchers to draw on a body of activities that can guide further research.

About the books

All the books in the series follow the same organisational principle:

Part 1: From Research to Implications

Part 1 provides an account of current research on the topic in question and outlines its implications for classroom practice.

Part 2: From Implications to Application

Part 2 focuses on transforming research outcomes into classroom practice by means of practical, immediately useable activities. Short introductions signpost the path from research into practice.

Part 3: From Application to Implementation

Part 3 contains methodological suggestions for how the activities in Part 2 could be used in the classroom, for example, different ways in which they could be integrated into the syllabus and applied to different teaching contexts.

Part 4: From Implementation to Research

Part 4 returns to research with suggestions for professional development projects and action research, often directly based on the materials in the book. Each book as a whole thus completes the cycle: research into practice and practice back into research.

About this book

The impact of new technologies on language learning is enormous and rapidly changing, requiring both educators and students to acquire new skills and strategies to access the potential that these tools can offer them. This book offers a comprehensive taxonomy and explanation of the digital literacies that students (and their teachers!) need to acquire if they are to access the educational opportunities that new technologies offer and become engaged citizens and effective employees in our digitally networked world. Literacies are organised into four broad groups: those literacies related to language and the communication of meaning (covering, for example, print literacy, multimedia literacy and mobile literacy); those related to information (covering search literacy, information literacy and filtering literacy); those related to connections (covering network literacy, participatory literacy and intercultural literacy); and one literacy related to (re-)design (namely remix literacy). A variety of engaging classroom activities is provided to familiarise learners and teachers with the full range of literacies. References are given to online resources which can support learners and teachers who may be unfamiliar with some of the technology. Activities have both digital literacy and language learning aims and suggestions are provided for integrating the activities into a language syllabus and adapting them for different teaching contexts, as well as for using them as a basis for action research. Worksheets are also available online at www.pearsoned.co.uk/hockly.

We hope that you will find the series exciting and above all valuable to your practice and research in language education!

Chris Candlin (Series General Adviser) and Jill Hadfield (Series Editor)

Acknowledgements

We offer sincere thanks to the students who've attended our classes as well as the participants who've attended our workshops, and who have given us the opportunity to develop our explanations of digital literacies and trial some of the activities included in this book. Special thanks are due to English Australia and Pearson for supporting digital literacies workshops delivered by Gavin and Mark in Australia in 2010, and by Nicky and Mark in Australia in 2012; to the British Council for supporting digital literacies workshops delivered by Gavin and Mark in Malaysia, Russia and Thailand in 2012; and to the Chinese Foreign Language Teaching and Research Press/Chinese Ministry of Education for supporting a digital literacies seminar delivered by Mark in China in 2012.

We would also like to thank those who have offered comments on sections of the text, or read early drafts, including Ben Beaton of Scotch College, Perth, Australia; Niamh Fitzpatrick of Presbyterian Ladies' College, Perth, Australia; Mirjam Hauck of the Open University, UK; and Tom O'Donoghue of The University of Western Australia. We offer particular thanks to our editors, Chris Candlin and Jill Hadfield, for their extensive comments on multiple drafts of our material and their warm support at all stages of the writing and editing process.

Finally, we'd like to thank all the teachers and trainers who form part of our PLNs, and from whom we have learned so much over the years. We hope this book captures something of the richness of our exchanges about the dynamic field of digital literacies, and will function as a useful resource within our PLNs as the field continues to grow and develop.

Publisher's acknowledgements

We are grateful to the following for permission to reproduce copyright material:

Figures

Figure on page 44 from http://www.tpck.org/, Reproduced by permission of the publisher, © 2012 by tpack.org; Figure on page 47 from A Brief Introduction to TPCK and SAMR, http://www.hippasus.com/rrpweblog/archives/2011/12/08/BriefIntroTPCKSAMR.pdf, Ruben R. Puentedura (2011); Figure on page 349, Reproduced by permission of SAGE Publications, London, Los Angeles, New Delhi and Singapore, from *All you need to know about action research*, 2nd, Sage (McNiff, J. and Whitehead, J. 2011) Figure 1.1, Copyright (© J McNiff and J Whitehead, 2011) www.sagepub.co.uk.

Screenshots

Screenshot on page 84 from Hurricane Irene claims lives and leaves trail of destruction, *The Guardian*, 29/08/2011 (Dominic Rushe), Copyright Guardian News & Media Ltd 2011, photograph by John Bazemore/AP/Press Association Images, copyright AP/Press Association Images; Photos in screenshots on pages 171 and 173 taken from www.flickr.com/photos/eltpics, by @sandymillin, used under a CC Atribution Non-Commercial licence, http://creativecommons.org/licenses/by-nc/3.0/; Screenshots on pages 171 and 173 from www.flickr.com/photos/eltpics, Reproduced with permission of Yahoo! Inc. © 2012 Yahoo! Inc. FLICKR, the Flickr logo, YAHOO! and the Yahoo! logo are registered trademarks of Yahoo! Inc.; Screenshot on page 174 from http://www.youtube.com/watch?v=KuXAlVLB_9M; Screenshots on pages 196 and 197 from www.google.com; Screenshot/poster on page 235 from nickyhockly.glogster.com/nickglog/ with permission of Nicky Hockly.

In some instances we have been unable to trace the owners of copyright material, and we would appreciate any information that would enable us to do so.

Chapter 1
From research to implications

We've always worried about the impact of new technologies on language, literacy, education and society at large. Socrates feared that writing, the new technology of his day, would lead to a decline in memorisation and an impoverishment of discussion. The Bible, ironically, includes one of the earliest complaints about books, wearily proclaiming that 'of making many books there is no end' (Ecclesiastes 12:12), while in ancient Rome Seneca warned that 'in reading of many books is distraction' (1917, p. 7). But it wasn't until the arrival of Gutenberg's printing press in the 1400s that the number of books really exploded – along with concerns about them. During the Renaissance, Dutch humanist Erasmus worried about printers flooding the world with 'stupid, ignorant, slanderous, scandalous, raving, irreligious and seditious books' (1964, p. 184). Martin Luther saw it this way:

> *The multitude of books is a great evil. There is no measure or limit to this fever for writing; every one must be an author; some out of vanity, to acquire celebrity and raise up a name; others for the sake of lucre and gain. (1857, p. 369)*

Complaints of being overloaded with trivia continued for centuries, with French theologian John Calvin bemoaning the 'confused forest of books' (cited in Blair, 2010, Kindle location 1348), German philosopher Gottfried Leibniz protesting the 'horrible mass of books' (ibid., Kindle location 1411) and English poet Alexander Pope grumbling about a 'deluge of authors' (1729, p. 55).

But it's not just books that once seemed iniquitous. The same pattern has repeated itself with the arrival of each new communications technology. The deleterious effects of the telegraph were trumpeted in the *Spectator* in 1889: 'The constant diffusion of statements in snippets . . . must in the end, one would think, deteriorate the intelligence of all to whom the telegraph appeal[s]' (cited in Morozov, 2011, Kindle location 4588). Postcards, it was claimed, would undermine letter writing. The telephone, it was feared, would encourage inappropriate social contacts. Comic books, it seemed, would lead to juvenile delinquency. And then came television, and CDs, and mobile phones . . .

With a few small changes, most of the comments quoted above could be drafted into the contemporary media assault on Wikipedia and YouTube, Facebook and Twitter, chat and text messaging. Like all past communications technologies, our new digital tools will be associated with changes in language, literacy, education and society. Indeed, they already are. Some observers perceive losses, such as a decline in more linear approaches to reading or more reflective approaches to writing. But others perceive gains, such as education through personal learning networks (PLNs), or collaborative projects based on collective intelligence. Eventually, the day will come when our new tools are so enmeshed in our routine language and literacy practices that we'll barely notice them any more. But that day is still some way off.

A framework of digital literacies

We're preparing students for a future whose outlines are, at best, hazy. We don't know what new jobs will exist. We don't know what new social and political problems will emerge. However, we're starting to develop a much clearer picture of the competencies needed to participate in digitally networked post-industrial economies and societies. Governments, ministries of education, employers and researchers are all calling for the promotion of twenty-first-century skills such as creativity and innovation; critical thinking and problem-solving; collaboration and teamwork; autonomy and flexibility; and lifelong learning. At the heart of this complex of skills is an ability to engage with digital technologies, which requires a command of the *digital literacies* necessary to use these technologies effectively to locate resources, communicate ideas, and build collaborations across personal, social, economic, political and cultural boundaries. In order to engage fully in social networks, gain employment in post-industrial knowledge economies, and assume roles as global citizens who are comfortable with negotiating intercultural differences, our students need a full suite of digital literacies at their disposal.

Digital literacies: the individual and social skills needed to effectively interpret, manage, share and create meaning in the growing range of digital communication channels.

Notwithstanding the views of politicians and pundits who cling to an older notion of literacy as a monolithic, print-based skillset, it is increasingly widely accepted that literacy is a plural concept (Kalantzis and Cope, 2012; Lankshear and Knobel, 2011; Pegrum, 2011), a point which has taken on added significance in the digital era. It has also become increasingly apparent that literacies are not just individual skills or competencies but social practices (Barton, 1994; Barton and Hamilton, 2000; Rheingold, 2012), another point which has become more salient thanks to the rise of the participatory *web 2.0* around the turn of the millennium. In the preceding decades we had already begun to talk of specific literacies like 'visual literacy', 'media literacy', 'information literacy' and 'multiliteracies', but with the advent of web 2.0 came an explosion of interest in new – especially digital – literacies. This has led to discussions of a whole slew of particular literacies ranging from 'remix literacy' (Lessig, 2007) and 'personal literacy' (Burniske, 2008) to 'attention literacy' (Rheingold, 2009b), 'network literacy' (Pegrum, 2010; Rheingold, 2009a) and 'mobile literacy' (Parry, 2011).

Web 2.0: a new generation of web-based tools like blogs, wikis and social networking sites, which focus on communication, sharing and collaboration, thus turning ordinary web users from passive consumers of information into active contributors to a shared culture (see Box 1.1).

'Reading is an unnatural act; we are no more evolved to read books than we are to use computers', Clay Shirky (2010b) reminds us. As he goes on to point out, we spend a great deal of time and effort developing reading (and, of course, writing) skills – in short, what we might call *print literacy* – in children, and it's now time to do the same with digital literacies. Language and literacy are tightly bound up with each other: partly because the very notion of literacy is grounded in language, and partly because all literacies are connected with the communication of meaning, whether through language or other, frequently complementary channels. Neither language nor literacy is disappearing. As James Gee and Elisabeth Hayes (2011) observe, language is actually 'powered up' or 'levelled up' by digital media. Digital literacy, then, is even more powerful and empowering than analogue literacy. We need to level up our teaching and our students' learning accordingly. For our language teaching to remain relevant, our lessons must encompass a wide variety of literacies which go well beyond traditional *print literacy*. To teach language solely through *print literacy* is, in the current era, to short-change our students on their present and future needs.

Box 1.1 What hardware and software do I need?

More on web 2.0
URL: goo.gl/LOOJM

In addition to an internet connection, teachers and students need adequate *hardware*. Gradually, *desktop computers* (which traditionally rely on hardwired internet connections) have lost market share to *laptops* (which mostly rely on wireless networks). In turn, laptops are now ceding space to *mobile handheld devices* (which rely on wireless and/or 3G and 4G networks). Mobile handheld devices encompass *tablets*, such as the iPad, and *mobile phones*, including *smartphones* like the iPhone, Android phones and BlackBerry phones. In high-tech educational contexts, there is a clear trend towards dismantling fixed computer labs and instead using laptops and mobile handheld devices, which are often student-owned rather than institutionally owned. Some institutions are starting to shift towards a *BYOD* (Bring Your Own Device) model, where each student brings their own device chosen from a range determined by the institution, or a *BYOT* (Bring Your Own Technology) model, where there are few if any restrictions on the range of web-enabled devices students can bring into the classroom to support their learning (see Chapter 3: *Teaching in technology-limited environments*). In low-tech contexts, some educators are also exploring the potential of mobile phones, as well as working with devices such as the inexpensive XO laptops developed by the *One Laptop Per Child* (OLPC) project to help address the global divide in digital access (see Box 1.4).

The *world wide web*, or simply *the web*, is one of the dominant services running on the internet. It is made of up of millions of interlinked *websites*. Nowadays many teachers primarily use free or low-cost *web 2.0* services in their lessons. The hardware devices mentioned above allow web access through *software* called a *web browser*; examples include Apple's Safari, Google's Chrome, Microsoft's Internet Explorer and Mozilla's Firefox. Although many mobile handheld devices also include web browsers, such devices increasingly work with *applications*, or *apps*, that is, small pieces of software which are downloaded from the internet, have specific and limited functionality (as opposed to the general functionality of a web browser), may run with or without web access, and are typically inexpensive or even free (see Chapter 1: *First focus: Language, Mobile literacy*).

Other common hardware includes *data projectors*, which project a computer's display onto a large screen, for example at the front of a classroom.

A more flexible option is offered by touch-sensitive *interactive whiteboards*, or *IWBs*, which, operating in conjunction with data projectors, can be used to display and interact with webpages or software running on the connected computer, as well as capturing and saving notes. *Clickers*, also known by the fuller name of *personal response systems*, allow student responses to questions to be displayed on a screen or smartboard. A new development with some educational potential is the emergence of *3D printers*.

The proliferation of digital hardware, software and internet connections, especially coupled with the availability of free or cheap web 2.0 services and mobile apps, is good news for teachers everywhere.

Neil Selwyn notes that there are *external* and *internal imperatives* for incorporating digital technologies into education. *External imperatives* concern the need to prepare our students for social life, employment and citizenship in the digitally networked world outside the classroom. It is largely due to such external imperatives, particularly economic ones, that school curricula around the world are beginning to emphasise the importance of digital competencies and new literacies (Belshaw, 2011; Selwyn, 2011). *Internal imperatives* concern the benefits digital technologies can offer within the classroom, chiefly by supporting constructivist, student-centred pedagogical approaches (see Box 2.1). Digital literacies, we suggest, are linked to both imperatives: they're essential skills our students need to acquire for full participation in the world beyond the classroom, but they can also enrich our students' learning inside the classroom.

In Chapter 1, we'll discuss the major literacies our students need to acquire (based on Pegrum, 2009 and 2011). The literacies are grouped loosely under four focus points – language, information, connections and (re-)design – and arranged loosely in order of increasing complexity under those focus points, as can be seen in Table 1.1. The considerations which have led to this particular ordering are examined in more detail later (see Chapter 3: *Choosing activities for different levels and contexts, Overall complexity*). The framework is not intended as a checklist of distinct literacies – many of these literacies blur into each other, as indeed do the four focus points – but rather as a map of key areas of emphasis we need to consider within the overall field of digital literacies. While many of the literacies involve elements of other literacies, those which are most obviously *macroliteracies* – that is, which pull together a number of other literacies – are shown in bold in the table. Whether we are teaching students about literacies or macroliteracies,

Table 1.1 Framework of digital literacies

increasing complexity		First focus: Language	Second focus: Information	Third focus: Connections	Fourth focus: (Re-)design
	*	Print literacy			
		Texting literacy			
	**	Hypertext literacy	Tagging literacy		
	***		Search literacy	**Personal literacy**	
		Multimedia literacy	Information literacy	Network literacy	
			Filtering literacy	Participatory literacy	
	****	**Gaming literacy**		Intercultural literacy	
		Mobile literacy			
	*****	Code literacy			**Remix literacy**

our task is to help them develop strategies to deal with each key area so they can make the most of the possibilities of digital media. Of course, some literacies involve skillsets that language teachers have been promoting for decades, but which have come to greater prominence in recent years. *Intercultural literacy*, for example, has become all the more important in a world where technology often highlights, rather than erases, cultural and other differences.

After these skills and associated strategies have been outlined in Chapter 1, Chapter 2 offers some practical starting points for those who are not very familiar with new technologies and new literacies. It includes numerous activities, often based on activities well known to teachers, where digital literacies can be fostered side by side with traditional literacy skills. If you're more confident, you may wish to try out some of the more challenging activities suggested. While the activities included in Chapter 2 are designed primarily for teachers and learners of English as an additional, other, second or foreign language (with the most common nomenclature varying across contexts), most are easily transferable to other language learning contexts with a little adjustment. Many are also relevant to mainstream language teaching in native-speaking contexts, and more generally to fields such as communications and new media studies.

Chapter 3 offers advice on incorporating digital literacies into varying learning environments, including detailed advice on how to put the Chapter 2 activities into practice in a range of contexts. Again, the focus is on English language teaching, but most of the material covered is relevant to a wide range of other language and communication contexts. Chapter 4 contains pointers on how to conduct action research, so that our teaching feeds into a research cycle and thereby benefits our own professional development as well as that of fellow language teachers. Most of the strategies suggested are appropriate not just for language teachers but all educators. The chapter concludes with suggestions on how we can build, or extend, a personal learning network which will support our lifelong learning about new technologies in education.

When it comes to new literacies and new technologies, it's a good idea to start small. Build familiarity with one literacy, or one technology, before going on to add to your repertoire. No starting point is too small. But what is absolutely imperative is to make a start. Our students are waiting!

First focus: Language

The first set of key literacies our students need is broadly connected with the communication of meaning through language, including the many channels that complement, supplement and, on occasion, supersede linguistic expression.

Print literacy (Chapter 2: Activities 3 and 4)

Print literacy, on which language teaching has traditionally focused, has lost little of its relevance offline and has even gained additional relevance online. As Henry Jenkins and his co-authors (2009, p. 29) note: 'Before students can engage with the new participatory culture, they must be able to read and write'. It's easy to forget that most digital communication still involves written language. Readers skim and scan extended texts, assess and analyse opinion pieces, and evaluate subtle cues of tone and intent in status updates. Writers carefully plan and compose blog entries, build persuasive arguments and counter-arguments on discussion boards, restructure and copy-edit their own and others' work on wikis, and express themselves succinctly in tweets. In some ways, traditional literacy skills can be trained better online than offline. Students can annotate e-books, using the inbuilt features of the Kindle or other digital readers; they can annotate online articles, using web services like Diigo (www.diigo.com) or apps like GoodReader (www.goodreader.net/goodreader.html); and they can share and discuss their annotations. They often find it motivating to write for an audience of peers or the wider public (e.g. Godwin-Jones, 2003) but, amid stiff competition for attention online, they must tailor their writing well if it's to have any hope of reaching its target audience and achieving its communicative goals.

> *Print literacy:* the ability to comprehend and create a variety of written texts, encompassing a knowledge of grammar, vocabulary and discourse features alongside reading and writing skills.

Naturally, paper and screen are not always interchangeable. There is still a place for the development of fine motor skills through writing by hand, an activity whose sensorimotor aspects may also have important cognitive benefits (e.g. Mangen and Velay, 2010), and for reading free from the cognitive demands of hypertext (see below). Similarly, we should be wary of substituting interaction for reflection, or eroding all linear reading and focused writing by endlessly multiplying communication channels (Carr, 2010). But with these provisos, we can, as language teachers, find many inventive ways to explore and exploit *print literacy* online. Indeed, it lies at the very heart of digital literacies.

Texting literacy (Chapter 2: Activities 5 and 6)

Of course, digital language has its own native inflections in the form of *netspeak*, *textspeak*, or *txtspk*, leading to a need for *texting literacy*. This kind of language emerged in online chatrooms and mobile text messaging, with some of its abbreviations serving speed and cost purposes, and some, alongside emoticons, helping to avoid misunderstandings in these 'thin', text-only channels. It's now taken on a life of its own as a new linguistic register which, like online communication in general, is located somewhere between speech and writing (Baron, 2008; Crystal, 2011). While still serving its original goals, textspeak can also be used by adults as well as children to signal 'coolness' or in-group membership (Pegrum, 2009), and to participate in a long tradition of language play (Crystal, 2008), as seen, for example, in the LOLcats meme (see Chapter 2: Activity 47, *LOLcats*).

Texting literacy: the ability to communicate effectively in *netspeak* or *textspeak* (also known as *txtspk*).

Research findings about the effects of textspeak on young people's language development, if initially surprising, are very clear. As Kemp (2011) notes in her review of empirical studies of texting, there is actually a positive correlation between students' use of textspeak and their standard literacy skills. After all, to bend language rules you have to know the rules to begin with (Crystal, 2008, 2011; Plester, Wood and Bowyer, 2009). Research, moreover, indicates that most young people are aware of the distinction between textspeak and standard language (Crystal, 2008; Lenhart *et al.*, 2008). Yet apparently slip-ups continue to occur, as in the notorious case of a Scottish schoolgirl who handed in an essay written entirely in textspeak, its compact opening line reading: 'My smmr hols wr CWOT' (in standard English: 'My summer holidays were a complete waste of time'; for a full account, see Pegrum, 2009). There's a danger that if students use textspeak in inappropriate contexts, it may be seen as signalling rebelliousness (ibid.) or, worse still, sloppiness and lack of education (Baym, 2010). This suggests that a codeswitching approach to *texting literacy*, similar to the approach sometimes taken to slang in the classroom, may be appropriate (cf. Crystal, 2011). Such an approach recognises the value of students' pre-existing language use, or desired language use, while training them to make judgements about when, where and how to switch into and out of textspeak.

On the other hand, we should remember that netspeak and textspeak are key components of a broader digital trend towards increased speed, quantity, fragmentation and ephemerality of writing. This in turn slots into a more long-standing trend towards what Naomi Baron (2008, 2011) calls 'linguistic "whatever-ism"', in which language rules and consistency are viewed as increasingly inconsequential. As language teachers, we can't avoid being affected by such developments.

Box 1.2 Am I teaching digital natives?

The common belief that the younger generation is more technologically adept than its elders is reflected in terms like *digital natives* (promoted by Marc Prensky) and *the net generation* (promoted by Don Tapscott). It's true that many young people are driven to connect with their peers online as a result of increasingly heavily scheduled and protected lives. It's also true that, without a pre-digital mindset, many of them may be very open to creative uses of technology. And finally, it's true that some are willing and able to spend enough time experimenting with digital technologies to develop considerable expertise, which teachers can draw on (see Box 2.2). However, empirical studies show that the notion of a homogeneous, digitally able generation is a myth.

First, obvious factors like socio-economic status, education level and location, as well as perhaps less obvious ones like gender, race and language, dramatically impact both digital access and skills, creating an ongoing *digital divide* (see Box 1.4). Of course, young people also vary in their personal interest in going online. Secondly, while many of them are adept at using technology for entertainment and social purposes, they often need guidance in using it for educational or professional purposes, and in developing a critical understanding of its affordances and pitfalls. As teachers, we can play a role in turning our students from what Gavin Dudeney calls *tech-comfy* into *tech-savvy* users of digital tools.

In recent years, the alternative terms *digital residents* and *digital visitors* have been proposed as a more accurate representation of the way that people of all ages, not just youth, make use of the web. As David White puts it, 'the Resident has a presence online which they are constantly developing while the Visitor logs on, performs a specific task and then logs off'.

- For more on digital natives and the net generation, see: Prensky (2012b); Tapscott (2009).

- For more on the critique of these concepts, see: Bennett, Maton and Kervin (2008); Dudeney (2009); Hague and Williamson (2009); Hargittai (2010); Thomas (2011).

- For more on digital residents and digital visitors, see: White (2008); White and Le Cornu (2011).

Hypertext literacy (Chapter 2: Activities 7 and 8)

If textspeak is a new linguistic register, hyperlinks are a new form of punctuation (Weinberger, 2009a) requiring the development of *hypertext literacy*. Rhetorically, links exert a subtle persuasiveness, highlighting a document's key points, reinforcing its major arguments, and offering a snapshot of its openness and credibility. Navigationally, links demand that readers decide whether to accept invitations to go beyond the current text and take responsibility for choosing their own narrative pathways on the wider web. Because hyperlinks sometimes create a misleading impression – with lots of links to similar sources, for example, initially making a document seem more factually grounded than it really is – they need a critical eye. Conversely, online documents with few or no links should also strike critical readers as suspicious. It's therefore important that, when it comes to creating their own texts, students learn how to deploy hyperlinks judiciously to enhance their communicative intent. They also need to be aware that, as Nick Carr (2010) notes, hyperlinks add to cognitive load (as readers are obliged to decide over and over whether or not to click) and may slow down reading, possibly reducing comprehension and impairing retention. Understanding this can help inform their decisions on when to read online or offline, and to what extent to punctuate their own texts with links. At the same time, they need to develop strategies for dealing with the increasingly common practice of hyperlinking sections of images or videos, which will inevitably lead them in the direction of *multimedia literacy*, and 'hardlinking' real-world objects through QR codes, which will lead them towards *mobile literacy* (see below).

Hypertext literacy: the ability to process hyperlinks appropriately and to use hyperlinks effectively to enhance a document or artefact.

Multimedia literacy: the ability to effectively interpret and create texts in multiple media, notably using images, sounds and video.

Multimedia literacy (Chapter 2: Activities 9–15)

In a world of screens, we no longer rely on language alone to carry the weight of our communication. Visual elements have assumed greater cultural prominence in recent decades, hence a long-standing focus on 'visual literacy' in literacies research. This literacy has now become even more vital as users are confronted with proliferating pictorial displays of information online, ranging from tag clouds and visual search results to digital stories, data visualisations and infographics; and it's central to assessing aesthetics and design, which have been found to unduly influence people's evaluation of websites (Danielson, 2006; Livingstone, 2009). Visual literacy, moreover, feeds into the ensemble of skills taught in recent years under the banner of 'media literacy' (Livingstone, 2009), which is designed to foster a critical (and occasionally participatory) approach to media, notably the mass media – whose presence is also growing ever stronger online.

Box 1.3 Does Facebook belong in my classroom?

Many of our students will be among Facebook's more than one billion users worldwide. Some educators, particularly at post-secondary level, choose to go where the students are, and use Facebook *groups* as mini-VLEs (see Box 1.10) for information dissemination and student collaboration, or Facebook *pages* as hubs for announcements and questions. Neither of these require teachers to *friend* students on the site, but to avoid perceptions of impropriety teachers running closed groups may invite a colleague to join as an observer. It's also a good idea to cover digital safety and privacy guidelines with students (see Box 1.9).

Some teachers prefer not to enter what is primarily their students' social space, and some institutions prefer their teachers not to blur professional boundaries by interacting with students on Facebook. Teachers may opt for alternative *social networking sites* like Grou.ps (grou.ps), Ning (www.ning.com) or the educationally oriented Edmodo (www. edmodo.com), all of which offer greater administrative control, or *microblogging* services like Twitter, where interaction is typically more public.

Note that the Terms of Service of many providers, including Facebook and Ning, set 13 as the minimum age for users, due to the requirements of the 1998 US Children's Online Privacy Protection Act (COPPA) regarding collection of personal information. While social networking sites for children and teens exist – examples include Club Penguin, Habbo (formerly Habbo Hotel) and Moshi Monsters, all of which have gaming or virtual world elements – they're not usually an appropriate platform for online classes. Note, too, that some countries block access to services like Facebook and Twitter (see Box 1.11), though local clones may exist.

- For more on the philosophy of Facebook, see: Kirkpatrick (2010).

- For more on how to use Facebook, see: Abram (2012); Belicove and Kraynak (2011); Vander Veer (2011).

- For more on Facebook in education, see: Fogg Phillips (2011); Levinson (2010); Merchant (2010a); Online College (2012).

However, because images, sounds and video are often intertwined, it is generally more helpful to think in terms of *multimedia literacy*, a concept that overlaps with the New London Group's (2000) 'multiliteracies' and Gunther Kress's (2003, 2010) 'multimodality'. *Multimedia literacy* has truly come of age on the internet, 'the first medium that can act like all media – it can be text, or audio, or video, or all of the above' (Rose, 2011, Kindle location 90). Rather than standing alone, text is often a complement to, or complemented by, other ways of communicating meaning. As David Crystal (2011) writes:

> In a multimedia world, it is not possible to focus exclusively on the spoken or written element, treating everything else as marginal – as non-linguistic extras. All the elements combine in a single communicative act, and their joint roles need to be considered. (Kindle location 4164)

Students have to learn not just to understand but to create multimedia messages, integrating text with images, sounds and video to suit a variety of communicative purposes and reach a range of target audiences. Key tools include podcasts and vodcasts as well as popular web-based animation services like Dvolver (www.dvolver.com), Voki (www.voki.com) and Xtranormal (www.xtranormal.com). Key techniques include data visualisation (Steele and Iliinsky, 2010), where patterns emerging from data are displayed, often as 'infographics' designed to convey complex information simply; digital storytelling (Alexander, 2011; Frazel, 2010; University of Houston, 2011), where multimedia narratives are typically built on a single platform; and transmedia storytelling (Jenkins, 2008; Transmedia Storytelling, 2012), where narratives are dispersed across multiple platforms. Because the stories presented to us by the culture and media industries increasingly take a transmedia format – 'Obi-Wan Kenobi is a transmedia character', says Henry Jenkins (2010), 'so is Barrack [sic] Obama' – this can help develop students' critical 'media literacy' skills. Students can also explore social sharing sites, including textsharing platforms like Scribd (www.scribd.com), photosharing platforms like Flickr (www.flickr.com) or Picasa (picasaweb.google.com), slidesharing platforms like Slideshare (www.slideshare.net), and videosharing platforms like YouTube (www.youtube.com) or TeacherTube (www.teachertube.com). On these sites, they can identify multimedia resources to repurpose for their own work, such as materials available in the public domain or under Creative Commons licences (see Box 1.12), while beginning to license and share their original work on the same platforms.

Gaming literacy (Chapter 2: Activities 16 and 17)

The rising use of multiple media points towards the emergence of new kinds of communication and learning spaces, which make new demands on language and literacy (e.g. Ensslin, 2012). With games now being taken seriously as a way to facilitate work and solve real-world problems (Dignan, 2011; McGonigal, 2011; Reeves and Leighton Read, 2009) as well as enhancing education (Gee, 2007a, 2007b; Prensky, 2007; Thomas and Seely Brown, 2011), there is a growing focus on 'game literacy' (Buckingham, 2008) or *gaming literacy* (Zimmerman, 2009). This is a macroliteracy – in other words, a literacy which draws on numerous other literacies – and involves linguistic, multimedia, spatial, kinaesthetic and other skills. What's more, the notion referred to by Gee (2007b) as 'projective identity' (that is, the often idealised identity people choose to project through their avatars in virtual environments) links it to *personal literacy* (see below). In coming years, gaming environments – as well as virtual worlds like Second Life, which isn't a game as such – may be seen as ideal learning spaces in which students can acquire digital literacies in addition to practising language and traditional literacies. Importantly, learning should be able to be transferred to and from the real world. Indeed, we may see elements of gaming environments and virtual worlds increasingly overlapping with the real world, necessitating a different inflection of digital literacies which we might refer to as *mobile literacy*.

Gaming literacy: the ability to effectively navigate, interact with and achieve goals in a gaming environment.

Mobile literacy: the ability to navigate, interpret information from, contribute information to, and communicate through the mobile internet, including an ability to orient oneself in the space of the *internet of things* (where information from real-world objects is integrated into the net) and *augmented reality* (where web-based information is overlaid on the real world).

Mobile literacy (Chapter 2: Activities 18–20)

Some of the most significant new developments in literacy are being driven by the emerging mobile web, underpinned by wireless technology and mobile devices like smartphones (including Android phones, BlackBerrys and the iPhone) and tablets (including the iPad). 'The future our students will inherit is one that will be mediated and stitched together by the mobile web', argues David Parry (2011, p. 16). He adds: 'Teaching mobile web literacy seems to me as crucial as teaching basic literacy'. This 'mobile web literacy' or 'mobile media literacy' (Collin *et al.*, 2011), or simply *mobile literacy*, is another macroliteracy. Besides print and multimedia literacy, it has to incorporate an understanding of information access (a mobile inflection of what we've called *search literacy* and *information literacy*, see below), hyperconnectivity (an inflection of *network literacy*, see below) and a new sense of space (Parry, 2011). The transformation of space is occurring as mobile technologies allow the web and the world to meet each other and begin to overlap, thanks to the *internet of things*, where data from real-world objects is shared through the internet, and *augmented reality*, where contextual web-based information is overlaid on visual displays of the real world (Johnson, Adams and Cummins, 2012; Johnson *et al.*, 2011; O'Reilly and Battelle, 2009). Today's proliferating *quick response (QR) codes*, two-dimensional barcodes which, when manually scanned with a mobile device, act as 'hardlinks' to webpages, media files or text-based information (Winter, 2011), may be a transitional stage towards more automated versions of augmented reality. Indeed, a *mixed reality* which blends the virtual and the real, through interfaces not dissimilar to gaming environments or virtual worlds, is beginning to arise around us.

Box 1.4 Does the digital divide still matter?

The *digital divide* (which was always less of a divide and more of a continuum) originally referred to the gap between those with access to adequate hardware, software and internet connections, and those without such access. There is still a global divide in access, which projects like OLPC (see Box 1.1) are trying to address. However, as access has spread in the developed world, the term *digital divide* has been repurposed to refer to the gap between those with the skills to make effective use of digital technologies, and those who lack such skills. Henry Jenkins refers to this as the *participation gap*, with those on the wrong side having fewer opportunities for full participation in society. Thus, in the ▶

developed world, the digital divide has become as much an educational issue as an economic one. Of course, education and economics are not unrelated, with young people's opportunities to develop digital skills outside formal schooling depending on a range of factors, many of them related to their home background (see Box 1.2). As educators, we have a key role to play in helping to upskill the less advantaged, less digitally literate students in our classrooms in order to narrow the gap.

■ For more on contemporary views of the digital divide, see: Haythornthwaite (2007); Helsper (2008); Selwyn and Facer (2007).

■ For more on the participation gap, see: Hargittai and Walejko (2008); Jenkins *et al.* (2009).

It's important for us to help students orient themselves in this new space. In fact, *m-learning*, or 'mobile learning', is already a rapidly growing area (Ally, 2009; Gagnon, 2010; Pachler, Bachmair and Cook, 2010), with mobile phones finding their way into more and more classrooms (Kolb, 2008, 2011; Nielsen and Webb, 2011). Importantly, mobile devices lend themselves to anywhere/anytime learning, that is, 'seamless learning' across formal and informal spaces (Looi *et al.*, 2010). The increasingly widespread term *u-learning*, or 'ubiquitous learning' (Bonk, 2009; Cope and Kalantzis, 2009), puts more emphasis on the situated and contextualised nature of the learning fostered by mobile devices, which makes them ideally suited to supporting personalised language teaching in real-world contexts.

M-learning: 'mobile learning', i.e. learning with mobile devices.

U-learning: 'ubiquitous learning', i.e. using mobile devices for contextualised learning, anywhere and at any time.

At the same time, we need to sensitise students to the differences between web-based digital experiences and the app-based experiences that are becoming more common with the proliferation of mobile devices (see Box 1.1). While offering considerable specialisation, personalisation and contextualisation, all of which have educational advantages, apps typically deliver less control, flexibility and creativity to end-users. Educational apps in particular are often *consumption apps*, based on traditional pedagogical approaches involving content transmission or drill and practice exercises; although *productive apps* oriented towards creation and networking are now appearing, they are still much rarer (Oakley, Pegrum and Faulkner, 2012).

What is more, the availability of apps may depend on a strict approvals process (see Box 1.11), most notably in the case of Apple's app store. A critical awareness of the pros and cons of our increasingly app-driven digital world is necessarily part of *mobile literacy*.

As with games and *gaming literacy*, we can help students develop *mobile literacy* at the same time as they develop language and more traditional literacies through their smart devices. This is a space to watch: as the technology develops, what new ways will we find of using our context-aware mobile devices to read, annotate and interact with the world around us? What new benefits and drawbacks will we encounter as we continue to shift towards an app-based model of digital communication and interaction? And what new inflections of literacy will this demand?

Code literacy (Chapter 2: Activities 21 and 22)

All of the literacies discussed above require some understanding of new technologies, including the ability to make effective use of common software, web 2.0 tools, and mobile apps, and to adapt to new software, tools and apps as they become available. Without it, it would be impossible for us to produce online documents, hypertexts or multimedia artefacts, much less to interact in games or through the mobile web. But beyond this kind of understanding, there is a need for a deeper level of *code literacy*. The ability to read and write computer code – including, nowadays, the ability to make mobile apps (Abelson, 2011; Prensky, 2012a) – gives us the flexibility to escape the pre-set options of commercial software (Prensky, 2012b) and even to bypass some political and social censorship (Newton, 2009). As Douglas Rushkoff (2010) puts it: 'If we don't learn to program, we risk being programmed ourselves' (Kindle location 1550). Even those who don't want or need to become programmers can still benefit from some understanding of how programming works and the kinds of biases and limitations it introduces into our software (Kelly, 2010; Lanier, 2010; Rushkoff, 2010). Eli Pariser (2011) sees it like this:

> *Especially at the beginning, learning the basics of programming is even more rewarding than learning a foreign language. . . . Mastery, as in any profession, takes much longer, but the payoff for a limited investment in coding is fairly large: It doesn't take long to become literate enough to understand what most basic bits of code are doing. (Kindle locations 3073 and 3075)*

Code literacy: the ability to read, write, critique and modify computer code in order to create or tailor software and media channels.

The skillset associated with *code literacy* is linked in important ways to the digital divide, which educational institutions are tasked with overcoming (see Box 1.4). In fact, as Scott McLeod (2012) reminds us, this is a new inflection of a rather older concern, as can be seen in these two quotes from the early 1990s:

> *Economically disadvantaged students, who often use the computer for remediation and basic skills, learn to do what the computer tells them, while more affluent students, who use it to learn programming and tool applications, learn to tell the computer what to do. (Neuman 1991, cited in McLeod, 2012)*

> *Those who cannot claim computers as their own tool for exploring the world never grasp the power of technology . . . . They are controlled by technology as adults – just as drill-and-practice routines controlled them as students. (Pillar, 1992, cited in McLeod, 2012)*

Certainly, there's a need for professional development in this area. This might include teachers learning how to set up productive partnerships with tech-savvy students, combining their own content and pedagogical expertise with students' technological knowledge (see Box 2.2). Ultimately, unless both teachers and students develop a certain level of *code literacy*, we are effectively handing control of our communicative options to a small elite of software designers in the employ of various commercial and political masters. As a result, all our other digital language and literacy skills may be compromised.

Second focus: Information

Now that contextually relevant information is increasingly available at our fingertips, thanks in part to the mobile web, memorising information is becoming less important than the skills of accessing, evaluating and managing it. These comprise a second set of key digital literacies.

An e-learning tag cloud
URL: goo.gl/e1Mgq

Tagging literacy (Chapter 2: Activities 23 and 24)

'Tagging' useful online resources is a way of keeping track of them by adding metadata in the form of descriptive terms, or 'tags'. These tags can be automatically compiled into user-generated indexes known as *folksonomies* and displayed as visual *tag clouds*, with the relative importance of the tags signalled by font size and density. Users can then click on the tags, which function as hyperlinks to lists of the saved resources. (Note that *word clouds*, which are a popular variation on tag clouds, show the relative frequency of words in a text but do not serve as hyperlinked indexes in the same way as tag clouds.) Unlike rigid taxonomies, folksonomies allow materials to be simultaneously classified in multiple ways (cf. Weinberger, 2007). They're malleable, extensible, and can be reconfigured by their creators at any time to generate a different view of the catalogued materials:

> *Imagine a library in which books and journals could be organized and re-organized at the click of a finger by subject, by topic, by date or by size and colour – or whatever category readers apply – and you begin to understand the magic of a folksonomy. (Merchant, 2010b, p. 96)*

Once they acquire the *tagging literacy* to navigate folksonomies, our students can use them as a complement to search engine results or traditional classification systems in libraries (now that user-generated folksonomies are beginning to appear alongside the Dewey Decimal or Library of Congress classifications in online catalogues). They can further hone their *tagging literacy* by using services like Delicious (www.delicious.com) and Diigo (www.diigo.com) to create their own folksonomies, in the process building on the traditional language and literacy skills needed to apply appropriate descriptive and classificatory labels. Individually created folksonomies can help them preserve their research trails and manage their resources, while the class folksonomies exploited by many teachers can promote what Bryan Alexander (2006, p. 36) calls 'collaborative information discovery'. And if students make their folksonomies public, they will be contributing to the global task of managing digital information, thereby developing their *participatory literacy* (see below).

Tagging literacy: the ability to interpret and create effective *folksonomies* (user-generated indexes of online resources represented visually as *tag clouds*) (see the QR code, An E-learning tag cloud).

Search literacy (Chapter 2: Activities 25 and 26)

Most of the time, lists of online resources are not simply provided to users; nor have resources always been collected in publicly available, user-friendly tag clouds. Students often need to start their online activities by searching for the information or materials they require.

Given the fundamental role of search engines in facilitating the flow of information online, it's not surprising that many people are confident they can use them well. Most people, unfortunately, are very wrong – and that's very dangerous (Jackson, 2009). Few people are skilled in choosing the most appropriate keywords for a search. Few know about the range of search engines available or the varying presentation formats of results. And few are fully aware of search engines' inherent limitations, notably their bias towards the commercial, the popular, the recent and, increasingly, the personally relevant (with Google now returning more personalised results based on its reading of an individual's likely interests; see Chapter 2: Activity 26, *Search me*, and Pariser, 2011, for further details). Studies have shown that young people's searches, in particular, tend to be rather haphazard (Livingstone 2009; Weigel, James and Gardner, 2009).

An acquaintance with *search literacy* can help our students to adopt appropriate research strategies. We might begin by helping them understand that relying solely on Google means giving one company licence to 'determine what is important, relevant, and true on the Web and in the world', as Siva Vaidhyanathan (2011, Kindle location 62) puts it. This is all the more problematic because Google's top non-commercial results largely come from one source, Wikipedia (see Box 1.6), leading to a narrow informational triumvirate of web-Google-Wikipedia (Carr, 2009). Students need encouragement to explore the full functionality of the full range of search services, from Google Advanced Search (www.google.com/advanced_search) to specialised search services (see Box 1.5). They need guidance in choosing search terms. They need help developing strategies for parsing search engines' muddled mixtures of decontextualised – or, worse, recontextualised – snippets of information (Carr, 2010; Mayer-Schönberger, 2009) and knowing when and how to dig deeper. Most importantly, perhaps, they need to realise they cannot just outsource their memories to search engines. Human remembering, unlike digital remembering, is a creative act which shapes, orders, makes sense of and, indeed, deletes information (for further details, see Aboujaoude, 2011; Carr, 2010; Jackson, 2009; Mayer-Schönberger, 2009). Some memorisation, as we'll see below, is crucial to *information literacy*. And some forgetting, of the kind search engines make so difficult, is essential to focusing our attention.

Search literacy: the ability to make effective use of a wide array of search engines and services, including a familiarity with their full functionality as well as their limitations.

Box 1.5 What are the alternatives to Google?

These are examples of different kinds of search services (see Chapter 2: Activity 25, *Search race* for more options; a fuller list may be found on the 'Search' page of the *E-language* wiki at e-language.wikispaces.com/search).

Specific content

Memeorandum (politics)	www.memeorandum.com
Technorati (blogs)	technorati.com

Specific media

flickrCC (CC photos)	flickrcc.bluemountains.net
Zanran (graphs, data)	zanran.com

Visual search

Quintura	www.quintura.com
Tag Galaxy	taggalaxy.de

Metasearch

Gnosh	www.gnosh.org
WebCrawler	www.webcrawler.com

Customisable search

Rollyo	www.rollyo.com

Box 1.6 Can we trust Wikipedia?

The one major review conducted of Wikipedia to date, Giles's 2005 *Nature* study comparing it to Britannica on the basis of 42 scientific entries, concluded that there were around three errors per Britannica article and four per Wikipedia article. Of course, Wikipedia is far more comprehensive and up to date than a traditional encyclopaedia. Nowadays, it may even be more accurate. As Amy Bruckman points out, ▶

'a popular, high profile Wikipedia page is the most accurate reference that has ever been created in the history of the written word' because it has been checked by hundreds, if not thousands, of editors. (Although falsification and vandalism do occur, with perpetrators ranging from ideologues with grudges to school students hoping to fool classmates the night before an assignment is due, they're typically repaired very quickly thanks to Wikipedia's history log and the vigilance of the Wikipedia community.) On the other hand, says Bruckman, an article on an obscure topic may be relatively unreliable (and any falsification or vandalism may go unnoticed for some time). What's crucial is knowing the difference between what is reliable and what is unreliable, and that's a matter of *information literacy*. One way of teaching this form of literacy is to ask our students, individually or in groups, to verify, modify and update – or even create – Wikipedia entries (with lower level learners of English starting with Simple English Wikipedia at simple.wikipedia.org). In this way, students can contribute to the accuracy, breadth and depth of a global reference at the same time as they are honing their digital literacy skills (see Chapter 2: Activity 7, *Sports linking* and Activity 41, *Our city on Wikipedia*).

■ For more discussion of Wikipedia, see: Bruckman (2011); Bruns (2008); Cummings (2009); Dalby (2009); Giles (2005); Lih (2009); O'Sullivan (2009); Reagle (2010).

■ For more on how to edit Wikipedia, see: Ayers, Matthews and Yates (2008); Broughton (2008).

Information literacy (Chapter 2: Activities 27 and 28)

'[I]f students do not understand the basic grammar of the Internet, they will be manipulated by people who do', warns Alan November (2010, p. 8). Building on *tagging* and *search literacy*, one of the most essential of contemporary literacies is *information literacy*. A term originally used by librarians to cover a range of search and evaluation skills (Bawden, 2008; Whitworth, 2009), we employ it more narrowly here to emphasise critical evaluation, drawing on the pedagogical traditions of 'critical literacy' and 'critical media literacy' with which it partly overlaps.

Information (critical) literacy: the ability to evaluate documents and artefacts by asking critical questions, assessing credibility, comparing sources, and tracking the origins of information.

Despite the growing availability of edited publications online, there are few gatekeepers – publishers, editors, librarians or teachers – patrolling the wider web. Clay Shirky, referring to online journalism, puts it like this: 'fact-checking is way down, and after-the-fact checking is way WAY up' (cited in Gillmor, 2010, Kindle location 777). The responsibility for after-the-fact checking of all documents and artefacts – not just the news – now falls to users. Our students must learn to ask critical questions about information found online; compare it to their existing baseline of knowledge (hence the need to have memorised widely accepted facts); and, where their baseline of knowledge is inadequate, they need to compare and contrast, or 'triangulate', multiple sources of information. One way to show the importance of *information literacy* is to begin with the critical analysis of spoof or bogus websites, which often catch students out (see Chapter 2: Activity 27, *Tree octopus*). It is important, as Howard Rheingold (2012) suggests, to '[p]romote the notion that more info literacy is a practical answer to the growing info pollution' (Kindle location 2017).

Bogus website resources
URL: goo.gl/ive5b

At the same time, we have to remind students that even the most credible online documents are often provisional and unstable. Stories are corrected or completed after publication on blogs (Jarvis, 2009b). Wiki entries offer a snapshot of discussions or arguments in progress (Bridle, 2010; Doctorow, 2006, 2008; Gleick, 2011). In this context, suggests David Weinberger (2009b), 'transparency is the new objectivity'. The credibility of information comes not (only) from an appeal to an external authority, but from engaged users being able to examine its origins and trace its development. Our students need to become adept at tracking information across multiple platforms, documents and, indeed, languages.

Box 1.7 Is there too much or too little information?

Past eras experienced waves of *information overload* before finding ways to adjust to and regulate it. In our own time, rising concerns about information and communication fatigue – as well as a rise in stress levels and attention disorders (see Box 1.13) – tell us we are again feeling overwhelmed, perhaps more than ever before. Linda Stone suggests we now find ourselves in a state of *continuous partial attention*. As we compete in the *attention economy*, it seems that attention itself has become our scarcest resource. Better ways to manage information, including searching and filtering techniques, are needed.

▶

But there's a growing danger of too much filtering, in part as a reaction to information overload. The net supports an unprecedented degree of *homophily* (essentially, the idea that birds of a feather flock together). Online, people can choose to isolate themselves in *echo chambers* or *information cocoons* where they only encounter others who are like them, and where their pre-existing views are always reinforced. This process is boosted by the automated personalisation seen, for example, in Google's search results or Facebook's news feed. As a consequence, there's an emerging danger of the public sphere splintering into separate publics with radically different worldviews and radically different sets of accepted 'facts'. It's vital for our students to learn to go beyond narrowly personalised spaces, explore diverse perspectives and bring a critical eye to the 'facts' they encounter.

■ For more on the history of information overload, see: Blair (2010); Gleick (2011); Powers (2010).

■ For more on contemporary information overload, see: boyd (2010b); Jackson (2009); Naish (2008); Stone (2008).

■ For more on homophily and echo chambers, see: Gee and Hayes (2011); Manjoo (2008); Pariser (2011); Sunstein (2007); Zuckerman (2008).

Filtering literacy (Chapter 2: Activities 29–32)

Tracking information is challenging when there is so much of it. There is a strong need for *filtering literacy* to reduce the digital flow to a manageable level. Some filtering strategies, such as setting up RSS (Really Simple Syndication) feeds, i.e. newsfeeds, or Google Alerts, are technological. Some, like identifying appropriate journalistic or pedagogical authorities, are editorial. Some are both. But more and more, sophisticated web users treat *filtering literacy* as a special inflection of *network literacy* (see below), with their trusted social and professional networks on services like Facebook and Twitter acting as 'decentralized relevancy filter[s]' (Sean Parker, cited in Kirkpatrick, 2010, p. 296) to 'curate' the information that flows to them on a daily basis (Bilton, 2010; Gillmor, 2010; Hagel, Seely Brown and Davison, 2010; Rheingold, 2012; Weinberger, 2011). Many of us already obtain a significant proportion of our news through our Facebook, Twitter and email contacts, and many of us turn to our social and professional networks for answers before we turn to search engines (Pegrum, 2010). As searching cedes more ground to networking in coming years – or becomes integrated with it in the *social search* services under development by the major search providers – it will be important for us to mentor our students in constructing personal learning networks, or *PLNs* (see Box 1.10). Because these PLNs will serve them as lifelong informational filters, it's vital that they are broad and diverse enough to ensure students don't become trapped in narrow echo chambers (see Box 1.7). For language students, the initial challenges of setting up multilingual PLNs will be more than compensated for by the richness of these networks in future years.

Filtering literacy: an inflection of *network literacy*, this is the ability to reduce information overload by using online social and professional networks as screening mechanisms.

Social search: a search service where results are ranked according to their relevance to users' online social and professional networks, e.g. on Facebook and Twitter.

PLNs: underpinned by *network literacy* and, more specifically, *filtering literacy*, and with a dedicated educational focus, 'personal learning networks' are trusted digital networks of people (experts and peers) and resources (sites and tools) which serve as sources of support and information, and which may be enriched by reciprocal sharing (see Box 1.10).

As they grapple with information overload (see Boxes 1.7 and 1.8), it may also be helpful for students to reflect from time to time on what Howard Rheingold calls 'attention literacy' (2009b) or 'infotention' (2012). It's all about striking a balance. As Rheingold (2010) notes: 'If I didn't follow online distractions, I couldn't keep up with my fields. If I didn't turn them off, I couldn't write books'. Taking time to consider the nature of attention is important for our students as present and future readers, writers, learners and thinkers.

Box 1.8 Does multitasking work?

Multitasking is not the magic bullet it seems to be. The human brain is not set up for parallel processing of tasks with similar cognitive demands, so what appears to be multitasking in fact involves switching rapidly between tasks. Studies show it is detrimental to both accuracy and efficiency, and may impair learning and recall. Although it may be possible to improve multitasking skills over time, there is still an upper limit hardwired into the brain. However, multitasking can also be seen as a coping strategy in the face of multiple, competing stimuli and it may have certain advantages for creativity, lateral thinking and group productivity. Conversely, some researchers suggest it is important to slow down occasionally or even switch off our streams of digital communication to make room for slower, more focused ways of reading, writing, thinking and learning. As teachers, we can help students reflect on when multitasking might be beneficial, when it might not, and when to switch off some of their digital tools (see Box 1.13).

■ For more on the limits of multitasking, see: Baron (2008); Jackson (2009); Kirn (2007); Rock (2009); Small and Vorgan (2008).

■ For more on how to work with multitasking, see: Anderson (2009); Davidson (2011); Gasser and Palfrey (2009); Gee and Hayes (2011); Rheingold (2012); Saveri (2009).

■ For more on slowing down, see: Brabazon (2009); Miedema (2009).

Third focus: Connections

In a digitally networked era, communicating meaning and managing information are intimately bound up with nurturing connections. Such connections are so important, in fact, that they necessitate a third set of digital literacy skills. As Nicholas Burbules (2009, p. 17) writes, 'people can be smarter because they have access to networked intelligence, whether it is technologically or socially distributed, or both'. It's up to us to help our students make the most of networked intelligence and its associated literacies.

Personal literacy (Chapter 2: Activities 33–37)

Before you can interact with a network, you need to establish your presence within it: hence the need for *personal literacy* (Burniske, 2008), which gives individuals the tools to shape their digital identities. When building your identity, says Nancy Baym (2010, p. 110), language and spelling matter (*print literacy*), but so do HTML and CSS (Cascading Style Sheets) (*code literacy*). 'Managing an online identity', warn Mary Madden and Aaron Smith (2010, p. 5), 'has become a multimedia affair' (*multimedia literacy*). *Personal literacy*, like gaming or mobile literacy, is very much a macroliteracy.

> *Personal literacy:* the ability to use digital tools to shape and project a desired online identity.

We now commonly hear of employers and colleges screening candidates online (e.g. Kirkpatrick, 2010; Kolb, 2010) or, similarly, clients checking out potential service providers (e.g. Madden and Smith, 2010). On the net, what you say and how you say it matters – and it matters that you say it yourself:

> *In the digital world, just as in the physical one, you are partly who others say you are.*

> *This is why you need to be at least one – and preferably the most prominent – of the voices talking about you. You can't allow others to define who you are, or control the way you are perceived. (Gillmor, 2010, Kindle location 2060)*

It's never too soon for our students to begin developing techniques for representing themselves appropriately. They probably won't find it easy to establish a public online voice in another language, much less in several languages, especially when it comes to integrating text and hypertext with multiple media and web design on platforms ranging from blogs, microblogs and wikis to photosharing, videosharing and social networking sites. They must also learn to protect their digital selves, and by extension their non-digital selves, from attack by cyberbullies, online predators and identity thieves (see Box 1.9), as well as from political or commercial censorship and surveillance (see Box 1.11).

Box 1.9 How can we promote digital safety and privacy?

All of us who spend time online need to keep in mind the intertwined issues of *safety*, *privacy* and *reputation management*. Attempting to protect students by blocking access to large swathes of the internet is

▶

not the answer: students, at least at higher levels, need to gain experience in safely navigating it. If they are unfortunate enough to encounter uncomfortable situations online, we need to provide support as well as building on any teachable moments that may arise. But we can begin by modelling good online behaviour and offering guidelines.

Digital safety resources
URL: goo.gl/EKfhU

Safety guidelines can help students develop strategies to protect themselves and their peers from *online predation*, a serious if rare phenomenon, and *cyberbullying*, a much more prevalent phenomenon which can be even more devastating than offline bullying because of the reach and persistence of comments or images spread online and via mobile phones. Fortunately, a growing bank of digital safety resources is available to educators (see QR code).

Privacy guidelines can help students limit the amount of personal information they share online, as well as how widely they share it. It's important to remind them to tighten up their privacy settings on social networking sites in particular. They'll then be less likely to fall prey to *identity theft*, while also being safer from *predators* and *bullies*. Many digital safety resources cover such privacy guidelines as well.

Reputation management guidelines can flag up the pros and cons of the *digital footprints*, or *data trails*, we all create online. On the negative side, the persistence of inappropriate status updates or photos – which, says Jeff Hancock, are a bit like digital tattoos (cited in boyd, 2009) – could damage chances of college entry or job interviews many years in the future. On the positive side, a PLE (see Box 1.10) containing evidence of creativity and technological skills, or a PLN (see Box 1.10) composed of a rich web of connections, might be helpful in establishing a good reputation. Of course, not all digital footprints are intentionally created: keeping an eye on privacy settings can help, though this won't offer total protection from governmental or corporate surveillance (see Box 1.11). Reputation management is something teachers should also consider: with employers, parents and students all Googling us, and with automated reputation systems like Klout (klout.com), PeerIndex (www.peerindex.com) and Proliphiq (www.proliphiq.com) beginning to emerge, we need to think about our online standing!

- For more on digital safety, see: Byron (2008); Internet Safety Technical Task Force (2008); Livingstone (2009).

- For more on digital privacy, see boyd (2010a); boyd (2011); Jarvis (2009a); Mayer-Schönberger (2009); Schneier (2010).

- For more on digital reputation, see: Levmore and Nussbaum (2010); Madden and Smith (2010); Solove (2007).

Network literacy (Chapter 2: Activities 38 and 39)

Naturally, digital identities are shaped through interaction with other digital identities in online networks. *Network literacy* is essential to navigating and capitalising on these interlinked social and professional networks. We've seen that personal learning networks serve as a way of filtering the tsunami of the internet, allowing us to remain informed and obtain specific information as needed. PLNs also herald a move away from standardised industrial models of education by promoting individual customisation of learning, breaking down barriers between the classroom and the world, and instigating lifelong professional development. Meanwhile, as our 'networked selves' (Papacharissi, 2011; Varnelis, 2008) come to function as nodes in digital networks, we gain access to channels through which we can reach target audiences, identify collaborators and supporters, and spread influence (Pegrum, 2010).

> *Network literacy:* the ability to deploy online social and professional networks to filter and obtain information (see also *filtering literacy*, above); to communicate with and inform others; to build collaboration and support; and to develop a reputation and spread influence.

Developing *network literacy* calls for educational intervention. As teachers, we can help our students enhance their information filters by hooking into educationally and professionally relevant networks as they set up blogrolls, Google Reader accounts, or Twitter lists; we can help them draw on and contribute to their incipient PLNs inside and outside school as they personalise their learning spaces and set themselves up for lifelong learning (see Box 1.10); and we can help them hone their *personal literacy* in order to raise their profiles, make their voices heard, and develop their reputations across the web.

Box 1.10 When, where and why should my students build PLNs (and PLEs)?

In our world of widespread connectivity and abundant information, more and more learning is taking place outside the formal spaces and times of education, and there are growing demands to customise it to individual needs. It's important for students to build up trusted *personal learning networks*, or *PLNs*, consisting of both living resources (experts, colleagues, peers) and material resources (websites, documents, artefacts, tools). Tended to, curated and expanded over a lifetime, PLNs can serve as information filters, learning spaces, and platforms for collaboration and dissemination. They are a core component of *connectivism*, an educational approach espoused by George Siemens.

A *personal learning environment*, or *PLE*, is a customised online study space that can be seen as a subset of an individual's wider PLN, in which focused learning occurs during a course of study. Such individually customised PLEs are at the opposite end of the spectrum from the homogeneous class spaces typical of institutional *virtual learning environments*, or *VLEs* (also called *learning management systems*, or *LMSs*). It is likely that in coming years the former will increasingly complement, and even partially supersede, the latter (see Chapter 3: *Building new learning spaces*), though some institutions are attempting to set up more flexible VLEs as a bridge between the two options.

A PLN can be built on any platform (such as Twitter, Facebook, a blog, website or wiki) where it's possible to gather together connections to people and resources. In fact, PLNs frequently range across multiple platforms. It's never too early to start building a PLN, or to begin enhancing one that already exists. We can guide students on how to broaden their PLNs by balancing the personal, social and professional elements in their networks, helping to ensure they don't become trapped in echo chambers (see Box 1.7). We can guide them on how to enrich their PLNs by actively contributing to as well as drawing from them. And as educators, we should also consider establishing our own PLNs, allowing us to engage in an ongoing process of professional development while modelling lifelong learning for our students (see Chapter 4: *Building and maintaining PLNs*).

- For more on PLNs and PLEs, see: Couros (2010); Drexler (2010); Ferriter, Ramsden and Sheninger (2011); McElvaney and Berge (2009); Pegrum (2010); Rheingold (2012); Richardson and Mancabelli (2011).

- For more on connectivism, see: Anderson and Dron (2011); Selwyn (2011); Siemens and Tittenberger (2009).

Participatory literacy (Chapter 2: Activities 40–43)

The more actively students contribute to online networks, the more *network literacy* begins to spill over into *participatory literacy*. In a networked era, suggests danah boyd (2010b), what matters is 'consuming to understand, producing to be relevant'. Or, as Dan Gillmor (2010) puts it: 'Being literate is also about creating, contributing and collaborating. In the Digital Age, participation is part of genuine literacy' (Kindle location 1389). This explains the widespread use of the term 'prosumer' (producer-consumer), coined by Alvin Toffler but reintroduced in a web 2.0 context by Ritzer and Jurgenson (2010) and others, and the alternative term 'produser' (producer-user), coined by Bruns (2008) to mitigate the commercial focus of the former term. Prosumer- or produser-style contributions to 'participatory culture' (Jenkins, 2008; Jenkins *et al.*, 2009) can begin on a simple level, with students honing a range of literacies as they edit Simple English Wikipedia entries (see Box 1.6), collaborate on Delicious or Diigo folksonomies (see Chapter 1: *Second focus: Information, Tagging literacy*), share links on Twitter, circulate photos on Flickr and videos on YouTube, or publish mobile apps – especially if they're encouraged to make their work reusable under Creative Commons licences (see Box 1.12). In the process students can develop lifelong skills, learning not only the value of contributing their 'cognitive surplus' (Shirky, 2010a) to collective projects, but also how to convey their meanings to diverse audiences and respond to their feedback. Of course, millions of students are already creating web content; as Alan November (2010, p. 32) notes: 'This is a major teachable moment'. And most of what we need to teach in this moment involves language and literacy, including many skills we've been teaching for decades, even if some of them have taken on new inflections in the digital era.

Participatory literacy: the ability to contribute to the collective intelligence of digital networks, and to leverage the collective intelligence of those networks in the service of personal and/or collective goals.

It's possible to create and share content whose value ranges 'from personal to communal to public to civic' (Shirky 2010a, p. 173). We might encourage our students to focus their attention towards the more public and civic end of the spectrum, where they can make contributions which extend from the local level (documenting neighbourhood problems) to the international level (participating in global political debates) (Lange, 2010). Students can be introduced to online platforms which seek to leverage networks for the public good, like Avaaz (www.avaaz.org), Change.org (www.change.org) and

TakingITGlobal (www.tigweb.org), and to the many ways that portable devices, especially, can be leveraged for what Liz Kolb (2008) calls 'mobile democracy' (Kindle location 3279). Certainly, a networked culture lets individuals and groups work together in ways that bypass traditional social, economic or political structures (Benkler, 2006, 2011; Castells, 2009; Shirky, 2008).

Yet there are dangers. There is a risk that 'slacktivism' (easy, one-click online activism which involves, for example, simply 'liking' a Facebook page, retweeting a news item, or sending an email) will partly replace more challenging and more effective real-world activism (e.g. Morozov, 2011). What is more, for a mixture of reasons, both governments and corporations are now seeking to curb the free communications and associations of the internet (see Box 1.11).

Box 1.11 Do I need to worry about censorship and surveillance?

Even if it's impossible to entirely rein in the internet, governments are gradually asserting sovereignty over it by regulating behaviour, limiting access, and monitoring users. While many countries still engage, regularly or intermittently, in online *censorship* of old media (newspapers and broadcasters) and social media (like Facebook, Flickr, Twitter, Wikipedia and YouTube), some authoritarian governments are moving increasingly from *censorship* to *surveillance*, having discovered that the internet is an ideal tool for identifying and tracking networks of dissidents. Even democratic governments, sometimes under the auspices of combating terrorism, crime and child pornography (all of which benefit from online networks), and sometimes in alliance with the twentieth-century culture industries, are seeking to introduce or strengthen laws limiting internet freedoms. The result is that, more than ever before, geography matters online. It determines what we can see, what we can do, and what might invite punishment. When we use the net to teach in different parts of the world, we have to check the availability and acceptability of the web resources and tools we're planning to use; and when we offer our students guidelines on *digital safety* and *digital privacy* (see Box 1.9), we have a responsibility to sensitise them to local laws.

Corporations engage in their own versions of censorship and surveillance. When technology companies seek to lock mobile users into *app stores* where all content has been pre-vetted, or web users into *walled gardens* such as social networking sites from which they can't freely extract their data, they have begun to play the role of censors. When telecommunications companies reject *net neutrality*, they restrict some users and uses of the internet in favour of others. And when search companies and social media companies monitor users, they promise better search results, more relevant newsfeeds and, above all, more targeted advertising. It's often been said that we're not Google's or Facebook's customers; we're their products, which they sell to advertisers. In short, we 'pay' for free services with our data, which is used to tailor the adverts we see and the environments we experience. At its extreme, this may lead to dangerously narrow echo chambers (see Box 1.7). Moreover, concerns have been raised about the limiting effects of a shift to an app-based rather than a web-based model of digital communication (see Chapter 1: *First focus: Language, Mobile literacy*). We must alert students to the consequences of the choices they make about whether to use the web or apps, and which web services or apps to use.

It's when governments and corporations collude that internet freedoms are most threatened. Of course, not all governments see eye to eye, not all corporations see eye to eye, and governments don't always see eye to eye with corporations. Political battles over internet access as a human right have begun, as have legal battles over who can access whose data, under which circumstances, and for what period of time. Meanwhile, across the internet, for their own varying and sometimes murky reasons, organisations ranging from the media whistleblower WikiLeaks to hacktivist groups like Anonymous and LulzSec have thrown down the gauntlet to both governments and corporations. This is a space to watch.

- For more on political control, see: Deibert *et al.* (2010); MacKinnon (2012); Morozov (2011); OpenNet Initiative (n.d.); Reporters Without Borders (n.d.).

- For more on commercial control, see: Chen (2011); Fuchs *et al.* (2011); Lanier (2010); Norman (2011); Pariser (2011); Vaidhyanathan (2011); Wu (2010); Zittrain (2008).

Note: There is considerable overlap between the references on political and commercial control in the above lists.

While teachers in many contexts will be wary of students straying into political or social activism, there may still be scope for inviting students to reflect on the societal impact and the personal consequences of participatory networking (for examples, see Pegrum, 2009), and perhaps even for them to become involved in addressing either small-scale local issues, or alternatively broad global issues such as the environment (see Chapter 2: Activity 43, *A good cause*). Despite the potential of networks to be used for nefarious ends, despite the dangers of activism sliding into ineffectual 'slacktivism', and despite the limitations introduced by governmental and corporate censorship and surveillance (see Box 1.11), online networking still holds some of the greatest promise for developing common solutions to shared planetary problems (Eagleman, 2010; Rheingold, 2012; Wright, 2010). Fostering *participatory literacy* in tandem with *intercultural literacy* (see below) can help prepare our students to assume roles as global citizens who are ready to participate in cross-cultural dialogues and debates, and to contribute to cross-cultural projects and initiatives.

Intercultural literacy (Chapter 2: Activities 44–46)

Today's proliferation of global connections underpinned by digital networks puts a premium on the skills of language teachers. After all, our work has always included helping students to build constructive cross-cultural relationships. But if this task has become easier technologically, it may have become harder psychologically. The internet, with its multiplying echo chambers (see Box 1.7), makes it easier for people (including students and, indeed, teachers) to find those who share their beliefs and biases – whether cultural, religious or political – and to ignore or vilify those who don't. 'Never underestimate the power of Twitter and Photoshop in the hands of people mobilized by prejudice', warns Evgeny Morozov (2011, Kindle location 4332).

Yet, as teachers, there's a lot we can do. First, it's important to continue teaching languages, giving non-native speakers access to what is still the structurally dominant language of the internet, namely English, and giving English native speakers access to at least some of the online conversations they'd otherwise miss (it's worth noting that English speakers had shrunk to 26.8 per cent of all net users as of May 2011; see 'Internet World Users', 2012). Secondly, it's important to continue helping students to develop the *intercultural literacy* to appreciate artefacts from other cultures, and to negotiate effective and constructive communication with members of those cultures. As Brian Street (2009, p. 30) points out: 'We can't assume that because the means of communication are now cross-cultural, the meanings are necessarily so'.

Intercultural literacy: the ability to interpret documents and artefacts from a range of cultural contexts, as well as to effectively communicate messages and interact constructively with interlocutors across different cultural contexts.

However, exposure to difference needs careful management. A long history of telecollaboration projects reveals that unless they are well prepared, well structured and well supported by teachers, cross-cultural interactions can lead to confusion, misunderstandings and, worse still, reinforcement of stereotypes and prejudices (Helm, Guth and Farrah, 2012; Lamy and Goodfellow, 2010; November, 2010). Fortunately, examples abound of successful partnerships between classrooms in different cities, states and countries. Some are set up through dedicated organisations like iEARN (www.iearn.org) or TakingITGlobal (www.tigweb.org), mentioned above; others are set up informally by pairs of teachers using interactive platforms like discussion boards, blogs or wikis, sometimes in the form of conversations built around podcasts, vodcasts or digital stories (for examples, see Bonk, 2009). Such collaborations allow students to learn from and about other cultures while acquiring the art of 'digital diplomacy', as they share their stories with members of cultures that are different from or even in conflict with their own (Solomon and Schrum, 2007, Kindle locations 1662–8, with reference to David Jakes).

More research is still needed on how to square the notion of *intercultural literacy* – underpinned by principles of cultural tolerance and relativism – with more absolutist cultural or faith-based perspectives. The promotion of an ethical pluralist stance, as described by Charles Ess (2009), might hold some promise. Meanwhile, David Weinberger (2012) suggests, optimistically, that the networked nature of digital knowledge is gradually making us 'more comfortable with unsettled differences':

> *Knowledge's new medium literally consists of linked differences: people saying different things, held together by hyperlinks. This runs against our traditional idea that knowledge consists of that about which there is no longer disagreement. (Slide 4)*

Yet he notes, too, that teaching people to 'love difference' is a major challenge (Weinberger, 2011). This needs to be a key research focus in coming years (see Chapter 4: *Conducting and sharing action research*) as we continue to promote greater intercultural understanding through language learning, a process made more urgent by the multiplying online connections of the digital era.

Fourth focus: (Re-)design

The focus of literacy over the past eighty years has shifted from 'convention' (e.g. learning to compose texts according to clearly established rules) through 'critique' (learning to problematise texts and stable textual conventions) to 'design' (learning to shape one's own texts in an unstable environment) (Kress, 2010). Nowadays we're called on to do much more than simply copy or critique past models: rather, we can contribute our own meanings to an increasingly fluid knowledge environment, often by building on others' texts and building in our own critique as we do so. In a digital culture, design often means re-design. For youth in particular, this process of re-designing meanings overlaps with processes of identity exploration, experimentation and construction (Alvermann, 2008; Dezuanni, 2010; Lange and Ito, 2010).

Remix literacy (Chapter 2: Activities 47–50)

Perhaps the best-known example of redesign is remix, which has become the hallmark of the digital era. Remix might involve changing the slogan on an advertisement to subvert the original message. It might involve photoshopping the image of a political figure into a pre-existing photo to cast new light on her politics. It might involve 'mashing up', or combining, two preexisting songs to create an unexpected dialogue between their lyrics. It might involve creatively dubbing or subtitling a film to surprise viewers. Remix is a knowing game in which truth claims are frequently unsettled. And like all games, it's about having fun along the way.

Remix has been described as 'a literacy for this generation' (Lessig, 2007) and as providing 'an educationally useful lens on culture and cultural production as well as on literacy and literacy education' (Knobel and Lankshear, 2008, p. 22). Certainly, the creation, circulation and interpretation of remixes depends on *remix literacy*, a macroliteracy which draws on all three skillsets covered so far: language-related skills like *print* and *multimedia literacy*, information-related skills like *tagging* and *information literacy*, and connection-related skills like *network* and *participatory literacy*. It can be seen as the ultimate proof of concept of web 2.0, because of the way it democratises content creation, critique, and the circulation of meaning – often in the form of *memes*, which are ideas or concepts that spread virally, especially through online networks, and impact mindsets and actions (Lankshear and Knobel, 2006) – while openly recognising that all new meanings are collaboratively built on a base of past meanings.

Remix literacy: the ability to create new meanings by sampling, modifying and/or combining pre-existing texts and artefacts, as well as circulating, interpreting, responding to and building on others' remixes within digital networks.

In opening up space for remix in our classrooms, we give students the opportunity to speak out about both major and minor issues that matter to them. The bigger issues might be social, political or environmental (with the last of these representing a relatively safe option in contexts where student social or political activism is risky or unwelcome). Because it entails a reconceptualisation and reworking of its constituent materials, remix presupposes a critical approach. But unlike the more traditional 'media literacy' (see Chapter 1: *First focus: Language, Multimedia literacy*) on which it builds, remix goes beyond critique by shifting the emphasis from consumption to production, thereby giving students agency and allowing them to propose their own alternative, sometimes even multiple, viewpoints.

Remix, in brief, is about culture as conversation. It's an idea which fits the current cultural and educational moment. It is time, suggest Mary Sheridan and Jennifer Rowsell (2010, p. 111), for teachers to help students go 'beyond the typical schooling practices of restating or critiquing' as they move towards production, which 'calls people to understand something in a unique way'. Lyndsay Grant (2010) puts it like this:

> [I]n a global remix culture, the power and relevance of critique itself may be due for critique. . . . While critique helps us uncover hidden interests and agendas, it is not so useful at helping us propose alternatives. An approach of re-design, on the other hand, is about constructing new ideas, artefacts and approaches – it is a forward-facing, proactive stance that does not just review others' work but makes its own contribution.

Remix, with its tendency to unsettle fixed perspectives and multiply viewpoints, is in some ways the sharp end of *participatory literacy*. Through remix, our students can learn to simultaneously critique and create in the process of 'producing to be relevant', as danah boyd was seen to say earlier.

As they hone this macroliteracy, they will find themselves exploiting most of the literacies covered in this chapter.

Box 1.12 How do I deal with copyright and plagiarism?

Digital *copyright* is a grey area. On the one hand, the culture industries, having succeeded in gradually extending copyright over the course of the twentieth century and into the twenty-first, are seeking political, legal and commercial support to enforce and even extend their rights online. On the other hand, after a century-long hiatus in which cultural production became increasingly professionalised and commercialised, we're seeing a re-emergence of amateur creativity: many net users want to play an active role in their own culture by quoting and transforming digital artefacts in line with the ethos of sharing and remixing that has grown up around web 2.0. While outright piracy is legally and morally dubious, the culture industries' push to enforce and extend their rights is having a chilling effect on emerging cultural creativity and commentary. A lot rests on the outcomes of ongoing legal battles.

Fortunately, net users – and educators – in many countries have *fair use* or *fair dealing* laws on their side, as well as specific educational copyright exemptions. They can also make use of works which are in the public domain, though these vary by jurisdiction, or works which have been placed under *Creative Commons (CC) licences* (creativecommons.org/licenses/). By the end of 2010, *CC licences* had been applied to over 400 million digital works by their creators (not including Wikipedia, which is also CC-licensed). These works include more than 100 million Flickr photos as well as many Scribd documents, Slideshare slides and YouTube videos. This opens up millions of resources for educational and other kinds of reuse. It is important that, as teachers, we explore our full rights (such as *fair use* or *fair dealing* rights) and options (such as using public domain or *Creative Commons* resources) in our given contexts, while simultaneously ensuring that we and our students work within local laws. After all, as timely as the wider war against the excesses of copyright may be, the classroom probably isn't the place to play out its battles.

While *copyright* is invoked legally, *plagiarism* is mostly invoked academically. Like copyright breaches, it's easier to commit but also easier to detect in a digital context. And again like copyright, plagiarism is an increasingly grey area, especially given the wider web 2.0 culture of borrowing and sharing, quoting and remixing, and implicit rather than explicit attribution. In the context of a participatory culture, and in view of literacy's growing emphasis on (re-)design, it may be time for educators to rethink traditional attitudes towards cultural referencing. Perhaps we should actively encourage thoughtful use of appropriation, even if we continue to insist on explicit attribution. At the same time we could approach assignments more imaginatively: requiring more personal input or synthesis from students; asking them to adopt a process approach to writing, where they submit successive drafts of work (see Chapter 3: *Choosing activities for different levels and contexts, Students' linguistic competence* and *Assessing digital work*); or engaging them in a trans-media approach, where they present work in different media formats or on different media platforms at different stages of a project. More creative approaches to plagiarism may ultimately open up innovative ways of teaching and learning better suited to contemporary cultural needs.

■ For more discussion of copyright and plagiarism, see: Blum (2009); Hyde (2011); Kress (2010); Lessig (2007); Lessig (2008); Patry (2009); Patry (2011); Sheridan and Rowsell (2010).

■ For more practical guides to copyright, see: Aufderheide and Jaszi (2011); Hobbs (2010).

■ For more on Creative Commons, see: Creative Commons (2011).

Many young people are already producing remixes and acquiring digital literacy skills in the process: as far back as 2006, 26 per cent of US 12–17-year-olds had remixed online content (Lenhart *et al.*, 2007), a figure which has certainly increased since then. But, given that much remixed material either lacks the critical edge necessary to make new meanings (Grant, 2010) or, worse, uses its critical edge to fashion negative propaganda (Morozov, 2011), there is considerable room for educational intervention. We can also invite students to reflect on when and how it might be appropriate to complement their (re-)designs with older strategies centred on conventional composition and critique. But, as teachers, we ourselves need to reflect on the limits placed on remix in typical educational contexts, where students' powers of critique and creativity are hemmed in by institutional fears over copyright and plagiarism (see Box 1.12) as well as requirements to turn out academically and publicly acceptable end products (Hobbs, 2011; McBride, 2011).

As a medium of cultural commentary, remix is continuing to grow in significance. In education, it offers an obvious way to harness our students' enthusiasm, focus their attention on important current issues, and help them develop the multiple literacies which feed into remix – while concurrently developing a familiarity with the hallmark macroliteracy of the digital era.

Looking ahead

Educational policies which curtail students' access to the wealth of digital information and communication they access regularly outside the classroom are sending a dangerous message to young people. For John Hartley (2009, p. 105), the message is 'that formal education's top priority is not to make [kids] digitally literate but to "protect" them from "inappropriate" content and online predators'. For Henry Jenkins (2009), the message is:

> that what they do in their online lives has nothing to do with the things they are learning in school; and that what they are learning in school has little or nothing of value to contribute to who they are once the bell rings.

Not only will this make literacies acquired outside the classroom seem more important than those learned within it, but it will open up a new digital divide between those whose socio-economic backgrounds permit them to acquire digital literacies in their own time, and those who are less fortunate (Lankshear and Knobel, 2008a; Pegrum, 2011). This cannot help but extend existing inequalities into the future, as 'those who aren't digitally literate will miss out on crucial educational and economic opportunities' (Susan Crawford, cited in Quitney Anderson and Rainie, 2010, p. 26).

Box 1.13 What do new technologies mean for people and the planet?

For all its benefits, technology use can have negative side effects for *human physical and mental health*. These include *internet addiction*, which, as a behavioural addiction, is still controversial among psychologists, but is already recognised and treated in rehabilitation centres in China and South Korea; the somewhat milder *sleep deprivation* noted by teachers among students who spend their nights gaming or texting; and rising *stress levels* as well as a proliferation of symptoms mirroring *attention disorders*, in both cases linked to information and communication overload (see Box 1.7). The most dramatic effects, however, may be yet to emerge from the rewiring of the brain (especially young brains) in technologically immersive environments. It will be years before we can draw up a balance sheet of the resulting pros and cons. In the meantime, we might encourage our students to take a more balanced approach to their use of technology – including switching it off from time to time – as well as modelling such an approach ourselves (see Box 1.8).

There are also negative effects on the *environment.* The manufacture and use of digital technologies is estimated to account for some 2–2.5 per cent of global carbon emissions, not dissimilar to the amount generated by the airline industry. There's also a crisis emerging around the growing *e-waste* dumps in the developing world, where toxic chemicals are leaching into the soil and poisoning the people (often young children) who try to scavenge spare parts and precious metals for resale. Fortunately, a range of political and commercial initiatives are now pushing in the direction of *green IT.* As a society, we certainly need to rethink our desire for disposable tools – computers, printers and phones – that we discard after only a few years. This is a conversation we should have with our students, as well as considering the consequences for our own lives.

- For more on technology's effects on the mind, see: Aboujaoude (2011); Greenfield (2008); Hallowell (2007); Small and Vorgan (2008); Turkle (2011).

- For more on technology's effects on the environment, see: Bily (2009); Dunn (2010); Grossman (2006).

As language teachers, we're well placed to promote digital literacies in the classroom, integrating them with traditional language and literacy teaching as we help equip our students with the full suite of literacies they will need as members of increasingly digitised social networks, as twenty-first-century employees, and as citizens of a world facing human and environmental challenges on a planetary scale (see Box 1.13). In the process, we can enrich our lessons, enhance our teaching spaces, and ensure we remain lifelong learners. The next chapter contains suggestions on where to begin.

Further reading

- For further theoretical reading on digital literacies, see: Baynham and Prinsloo (2009); Carrington and Robinson (2009); Coiro *et al.* (2008); Gee and Hayes (2011); Kalantzis and Cope (2012); Lankshear and Knobel (2006); Lankshear and Knobel (2008b). (See also: Chapter 2: *Further reading.*)

Chapter 2
From implications to application

If the first step for teachers is to recognise new literacies, the second is to integrate them into everyday lessons. After introducing two mutually supporting frameworks for incorporating new technologies into teaching, this chapter suggests many examples of activities under each of the four main focus points described in the last chapter (see Chapter 1: *A framework of digital literacies*). While the main emphasis is on teaching and learning English, most activities can be easily adapted for different language learning or communication contexts. As a teacher, you can pick and choose from the activities, adapting them to your own context and confidence level, as you begin integrating digital literacies with your teaching of language and conventional literacy skills.

Box 2.1 Will new technologies improve my students' learning?

Conclusive evidence of whether new technologies improve teaching and learning is elusive. The *No Significant Difference* phenomenon, established in Thomas Russell's review of hundreds of studies dating back to 1928, shows that new technologies generally do little harm. Actual improvements are much harder to demonstrate. Researchers note that it all depends on what we measure. Educational benefits may not always be reflected in traditional assessments: an exam focused on print literacy, for example, tells us little about students' digital literacies (see Chapter 3: *Assessing digital work*, for ideas on assessing other literacies).

Nevertheless, those studies which do find significant differences tend to find improvements with the use of technology. This is the conclusion reached in Russell's review of studies from the past few decades, as well as in a landmark 2009 US Department of Education report, *Evaluation of Evidence-Based Practices in Online Learning*, based on a review of over

1,000 empirical studies, which found small improvements in online learning relative to face-to-face learning, with greater improvements still in blended learning (see Box 2.2). But it has been suggested that improvements in technology-supported courses may be due to the enthusiasm of teachers or the (re-)design of the courses, rather than the technology itself.

It's apparent that new technologies can be repurposed to support very different pedagogical approaches, but the affordances of the technologies do encourage some uses rather than others. The informational orientation of web 1.0, for example, sat well with transmission and behaviourist approaches, while the interactive tools of web 2.0 sit comfortably with contemporary collaborative, learner-centred approaches like social constructivism, inquiry-based learning and problem-based learning. Similarly, as noted earlier, many mobile educational apps are oriented towards consumption, being based on information transmission or drill and practice exercises, though productive apps which mimic or parallel the creativity and collaboration of web 2.0 are now appearing (see Chapter 1: *First focus: Language, Mobile literacy*). To the extent that web 2.0 tools – and productive mobile apps – bring educational benefits, it's more about the accompanying pedagogical approaches than the tools themselves.

- For more on the No Significant Difference phenomenon, see: Russell (2010).

- For more on the difficulties of assessing the impact of new technologies on education, see: Beins (2011); Egbert *et al.* (2011); Liu *et al.* (2012); Livingstone (2009); Richardson and Mancabelli (2011); Selwyn (2011).

- For more on the fit between web 2.0 and contemporary pedagogy, see: Pegrum (2009).

The TPACK framework for integrating technology use

The best-known model for incorporating new technologies into teaching is probably Mishra and Koehler's (2006) TPACK (originally TPCK) framework, which depicts teachers' integrated Technological, Pedagogical and Content Knowledge. Effectively, it suggests teachers should be aiming to reach a point where their traditional content and pedagogical knowledge is enhanced by technological knowledge. Perhaps the most important message of the

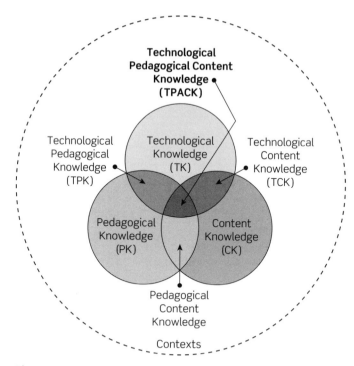

The TPACK Framework
Source: www.tpck.org

TPACK framework is that teachers remain content and pedagogical experts; technological expertise is an additional dimension which complements rather than replacing or superseding their existing knowledge and skills base. This important realisation should help lay to rest some common fears teachers hold about new technologies (see Box 2.2). Naturally, as the framework also suggests, the optimal educational effects come from the integration of teachers' CK, PK and TK. Given that certain technologies sit most easily with certain pedagogies (see Box 2.1), there is some circularity of influence in the overall teaching ecology, but as a general rule we would argue that content and pedagogy should take primacy over technology in curriculum design and lesson planning.

The TPACK model is helpful in framing technology integration in both preservice teacher training and in-service professional development courses. But because emerging technologies are inherently unstable and constantly changing, teachers' TK – and, by extension, their integrated TPACK – will have to continue to develop outside formal courses (Koehler and Mishra, 2008). To help deal with this need for ongoing learning, PLNs are likely to become an ever more common aspect of teachers' daily practice (see Box 2.2).

Box 2.2 Should I be worried about teaching with new technologies?

These are some common beliefs held by teachers who are worried about new technologies. Do you recognise any of them?

'Digital technologies will replace pedagogy.' Absolutely not. Content and pedagogy come before technology. We must decide on our content and pedagogical aims before determining whether our students should use pens or keyboards, write essays or blogs, or design posters or videos.

'Digital technologies will replace face-to-face teaching.' Face-to-face and online learning both have their advantages. Research overwhelmingly recommends *blended learning* models, which capitalise on their complementary strengths (see Box 2.1).

'Digital technologies will replace teachers.' In some transmission and behaviourist educational approaches, this is possible up to a point. In contemporary collaborative approaches, digital learning spaces may partly replace physical classrooms, but both teachers and students are still very much present and interacting within these spaces.

'Digital technologies aren't designed for education.' That's largely true, but they can be very effectively repurposed for education by teachers who integrate them into their TPACK.

'Digital technologies cause delays and glitches.' Sometimes they do. There's often a temporary slowdown when we first introduce new technologies to do what we're used to doing in an analogue way. Sometimes, too, technologies fail – which was as true of tape recorders and overhead projectors as it is of computers and digital projectors. Experienced teachers have back-up plans.

'Students know more than teachers about digital technologies.' Despite misleading terms like *digital natives* and *the net generation*, students' digital skills are patchy and many of them need support in using technology for educational purposes (see Box 1.2). However, those students with more advanced technological skills can be empowered to play key roles (as technological experts) in productive learning partnerships with teachers (the content and pedagogical experts). This links up with what Marc Prensky calls *partnering pedagogy* in his 2010 book *Teaching Digital Natives*. As teachers, we can model lifelong learning as we improve the technological component of our TPACK through on-the-job

▶

experience, which may include learning about technology from some of our students.

'Students want to use digital technologies all the time.' Numerous surveys have shown that most students prefer a moderate amount of technology use in their education, but they do resent arbitrary educational policies which shut them off from the wealth of online resources and communication channels – their incipient PLNs (see Box 1.10) – which they are used to accessing outside the classroom on mobile or other devices.

'Teachers don't get enough training on digital technologies.' While it's true that pre-service teacher education has only recently begun to focus on digital technologies, in-service professional development courses are becoming more common. But most teachers learn about new technologies in a variety of other ways as well: by experimenting with one tool at a time and gradually building up a repertoire, by learning from digitally able students and, above all, by seeking ideas and support through their PLNs (see Chapter 4: *Building and maintaining PLNs*). Once they see the possibilities for enriching their classes, many teachers begin to find these learning experiences addictive!

The SAMR model for evaluating technology use

The SAMR model, developed by Ruben Puentedura (2011), can be used as a complement to the TPACK framework. It serves as a reminder that some uses of new technologies lead at most to *enhancement* of education, while other uses lead to real *transformation*.

On the lower level, *enhancement*, some uses of technology may involve *substitution* which adds little to the task at hand, like typing an essay on a computer instead of writing it by hand, or emailing an assignment to a teacher instead of physically handing it in. Other uses of technology on this level involve *augmentation*, such as employing word processing tools like spellcheckers, text search, or formatting options.

On the higher level, *transformation*, some uses of technology lead to *modification*, where a task is significantly reshaped, such as through the embedding of multimedia artefacts to complement text-based communication in a reflective diary on a blogging platform (see e.g. Activity 35, *Personal*

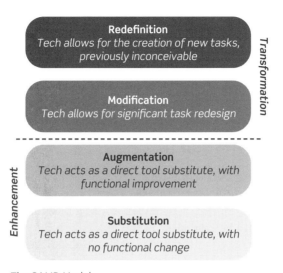

The SAMR Model
Source: Puentedura, 2011

blogging). Finally, the greatest *transformation* is likely to occur through uses of technology which involve a *redefinition*, that is, which allow for completely new tasks that were previously impossible; one example might be the kind of collaborative process writing – and perhaps even multimodal composition – enabled by wikis (see e.g. Activity 40, *Our city guide*). (For further suggestions of tasks at different levels of SAMR, see Gregory, 2010; Hos-McGrane, 2011.)

While the educational value of substitutional and augmentative uses of technologies is limited, they may offer benefits in terms of flexibility and convenience. Indeed, such uses underpin the recently popular notion of *flipped classrooms* (e.g. Thompson, 2011; Tucker, 2012), where traditional content transmission is removed from classroom time – students are asked, for example, to watch instructional videos or listen to lecture podcasts in their own time – so that classroom sessions can be devoted to student inter-action and intensive teacher support. Aided by the rapid development of the Khan Academy (www.khanacademy.org) and the growing provision of open educational resources globally, including free materials on platforms like iTunes U (www.apple.com/education/itunes-u/) and TED (www.ted.com), flipped classrooms are emerging as a valuable model of blended learning.

However, teachers who want to make creative use of new technologies to support collaborative, learner-centred teaching and learning approaches need to orient their TK – as well as their TCK, TPK, and of course TPACK –

towards more transformational ways of integrating those technologies. Wherever possible, the activities outlined in this chapter use technologies in ways that modify or redefine classroom tasks. We thus embrace a transformational approach to the development of traditional language and literacy skills alongside digital literacies.

The digital activities grid

The best way to begin exploring new literacies and new technologies is to start small (as we suggested in Chapter 1). Consider working with one or two new literacies, and a couple of associated technologies, at any given time. The activities in this chapter offer some guidelines on where, as a technologically inexperienced teacher, you can begin experimenting with new literacies and new technologies, and where, as a more experienced teacher, you can further develop the integration of new literacies and new technologies into your language lessons. While some activities privilege one particular digital literacy, some incorporate several new literacies. Between them, they make use of a wide variety of new technologies, mostly in the form of web 2.0 tools and related mobile apps (see Box 1.10 and Table 2.2). All of them sit comfortably alongside, and serve as a complement to, traditional language teaching and learning goals.

The *Digital activities grid*, shown in Table 2.1, is organised according to the main literacy, *Literacy 1*, underpinning each activity. These literacies are presented under the same focus points and in the same order as in the *Framework of digital literacies* (see Chapter 1, Table 1.1). Where an activity incorporates a second or third literacy, these are listed under *Literacy 2*. The *Activity* column gives the title of each activity as well as the activity number, which you can use to find it in the pages that follow. The stars in this column indicate the level of complexity of the literacy involved (see Chapter 3: *Choosing activities for different levels and contexts, Overall complexity*); where there is more than one literacy involved in a particular activity, the most complex literacy determines the overall rating of the activity. The two introductory activities, which do not directly involve digital literacies or technologies, are unrated. The *Tech* column indicates which of the following versions a particular activity has available:

- *High-tech (H)*: suitable for a classroom where the teacher has an internet-enabled computer connected to a data projector, and students have access to enough internet-enabled computers or mobile devices to allow them to work in small groups, pairs, or even individually.

- *Low-tech (L)*: suitable for a classroom where the teacher has an internet-enabled computer connected to a data projector, but students do not have access to internet-enabled computers or mobile devices.

- *No-tech (N)*: suitable for a classroom where there is no internet-enabled computer available, although some of these activities require the teacher to access an internet-enabled computer outside the classroom and print out materials to bring to class.

Most activities assume there is a board – a whiteboard or blackboard – available in the classroom. Activities that involve the internet assume that a web browser is available on the internet-enabled devices; the best options when using web 2.0 tools include Chrome, Firefox or, on an Apple device, Safari. The *Topic* column gives the main topic or topics of each activity, while subsequent columns list activity *Aims* and indicate the *Language* focus (generally vocabulary, grammar, functions and skills). The final column lists the suggested *Time* for each activity. Beneath the *Digital activities grid* is a *Digital tools grid* (Table 2.2) showing key technological tools, loosely grouped into tool types, along with the main related activities in which they are used or discussed; some teachers may wish to start here.

Wherever an activity requires or suggests that teachers and/or students should create digital documents or artefacts, *Tech support* links for all the major tools needed are provided alongside the activity itself. These typically give an overview of the tool in question (e.g. wikis) as well as links to the help pages of recommended services (e.g. PBworks or Wikispaces). This allows teachers to judge from the outset how much technological knowledge is required. If our text is used primarily to develop students' digital literacies (see Chapter 3: *Incorporating activities into the syllabus and timetable, The digital literacies-driven approach*), the *Tech support* sections can be used to support the development of students' technological competence. If our text is used to develop teachers' digital literacies, the *Tech support* sections can be used to build teachers' own technological competence (see Chapter 3: *Choosing activities for different levels and contexts, Teachers' technological competence*).

Activities 1–50 follow immediately after the *Digital tools grid*. Worksheets are provided as appropriate: you will find them at the end of each related activity, or online at www.pearsoned.co.uk/hockly. Answer keys can be found in the Appendix at the end of the text, or at the same URL. All information regarding websites, apps and other digital resources was correct and current at the time of publication, but please note that the availability, format and content of digital materials may change from time to time.

Table 2.1 Digital activities grid

	Literacy 1	Literacy 2	Activity	Tech	Topic
INTRO			1 Technology past & present	H L N	Common technologies
			2 Being digitally literate	H L N	Technology habits
FIRST FOCUS: LANGUAGE	print		3 Writing the news*	H L N	Odd news
		information	4 Extreme weather***	H L N	Weather, environment
	texting		5 Cryptic messages*	H N	Textspeak
		print	6 Codeswitching*	H N	Textspeak
	hypertext		7 Sports linking**	H L N	Sports
		search; information	8 Building links***	H	Controversies

Aims	Language	Time
To raise awareness of and introduce the topic of digital literacies	Vocabulary: Common technologies Grammar: Can/can't Functions: Discussing abilities Skills: Reading, speaking	60 mins
To raise awareness of digital literacies and reliance on technology	Vocabulary: Gadgets; the internet Grammar: Adverbs of frequency; present simple tense; question forms Functions: Discussing habits and daily routines Skills: Reading, speaking, writing	45 mins
To examine a particular online text genre and recreate it	Vocabulary: General Grammar: Narrative (past) tenses Functions: Narrating Skills: Reading, speaking, writing	90 mins
To raise awareness of how to convey a message via different genres of online text	Vocabulary: Weather, environment Grammar: Present simple tense (for facts); past simple tense (for news events) Register: Formal versus informal communication Functions: Giving opinions; discussing facts versus opinions Skills: Reading, speaking, writing	60 mins
To raise awareness of L2 textspeak conventions	Vocabulary: Textspeak, abbreviations and emoticons Register: Informal communication Functions: Discussing; giving opinions Skills: Reading, speaking, writing	45 mins
To raise awareness of codeswitching	Vocabulary: Textspeak, abbreviations and emoticons Register: Informal versus formal communication Skills: Reading, speaking	60 mins
To raise awareness of the appropriate use of hyperlinks in online texts, and the effects of hyperlinks on reading	Vocabulary: Sports; biographies Grammar: Narrative tenses Functions: Narrating; discussing Skills: Reading, speaking, writing	60 mins
To find supporting evidence for a point of view, and to raise awareness of the role hyperlinked materials play in learning	Vocabulary: Controversial topics Functions: Expressing agreement and disagreement; expressing opinions Skills: Reading, speaking	90 mins

Literacy 1	Literacy 2	Activity	Tech	Topic
multimedia		9 Food boards***	H L N	Foods, recipes
	search	10 Copycat***	H L N	Animals
		11 Envisioning the facts***	H L N	Information overload
		12 Sales techniques***	H	Advertising
		13 Showcasing hobbies***	H L	Hobbies
		14 Selling English***	H L	Advertising
		15 Transmedia stories***	H	Adventure stories
gaming	personal	16 Avatars****	H L N	Appearance, personality
		17 Choose your own adventure****	H L	Adventure games

FIRST FOCUS: LANGUAGE

Aims	Language	Time
To create online multimedia boards	Vocabulary: Food; recipes Grammar: Sequencing adverbs Functions: Describing a process Skills: Writing, speaking, reading	60 mins
To raise awareness of copyright and the appropriate use of digital images	Vocabulary: Animals (or any lexical sets) Grammar: Can/can't; present simple tense Functions: Describing (animals) Skills: Listening, writing	45 mins
To produce an infographic about technology use	Vocabulary: Information, facts and figures Grammar: Present simple tense (for facts); question forms Functions: Presenting factual information Skills: Reading, writing	90 mins
To produce an advertisement in the form of a vodcast	Vocabulary: Advertisements Functions: Describing objects and functions Skills: Speaking, writing	120 mins
To produce an audio-visual slideshow	Grammar: Present simple tense Functions: Describing objects and actions; giving opinions; giving instructions Skills: Listening, speaking, reading, writing	90 mins
To create an advertising collage in the form of a vodcast	Vocabulary: Advertising; filming Grammar: Comparative and superlative adjectives Functions: Discussing Skills: Reading, speaking, writing	90 mins
To produce a transmedia episode of a popular online story	Grammar: Narrative (present and past) tenses Functions: Narrating Skills: Reading, speaking, writing	180 mins
To raise awareness of online identity and virtual worlds/games	Vocabulary: Appearance; personality Grammar: Is; has/have got Functions: Describing people Skills: Speaking, reading, writing, listening	60 mins
To raise awareness of and implement basic game design	Vocabulary: Mystery, adventure and crime Grammar: Present simple tense; narrative tenses Functions: Narrating Skills: Writing, reading, speaking	90 mins

	Literacy 1	Literacy 2	Activity	Tech	Topic
FIRST FOCUS: LANGUAGE	mobile	multimedia; gaming	18 History hunt****	H L	Local history
		multimedia; personal	19 A picture a day****	H L	Daily life
			20 Mobile rules****	H L N	Mobile phone rules
	code		21 HTML basics*****	H L	Animals
		multimedia	22 HTML advanced*****	H L	Animals
SECOND FOCUS: INFORMATION	tagging	multimedia	23 Travel clouds***	H L	Travel
			24 Travel tags***	H L N	Travel
	search		25 Search race***	H L	Pollution, environment
		information	26 Search me***	H L N	Personalised search

Aims	Language	Time
To create a local history quiz in the form of a multimedia mobile app	Vocabulary: Buildings; historical events Grammar: Passive voice; past simple tense; question forms Skills: Reading, writing, speaking, listening	180 mins
To document daily life through a series of photos	Vocabulary: Any Grammar: Any Functions: Discussing daily routines, habits and customs Skills: Speaking, writing	90 mins
To raise awareness of the impact of mobile devices on learning, and to negotiate a fair use policy for class	Vocabulary: Mobile devices; learning; habits Grammar: Modal verbs (for permission and obligation) Functions: Giving opinions; expressing agreement and disagreement; discussing rules Skills: Speaking, writing, reading	60 mins
To raise awareness of HTML and how it works	Vocabulary: Animals; formatting of documents Skills: Reading, writing	60 mins
To raise awareness of HTML and media embedding	Vocabulary: Animals Skills: Reading, writing	60 mins
To raise awareness of the concept of tag clouds by exploring word clouds, and to investigate how key words in the text can be visually represented in a word cloud	Vocabulary: Travel and tourism; cities Grammar: Present simple tense (for facts) Functions: Describing a town or city Skills: Reading, writing, speaking	60 mins
To increase familiarity with the concept of tag clouds	Vocabulary: Travel and tourism; cities Grammar: Present simple tense (for facts); parts of speech Functions: Describing a town or city Skills: Reading, speaking, writing	60 mins
To explore a variety of search engines	Vocabulary: Pollution; environment Grammar: Present simple tense; passive voice Functions: Expressing likes and dislikes Skills: Reading, writing, speaking, listening	60 mins
To raise awareness of how search engines filter results for individuals, and how this can impact on their studies/work	Grammar: Modal verbs (for probability) Functions: Expressing probability Skills: Speaking, reading, writing	60 mins

Literacy 1	Literacy 2	Activity	Tech	Topic
information		27 Tree octopus***	H L N	Endangered animals
	search	28 Fun facts***	H L N	Unusual facts
filtering	network	29 News in my networks***	H L N	News
		30 Connecting people***	H L N	Social circles
		31 My digital life***	H L N	Technologies
	network	32 Turn off, tune out***	H L N	Digital communications

SECOND FOCUS: INFORMATION

Aims	Language	Time
To raise awareness of the importance of evaluating information on websites, by visiting a number of spoof websites	Vocabulary: Endangered animals and habitats; websites Grammar: Present simple tense (for scientific facts) Functions: Giving opinions Skills: Reading, speaking	60 mins
To raise awareness of how to check online sources	Vocabulary: Animals Grammar: Present simple tense (for facts) Functions: Expressing opinions; discussing facts versus opinions Skills: Reading, listening, speaking	45 mins
To develop the ability to filter information, and to discuss news and current affairs	Vocabulary: News and current affairs Grammar: Past tenses; reporting verbs; passive voice Functions: Discussing current affairs; giving opinions Skills: Reading, speaking	90 mins
To explore the idea of filtering information through social connections	Vocabulary: Personal skills; interests and hobbies Grammar: Present simple tense; can/can't Functions: Discussing abilities and interests Skills: Speaking, writing	60 mins
To discuss attention and offer advice on how to improve it	Vocabulary: Technologies; habits and daily routines Grammar: Present simple tense Functions: Describing routines Skills: Listening, speaking, reading, writing	60 mins
To raise awareness of how multiple information and communication channels can affect our daily lives, and explore ways of filtering out digital distractions	Vocabulary: Technology, gadgets and the internet Grammar: Past tenses Functions: Discussing Skills: Writing, speaking	60 mins

THIRD FOCUS: CONNECTIONS

Literacy 1	Literacy 2	Activity	Tech	Topic
personal	network	33 Faking it***	H L N	Famous people
	multimedia	34 Online me***	H L N	Personal information
	print; multimedia	35 Personal blogging***	H L N	Hobbies, interests
	network	36 Setting the scene***	N	Digital safety
		37 Footprints in the wires***	H L N	Digital identity
network	multimedia	38 Going viral***	H L	Viral videos
	filtering	39 A class PLN***	H	PLNs

Aims	Language	Time
To raise awareness of social networking profiles, online identity and identity management	Vocabulary: Famous people and biographies; personal information Grammar: Present simple tense Functions: Giving personal information; discussing Skills: Reading, writing, speaking	60 mins
To raise awareness of online identity, and how to present yourself online	Vocabulary: Personal information; hobbies and interests Grammar: Present simple tense; would Functions: Talking about yourself; discussing what you would or wouldn't do Skills: Speaking, writing, reading	60 mins
To raise awareness of the value of blogging	Vocabulary: Hobbies and interests Grammar: Present simple tense; adverbs of frequency; question forms Functions: Describing hobbies and interests Skills: Writing, reading, speaking, listening	90 mins
To help students learn to deal with challenging or inappropriate online behaviour	Grammar: Should; second conditional Functions: Giving advice and making suggestions Skills: Reading, speaking	60 mins
To create a poster with advice on managing digital footprints	Vocabulary: Internet scams; technology; online identity Grammar: Past simple tense; narrative tenses; should; second conditional Functions: Giving advice and making suggestions; discussing Skills: Speaking, listening, reading, writing	90 mins
To encourage students to explore the phenomenon of viral videos, and to contribute their views to a public forum	Vocabulary: Videos and filming Grammar: Present simple tense; verbs of liking and disliking Functions: Expressing likes and dislikes; giving opinions Skills: Listening, speaking, writing, reading	60 mins
To help students understand the value of learning through others in networks outside the classroom	Vocabulary: Any Grammar: Any Functions: Expressing likes and dislikes; giving opinions Skills: Speaking, reading, writing	60 mins

Literacy 1	Literacy 2	Activity	Tech	Topic
participatory	print	40 Our city guide***	H L N	Travel, tourism
		41 Our city on Wikipedia***	H L N	Travel, tourism
	multimedia	42 Flickr vocabulary book***	H L	General
		43 A good cause***	H L N	Global & local issues
intercultural	multimedia	44 Vox pop****	H L N	Culture
		45 Global dancing****	H L	Countries
	print	46 Travel tips****	H L N	Travel advice

THIRD FOCUS: CONNECTIONS

Aims	Language	Time
To encourage students to contribute to a class wiki	Vocabulary: Travel, tourism and cities Grammar: Present simple tense; past simple tense (for historical facts) Functions: Describing city sites, history, food, etc. Skills: Writing, reading	60 mins
To show students how to contribute to a public wiki	Vocabulary: Travel, tourism and cities Grammar: Present simple tense; past simple tense (for historical facts) Functions: Stating facts Skills: Writing, reading	60 mins
To produce an online vocabulary source	Vocabulary: Any Grammar: Any Skills: Writing	90 mins
To encourage students to explore the world of online campaigning and transpose it to their own contexts	Vocabulary: Global and local issues; current affairs Grammar: Present simple tense; comparative and superlative adjectives (for ranking) Functions: Discussing current affairs and issues; expressing opinions Skills: Speaking, listening, reading, writing	60 mins
To make a vodcast about culture	Vocabulary: Food; weather; music; entertainment; physical appearances Grammar: Present simple tense Functions: Making suggestions; discussing Skills: Listening, speaking, writing	60 mins
To introduce the topic of countries, cultures and travel	Vocabulary: Countries, cultures, travel, languages and customs Grammar: Present simple tense; past simple tense Functions: Giving opinions; discussing Skills: Speaking	90 mins
To consider cultural norms in different societies	Vocabulary: Travel, culture, behaviour, customs and food Grammar: Modal verbs (for permission and obligation) Functions: Giving advice and making suggestions; discussing rules Skills: Speaking, reading, writing	90 mins

Literacy 1	Literacy 2	Activity	Tech	Topic
remix	texting; multimedia	47 LOLcats*****	H L N	Cats
		48 Texting Hillary*****	H L	Popular culture
	multimedia	49 I'mma let you finish*****	H L N	Celebrities, famous people
		50 Movie mashup*****	H L	Cinema

FOURTH FOCUS: (RE-)DESIGN

Aims	Language	Time
To explore and respond to an internet meme, and to begin learning about remix	Vocabulary: Cats Grammar: Present simple tense Register: Informal versus standard communication Functions: Giving opinions; discussing Skills: Reading, speaking, writing	60 mins
To further explore internet memes and the phenomenon of remix	Vocabulary: Mobile phones; textspeak Grammar: Present simple tense Register: Informal communication Functions: Giving opinions; discussing Skills: Reading, speaking, writing	60 mins
To further explore internet memes and the phenomenon of remix	Vocabulary: Celebrities and famous people; music; textspeak Grammar: Present simple tense Register: Informal communication Functions: Giving opinions; discussing Skills: Reading, speaking, writing	60 mins
To create a remix by adding original subtitles to a film trailer	Vocabulary: Cinema and films Grammar: Present simple tense; present continuous tense Functions: Creating dialogues and narratives; describing scenes Skills: Writing, speaking	60 mins

Table 2.2 Digital tools grid

Key types of software, web tools & apps	Key examples of software, web tools & apps	Key activities where they may be used or discussed
Aggregators	Flipboard Netvibes Symbaloo	29 25 25
Avatar creators	Build Your Wild Self CYOS Meez	16 16 16
Blogs	Blogger Edublogs	3, 4, 8, 10, 18, 22, 24, 31, 32, 34, 48, 49 3, 4, 8, 10, 18, 22, 24, 31, 32, 34, 35, 48, 49
Digital storytelling	Capzles Tiki-Toki	43 43
Document sharing	Google Docs	33
Gaming	Club Penguin Habbo Moshi Monsters Pick a Path The Sims World of Warcraft	16 16 16 17 16 16
HTML generators	Easy HTML Tag Generator Online HTML Code Generator Quackit	21, 22 21 21
Infographics	Easel.ly Piktochart	11 11
Mapping	Google Maps	18
Microblogging	Twitter	4, 16, 25, 28, 29, 30, 39
Mobile learning	Foursquare SCVNGR Wikitude	18 18 18
Multimedia sharing	Glogster (EDU) VoiceThread	18, 33, 34, 36, 37, 43 13, 15, 43
Photosharing	Flickr Instagram Pinterest Posterous Spaces Smilebox	10, 13, 15, 17, 22, 24, 25, 37, 42, 47 19 9 19 19

Key types of software, web tools & apps	Key examples of software, web tools & apps	Key activities where they may be used or discussed
Podcasting [audio editing]	Audacity GarageBand	43 43
Polling	SurveyMonkey	2, 11
Presentation software	Keynote PowerPoint Prezi	8, 11, 13, 15, 31, 37, 47, 48, 49 8, 11, 13, 15, 16, 17, 31, 37, 47, 48, 49 8, 11, 13, 15, 31, 37
Quizzes	Quizlet QuizStar	18 46
Search	General Google (Advanced) Google Images	25 15, 25, 26 10, 13, 15, 47
Social networking	Edmodo Facebook Historical Facebook Lesson LinkedIn My Fake Wall The Wall Machine	30, 39 4, 16, 20, 25, 29, 30, 31, 32, 33, 36, 39 33 16, 33 33 33
Subtitling	CaptionTube Overstream Subtitle Horse	50 50 50
Virtual worlds	Second Life	16
Vodcasting [video editing]	iMovie Movie Maker	12, 14, 15, 38, 43 12, 14, 15, 38, 43
Vodcasting [videosharing]	Vimeo YouTube	12, 14, 38, 44 12, 14, 17, 22, 25, 37, 38, 44, 50
Wikis	PBworks (Simple English) Wikipedia Wikispaces	7, 8, 18, 20, 31, 32, 34, 40, 46 7, 16, 23, 25, 40, 41 7, 8, 18, 20, 31, 32, 34, 40, 46
Word cloud generators	TagCrowd Tagxedo Wordle	23 23 23
Word processing software	Apple Pages Microsoft Word	8, 10, 11, 16, 21, 23, 24, 30, 38, 40, 41, 50 8, 10, 11, 16, 21, 23, 24, 30, 38, 40, 41, 50
Other	ImageCodr TED/TEDiSUB	10 26, 38

Activity 1: Technology past and present

Students reflect on past and present technologies, and the skills we need to be able to use them.

This activity raises awareness of digital literacy skills by placing them in the context of technologies in general, both past and present. When integrating digital literacies into the syllabus, this activity is a good starting point. It also functions as a diagnostic activity for both students and teachers.

Literacy: **Digital literacies**

Topic: Common technologies

Aim: To raise awareness of and introduce the topic of digital literacies

Level: Lower intermediate +

Time: 60 minutes

Language	
Areas	*Vocabulary:* Common technologies *Grammar:* Can/can't
Functions	Discussing abilities
Skills	Reading, speaking

Resources	
High-tech	*Documents:* Online worksheet (www.pearsoned.co.uk/hockly)
Low-tech	*Documents:* Printed worksheet (follows Activity)
No-tech	*Documents:* Printed worksheet (follows Activity)

Procedure

1. Put the following words on the board, or use images of each object (see Activity 10, *Copycat* for how to find Creative Commons-licensed images):

   - map
   - clock

- car
- refrigerator
- TV
- internet

Ask students to work individually to put these words into two categories (they need to decide on the categories). Put students into pairs to compare their categories and explain their choices. Get feedback on the categories they've chosen. Note that there is no single correct answer here; it simply gives students a chance to think about the words/images by creating personalised categories or groupings.

2. Ask students what these words all have in common (*they are all technologies that have changed our lives*). Ask students to work in pairs to put the words into chronological order, depending on when each technology was invented, and to think of one advantage and one disadvantage that each technology has brought us.

3. For feedback, put the following grid on the board. The advantages and disadvantages below are suggestions – students may come up with different ideas, which you should add to the grid.

Technology	Advantage	Disadvantage
Map	Maps help us find our way	Some maps are difficult to read
Clock	Clocks help us divide up our day	We become too concerned about time
Car	Cars make getting around much faster	Cars use petrol and pollute the environment
Refrigerator	We can keep food fresh	We sometimes overeat because we have easy access to food
TV	We can watch excellent programmes and news	Some people spend too much time watching TV
Internet	We have instant access to news, information and friends	Some people find it difficult to switch off, and become addicted to the internet

4. Add a third column (*Skills needed to use this technology*) to the grid on the board:

Technology	Skills needed to use this technology
Map	Understand how to show geography visually
Clock	Understand how to show time visually
Car	Know how to drive
Refrigerator	Know how long certain foods will last in the fridge (e.g. meat)
TV	Know how to use a remote control, change channels, record programmes, etc.
Internet	

Elicit some of the skills needed to use each of these technologies, and fill in the grid. Leave the skills needed to use the internet blank for the moment. Ask students to discuss this in pairs, and to come up with two or three skills. You may want to give them a couple of items from **Activity 1 Worksheet – Internet skills**, to get them started.

5. Ask students to refer to the worksheet and to individually tick the skills they are confident with. Then ask students to compare their worksheet checklists in pairs or small groups. Ask them to consider what skills their pair or small group is most and least confident with.

6. Conduct feedback. Explain to students that you plan to integrate an element of digital literacy skills into their English classes (see Chapter 3: *Incorporating activities into the syllabus and timetable*). Ask for their views and opinions on this. You may want to emphasise that this will not become the main focus of their English classes, but that it's very important for them to develop the language and other skills they need to make effective use of technologies in English. This is more and more important, for example, for college and university entry, and for many careers. Ask each student to add their name to their worksheet, and to hand it in to you. Students can send you the online worksheet by email (high-tech version), or simply give you the printed worksheet (low-tech and no-tech versions).

7. Each of the statements on the worksheet maps on to specific activities in this text (see Appendix: Answer keys). After class, carefully go through these worksheets to see how well developed individual students' digital literacies are, and also how well developed the skills are in the class over-all. Having a clear idea from the outset of the level of your students' digital literacy skills will help you with integrating these activities into your syllabus. It will also help you pair up students, as for certain tasks you can put individuals with stronger technological skills together with those with less developed skills. After you have worked on developing your students' digital literacies over a period of time (e.g. an academic year), you could ask students to fill in the worksheet checklist again. Then give them back their original worksheets, and let them compare what skills they have developed in the interim.

Extension

Encourage students to add their completed checklists to their e-portfolios (see Chapter 3: *Assessing digital work, Assessing through e-portfolios*) and review them regularly, so that they can keep track of their improving digital skills (high-tech version).

Activity 1 Worksheet – Internet skills

What skills do we need to use computers and the internet effectively? Below are some suggestions. Tick the box if you feel confident with each skill. Leave blank the skills you are unsure about. These skills are also called *digital literacies*.

I can . . .

☐ use digital technologies in my daily life (e.g. a mobile phone, a computer . . .)

☐ create different types of online texts (e.g. blog posts, status updates, tweets . . .)

☐ write mobile phone text messages in my own language and in English

☐ recognise when I should and shouldn't use *textspeak* (abbreviated SMS language)

☐ create an online text with an appropriate number of hyperlinks

☐ understand how the use of hyperlinks can influence a reader's opinion

☐ create a multimedia noticeboard

☐ find online images that I am free to use

☐ produce an *infographic* (a display of facts and figures on a given topic)

☐ understand how online images can be used to create or manipulate opinions

☐ combine media (e.g. images, audio and video) into a digital product

☐ create an online *avatar* (character)

☐ create a simple online game

☐ use multiple media (images, audio and video) on a mobile phone

☐ share multimedia artefacts (images, audio and video) with others online

☐ use my own mobile devices for learning

☐ recognise when it's appropriate or inappropriate to use mobile devices in class

☐ understand HTML code

☐ interpret word clouds

☐ navigate tag clouds

☐ use a variety of search engines for different types of online searches

☐ understand personalised search

☐ evaluate information I find online

☐ filter online information to find what is useful and relevant to me

☐ cope with digital distractions

☐ manage my own online identity or identities

☐ set up a personal blog

☐ deal with difficult people or situations online

☐ manage my digital footprint

☐ understand and follow a 'viral' image or video

☐ set up and use a PLN (Personal Learning Network)

☐ contribute to collaborative online projects (e.g. wikis, photosharing sites . . .)

☐ interpret media artefacts produced in different cultural contexts

☐ understand and contribute to an internet *meme* (an idea or concept spread virally online, e.g. LOLcats)

☐ create a *mashup* or *remix* (a media artefact created by combining and/or altering pre-existing artefacts)

Activity 2: Being digitally literate

Students discuss their uses of various technologies and websites.

This activity introduces the theme of digital literacies and skills by examining how students currently use gadgets and what they do online. It follows on well from Activity 1, *Technology past and present.*

Literacy:	**Digital literacies**
Topic:	Technology habits
Aim:	To raise awareness of digital literacies and reliance on technology
Level:	Intermediate +
Time:	45 minutes + homework
Tech support:	Polling:

- General: e-language.wikispaces.com/polling
- SurveyMonkey: help.surveymonkey.com

Language	
Areas	*Vocabulary:* Gadgets; the internet *Grammar:* Adverbs of frequency; present simple tense; question forms
Functions	Discussing habits and daily routines
Skills	Reading, speaking, writing

Resources	
High-tech	*Equipment:* Internet-enabled student computers or mobile devices (one each) *Documents:* Online worksheet (www.pearsoned.co.uk/hockly)
Low-tech	*Documents:* Printed worksheet (follows Activity)
No-tech	*Documents:* Printed worksheet (follows Activity)

Procedure

1. Introduce the topic by telling students about a typical day in your 'digital life', referring, as far as possible, to points mentioned on **Activity 2 Worksheet – Digital me**. If you can, bring in some of the devices you use on a daily basis and let students see them. Encourage them to ask questions.

2. Divide the class into pairs and assign each student a role (A or B). Once each student has looked at their own questions, pairs should work through the questions together. Give them plenty of time to do this. Some of the questions should elicit longer answers as students get into the details of their digital lives.

3. Conduct feedback as a whole group. Elicit stories and anecdotes from the group as you go through the questions.

4. Open the discussion up to a wider set of issues. Suggested topics include:

   - Do you rely on technology too much each day?
   - Do you spend too much time with gadgets and not enough with people?
   - What would you do without your mobile phone for a day?
   - What would you do without the internet for a day?
   - What technologies would you like to use in class?
   - Do you think mobile phones should be turned off in class?

Variation

If you have time, you could make the worksheet into an online survey using a tool such as SurveyMonkey (www.surveymonkey.com). In addition to the speaking activity you could then get students to complete the survey online, perhaps as part of a homework assignment (high-tech version). This would provide a set of statistics that would be useful for a writing task of the kind found in exams such as IELTS.

Extension

Set students a homework writing task in which they describe a day in the life of a 'digital resident' (see Box 1.2), explaining what gadgets they have, and how they use them each day.

Activity 2 Worksheet – Digital me

Student A

Look at these questions and think about your own answers. Now ask your partner the questions. If you can answer 'yes' to any of the questions, give more details.

1. Do you check your email first thing in the morning?

2. When going out in town do you first check the web for suggestions?

3. Do you share your digital photos online for friends and family to see?

4. Do you often use your credit card to pay online?

5. Do you often download or buy music online?

6. Do you read blogs often?

7. Do you post comments on other people's blogs?

8. Do you have your own blog that you update regularly?

Student B

Look at these questions and think about your own answers. Now ask your partner the questions. If you can answer 'yes' to any of the questions, give more details.

1. Do you often chat with friends/colleagues online?

2. Do you often share amusing websites with friends/colleagues?

3. Do you have five or more friends you met online?

4. Did you meet your partner online?

5. Have you ever edited a Wikipedia entry?

6. Do you use your mobile phone primarily for texting?

7. Do you get your news online, rather than from a newspaper?

8. Do you usually watch live TV, or record it to watch later?

Activity 3: Writing the news

Students read and write short news articles based on odd news stories.

This activity deconstructs a particular online text genre and then asks students to recreate it. It encourages students to analyse how a text is put together and delivered online. It shows that traditional print literacy skills can also be trained online.

Literacy:	**Print literacy** (complexity: *)
Topic:	Odd news
Aim:	To examine a particular online text genre and recreate it
Level:	Intermediate +
Time:	90 minutes
Tech support:	Blogs:

- General: e-language.wikispaces.com/blogs
- Blogger: support.google.com/blogger/?hl=en
- Edublogs: help.edublogs.org

Language	
Areas	*Vocabulary:* General *Grammar:* Narrative (past) tenses
Functions	Narrating
Skills	Reading, speaking, writing

Resources	
High-tech	*Equipment:* One internet-enabled teacher computer and data projector; internet-enabled student computers or mobile devices (one per group) *Tools (optional):* Individual blogs (see Activity 35, *Personal blogging*) *Documents:* Online news stories

Low-tech	*Equipment:* One internet-enabled teacher computer and data projector *Tools (optional):* Class blog (see Activity 4, *Extreme weather* or Activity 10, *Copycat*) *Documents:* Printed news stories
No-tech	*Documents:* Printed news stories

Digital risks

As with all websites, there is a small risk of inappropriate advertising or other content appearing around the materials you plan to use. Review the news stories before taking them to class, or print them out for a safer working environment if you are worried about this.

Procedure

Before class

- Choose four headlines from the Yahoo Oddly Enough section (uk.news. yahoo.com/oddly-enough/) for use in Step 2, and ensure the stories are suitable for your students.

- Print out the stories which accompany the four headlines, for use in Step 5 (no-tech version).

1. Ask students whether they saw or heard the news before coming to class. What were the top stories, and what were they about? Which news sources did they watch/listen to/read? Were there any variations in the way stories were presented: on the television, on radio, in print media, on the net?

2. Divide the class into four groups and show the four headlines you have chosen from the Yahoo Oddly Enough section (as described above) on the projector screen (high-tech and low-tech versions) or write them on the board (no-tech version). Assign one headline to each group and tell students that they need to decide what their story is about, and that they also need to note down six words they would expect to find in their given story.

3. Redivide the groups so that there is one member from each of the original groups in the new ones. Each student should tell their group what they decided about their story, and the words they thought of.

4. Get the class back into their original groups and ask for some feedback from each group about the likely content of the story they discussed. As each group tells their story, note down the six words they decided would be in their story – you will use them later in the class.

5. Give the students an opportunity to read the stories online (high-tech version) or printed out (low-tech and no-tech versions) and compare the real stories with what they thought. Ask them to check whether their words are in the original stories. Conduct feedback.

6. Now examine one of the four stories for structure and content. Get students to deconstruct the story to see how it's put together, and what content is in the story. They should think about the following:

   - **structure**
     headline
     writer
     date
     story: paragraphs, order of events
   - **content (the six 'w's of journalism)**
     who is it about?
     what happened?
     where did it take place?
     when did it take place?
     why did it happen?
     ho**w** did it happen?
   - **presentation**
     photos?
     videos?
     supporting links?
     adverts?

7. Now jumble up the 24 words generated by your students and give six to each group. Their task is to construct a new story from these six words, bearing in mind the structure and content rules they have just discussed. If students have set up individual blogs (see Activity 35, *Personal blogging*) these stories can be added there, illustrated with images and links, and then other students can be invited to comment (high-tech version). If you have already set up a class blog (see Activity 4, *Extreme weather*

or Activity 10, *Copycat*) the stories can be added there using the teacher computer (low-tech version). Alternatively, the stories can simply be written on paper and shared between students or posted on a classroom wall (no-tech version).

Extension

Encourage students to add their stories to their e-portfolios, or to add hyperlinks from their e-portfolios to their blog posts (see Chapter 3: *Assessing digital work, Assessing through e-portfolios*) (high-tech version).

Activity 4: Extreme weather

Students analyse a variety of online text sources and consider the conventions of each.

Online print literacy, although closely related to traditional print literacy, has some significantly different features. The online medium can affect the message. This activity raises awareness of different genres of online text, and encourages students to create their own.

Literacy: **Print literacy** and **Information literacy** (complexity: ***)

Topic: Weather and environment

Aim: To raise awareness of how to convey a message via different genres of online text

Level: Upper intermediate +

Time: 60 minutes

Tech support: Blogs:

- General: e-language.wikispaces.com/blogs
- Blogger: support.google.com/blogger/?hl=en
- Edublogs: help.edublogs.org

Microblogging:

- General: e-language.wikispaces.com/microblogging
- Twitter: support.twitter.com

Social networking:

- General: e-language.wikispaces.com/social-networking
- Facebook: www.facebook.com/help/

Language	
Areas	*Vocabulary:* Weather, environment and climate change *Grammar:* Present simple tense (for facts); past simple tense (for news events) *Register:* Formal versus informal communication
Functions	Giving opinions; discussing facts versus opinions
Skills	Reading, speaking, writing

Resources	
High-tech	*Equipment:* One internet-enabled teacher computer and data projector; internet-enabled student computers or mobile devices (one per pair) *Tools:* Class blog (e.g. Blogger or Edublogs); Twitter account; Facebook group *Documents:* Online worksheet (www.pearsoned.co.uk/hockly)
Low-tech	*Equipment:* One internet-enabled teacher computer and data projector *Documents:* Printed worksheet (follows Activity)
No-tech	*Documents:* Printed images of extreme weather; printed worksheet (follows Activity)

Digital risks

- Most web 2.0 services, including blogs, offer different levels of privacy. With young learners, or in contexts where learners reveal their identities, it may be best to make blogs entirely private. With older students and less personally sensitive content, it may be appropriate to make blogs partly or wholly public, so that they can be viewed by others and may even receive feedback. (For other, similar discussions of privacy settings, see Activity 7, *Sports linking* on wikis, Activity 34, *Online me* on Glogster and Activity 44, *Vox pop* on vodcasts.)

- Privacy is a particular issue with certain web 2.0 services like social networking sites. Some students may be reluctant to use tools such as Facebook or the microblogging service Twitter. This is worth discussing directly with students (for more detailed guidelines, see Box 1.3; Box 1.9; Activity 33, *Faking it*).

Procedure

Before class

- Find pictures of extreme weather, as suggested in Step 1, and bookmark the pages (high-tech and low-tech versions) or print them out (no-tech version).

- Ensure that students are familiar with blogs, microblogging (especially Twitter and tweets) and social networking (especially Facebook and status updates), so that they can recognise, analyse and create texts for these kinds of web 2.0 services in Step 5.

- Set up a class blog, a class Twitter account and a class Facebook group for use in Step 5 (high-tech version).

1. Show students four or five pictures of extreme weather such as hurricanes, floods, droughts, landslides or bush fires (see Activity 10, *Copycat* for how to find Creative Commons-licensed pictures). Show the images on the projector screen (high-tech and low-tech versions) or put the printed images on the board (no-tech version). Elicit the weather vocabulary for each picture and write it on the board. Ask students what these pictures have in common (*most scientists agree that these phenomena are caused in part by climate change*).

2. Tell students that they are going to read extracts from several online sources about climate change and extreme weather. Ask students to refer to **Activity 4 Worksheet – Extreme weather** and to complete Task 1 in pairs.

3. Put the following words on the board:

      news website   personal blog   Twitter   Facebook

   Check the answers to Task 1 (see Appendix: Answer keys) with the group. Discuss the similarities and differences between these sources/services, and how the style of each varies from formal to informal depending on the purpose, the writer and the audience. Discuss what sort of information is appropriate or inappropriate for each of these sources.

4. Put students into small groups, and ask them to discuss Task 2 on the worksheet. Conduct feedback.

5. Ask students to complete Task 3 on the worksheet. Blog posts can be shared on a class blog (which can be set up for free with Blogger or Edublogs), tweets can be shared on a class Twitter feed, and status

updates can be shared in a class Facebook group (high-tech version). Alternatively, all of the texts can be created on paper and shared among students (low-tech and no-tech versions).

Extension

Encourage students to add their texts to their e-portfolios and/or to add hyperlinks from their e-portfolios to their blog posts (see Chapter 3: *Assessing digital work, Assessing through e-portfolios*) (high-tech version).

Activity 4 Worksheet – Extreme weather

1. Extreme weather phenomena

Read the extracts below and answer these questions:

- What extreme weather or environmental phenomenon does each extract refer to?

- What is the source of each extract – a news website, a personal blog, a tweet (from Twitter), or a status update (from Facebook)?

- Who has written each extract? Who is each extract written *for*?

- Is the information in each extract fact or personal opinion, or a mixture of both?

Extract 1

The Green Man

MONDAY, SEPTEMBER 3, 2012

Welcome to my blog!

Hello and welcome to my blog. Everyone knows that climate change is affecting us more and more, but what can we do about it? As an expert in the field of meteorology, I use my blog to look at the evidence, and what climate change is doing to communities around the world. My first post looks at the effects of low and non-existent rainfall in areas of East Africa, and how this is leading to conflicts over land and water.... [read more]

Posted by The Green Man at 5:09 AM   No comments:

Extract 2

greenmanbc
Why is this government still in denial about #climatechange?
Get real! Evidence - Maldives disappearing under sea
bit.ly/Dnh

Extract 3

Hurricane Irene claims lives and leaves trail of destruction

Millions across eastern seaboard left without power and at risk of flooding despite hurricane being downgraded to tropical storm

Dominic Rushe in New York

🐦 Follow

guardian.co.uk, Monday 29 August 2011 00.02 BST

A woman rescues belongings from houses damaged by Hurricane Irene in Columbia, North Carolina. Photograph: John Bazemore/AP

New York breathed a sigh of relief on Sunday after hurricane Irene passed over without major damage to the city, but the storm still caused deaths, serious floods and power blackouts affecting more than a million people as it swept up the north-eastern seaboard of the United States.

Irene weakened quickly after making landfall near Atlantic City, New Jersey, at about 5.30am local time. By the time it made landfall again, at Coney Island four hours later, it had been downgraded by the

Extract 4

 Nicky Hockly shared a link.
September 5, 2011 🔒 Only Me

Article describes how bush fires in Australia are linked to climate change
http://www.time.com/time/health/article/0,8599,1878220,00.html

 Why Global Warming May Be Fueling Australia's Fires
www.time.com

Police suspect arsonists set some of the Australian wildfires. But their deadliness and intensity may have had more to do with climate change.

Like · Comment · Share

2. Online texts

(a) Which of these online sources or services do you regularly read? Have you ever written or published anything through any of these sources or services? If so, what? Which of these services do you *not* want to use, and why?

> news website   personal blog   Twitter   Facebook

(b) Can you list three advantages and three disadvantages of each of these sources or services for:

(i) readers

(ii) writers

3. Creating online texts

Work in pairs. Choose one area of extreme weather or climate change (e.g. hurricanes, floods, droughts, landslides, bush fires, rising sea levels, etc.). Create the following online texts about your chosen topic:

- a short blog entry (100–150 words)

- a tweet (maximum 140 characters)

- a Facebook status update

Exchange your texts with another pair. Then look at their online texts, and consider the language and information included:

- Is the message of each text clear?

- Does each text have the appropriate level of formality/informality?

- Is the length of each text appropriate?

- Is the amount of detail in each text appropriate?

- Is the number of links to additional online information in each text appropriate?

- In each case, does the message match the medium?

Share your texts with the rest of your classmates, online or on paper.

Activity 5: Cryptic messages

Students decipher the textspeak used in SMS messages and discuss its appropriacy.

An awareness of textspeak is helpful for students if they are to take part in web 2.0 culture in English (see e.g. Activity 47, *LOLcats* and Activity 48, *Texting Hillary*). Text messaging linguistic conventions will frequently exist in the students' L1s, which can provide a useful point of comparison with English textspeak.

Literacy: **Texting literacy** (complexity: *)

Topic: Textspeak

Aim: To raise awareness of L2 textspeak conventions

Level: Intermediate +

Time: 45 minutes

Language	
Areas	*Vocabulary:* Textspeak, abbreviations and emoticons *Register:* Informal communication
Functions	Discussing; giving opinions
Skills	Reading, speaking, writing

Resources	
High-tech	*Equipment:* Teacher mobile phone; student mobile phones (one each) *Documents:* Online worksheet (www.pearsoned.co.uk/hockly)
Low-tech	Not available for this activity
No-tech	*Documents:* Printed worksheet (follows Activity)

Digital risks

- Using a personal mobile phone to communicate with students may be forbidden or frowned upon in some educational contexts. In this case, use the no-tech version of this activity.

- Students may have to personally pay for any text messages they send during class, which could be prohibitive for some. The no-tech version of this activity provides a suitable alternative.

Procedure

Before class

- If all of your students have mobile phones and are allowed and willing to use them in class, collect their phone numbers in advance of the class. Send them the messages in Task 1 of **Activity 5 Worksheet – Cryptic messages** from your own phone just before class begins, for use in Step 3 (high-tech version).

1. Ask students about their mobile/cell phones. What do they use them for? How often? Do they send SMS (text) messages? What are the advantages of using *textspeak* in such messages (e.g. speed, cost, informality, playfulness)? Can they give an example of a text message in their native language?

2. Show the following mobile phone text message on the projector screen (high-tech version) or write it on the board (no-tech version):

   Thx 4 gr8 eve & dinner :) Gd 2 c Steve&Jill 2. C u soon. xxx Sue

   Tell students you recently received this message from a friend. What is it about? Can they decipher the text message in pairs?

   Give feedback, pointing out some of the features of text messages in English, such as:
   - common abbreviations: 'Thx' = 'thanks', 'c u' = 'see you', 'gd' = 'good'
   - common uses of numbers: 'gr8' = 'great' , '2' = 'to'
   - emoticons: :) = a smiley face
   - symbols: '&' = 'and', 'xxx' = 'kisses'

3. Ask students to look at the phone messages you sent them before class and to work in pairs to interpret them (high-tech version). Alternatively,

refer them to Task 1 on the printed worksheet and ask them to complete it in pairs (no-tech version). Provide feedback.

4. Ask pairs to choose *one* of the appropriate text messages from the worksheet, and to compose a reply. Ask students to send their replies to you via their phones (high-tech version) or write their replies on the board (no-tech version).

5. Reply to the students, indicating any issues with their messages (high-tech version) or ask students to work in pairs to decipher all the messages on the board, and to match them to the original messages in Task 1 on the worksheet (no-tech version). Provide feedback.

6. Ask students to discuss Task 2 from the worksheet (see Appendix: Answer keys), either in small groups or as a whole class.

7. Work through Task 3 on the worksheet as a whole class.

Activity 5 Worksheet – Cryptic messages

1. Look at these textspeak messages. Write them in standard English.

   - Wot u up 2 2day?
   - Had gr8 time w friends on hols
   - Pls send me info re: ur Eng courses 4 nxt yr
   - OK, midday gd. C u there!
   - i want 2 apply 4 job in ydays nwspaper

   What is the context for each message? Which two messages are *not* appropriate as SMS texts?

2. Look at the emoticons below. Can you work out what they mean in English? Which are also used in your language? Which are not?

Emoticon	Meaning in English	Used in your language? (✔ or ✗)	Alternative emoticon in your language?
:) or :-)			
:p or :-p			
:o or :-o			
:(or :-(or =(			
:/ or :-/			
:s or :-s			
:@ or :-@			
:D or :-D			
:* or :-*			

3. Discuss:

- How many text messages do you send per day in your native language? Per week?
- Who do you text? When and why?
- Can you give an example of an emoticon which is the same in your language as in English? Can you give an example which is different?
- Can you give an example of a textspeak abbreviation which works the same way in your language as in English? Can you give an example which is different?
- In what situations is text messaging considered OK in your native language? Do you think this is the same in English?
- In what situations is text messaging *not* considered OK in your native language? Do you think this is the same in English?
- For homework, send your teacher a text message in English telling him or her what you thought of the class!

Activity 6: Codeswitching

Students identify appropriate uses of textspeak.

This activity aims to raise students' awareness of the use of textspeak in formal and informal settings. It looks at register and appropriacy, encouraging students to examine both standard language and textspeak, and to think about how they switch between them in their lives. This activity works well with Activity 5, *Cryptic messages*, Activity 47, *LOLcats* and/or Activity 48, *Texting Hillary*.

Literacy: **Texting literacy** and **Print literacy** (complexity: *)

Topic: Textspeak

Aim: To raise awareness of codeswitching

Level: Upper intermediate +

Time: 60 minutes

Language	
Areas	*Vocabulary:* Textspeak, abbreviations and emoticons *Register:* Informal versus formal communication
Skills	Reading, speaking

Resources	
High-tech	*Equipment:* One internet-enabled teacher computer and data projector; internet-enabled student computers or mobile devices (one per group) *Documents:* Online worksheets (www.pearsoned.co.uk/hockly)
Low-tech	Not available for this activity
No-tech	*Documents:* Printed websites; printed worksheets (follows Activity)

Procedure

Before class

- Print out the articles for use in Step 5 (no-tech version).

1. Display '2B / -2B = ?' on the projector screen (high-tech version) or write it on the board (no-tech version) and ask your students whether they know what it means. If they don't immediately see it, tell them it is a famous quotation from Shakespeare, rewritten as an SMS message. (*To be or not to be? That is the question.*)

2. Tell students they are going to read an essay a student wrote for her teacher. The essay was written in the first class after the long summer break, and it describes the student's summer holidays. Show them the text on **Activity 6 Worksheet A – Summer holidays** and give them a few minutes to try to decipher it. For the moment don't give them any help. Conduct feedback and get their general impressions, both about the text itself and its meaning.

3. Refer students to the grid on **Activity 6 Worksheet B – Cracking the code** and ask them to read through the text again and try to decipher it. This is a demanding exercise, so you should give students plenty of time to attempt it, but beware of potential frustration. Conduct feedback on the standard English text as a whole class (see Appendix: Answer keys), finding out whether similar abbreviations exist in the other languages spoken by students in the class.

4. Tell your students that a search for this text on Google generates over 27,000 hits. What do students think the focus of these stories is? (*Most of the stories are negative about the use of textspeak and critical of what the authors see as falling literacy standards.*)

5. Divide the class into two groups. Group 1 will be investigating positive reactions to the text; Group 2 will research negative reactions to it. Depending on the search skills of your class, you can either let them find suitable resources themselves (see Activity 25, *Search race* for guidance on search skills and search engines), or direct them to the following texts (though you may find other more recent and more appropriate texts yourself):

Positive

- Delingpole, J. (2008) 2 txt or not 2 txt – That's the gr8 db8. *Mail Online.* www.dailymail.co.uk/home/books/article-1036290/2-txt-2-txt-- thats-gr8-db8.html

- Ward, L. (2004) Texting 'is no bar to literacy'. *The Guardian.* www.guardian. co.uk/technology/2004/dec/23/schools.mobilephones
- North, M. (2003) My summr hols wr CWOT. B4, we usd 2 go 2NY 2C my bro, his GF &. *The Times Higher Education Supplement.* www. timeshighereducation.co.uk/story.asp?storyCode=179327&section code=26

Negative

- Reuters (2003) Text message essay baffles British teacher. *CNN.* edition.cnn.com/2003/EDUCATION/03/03/offbeat.text.essay.reut/
- Cramb, A. (2003) Girl writes English essay in phone text shorthand. *The Telegraph.* www.telegraph.co.uk/news/uknews/1423572/Girl-writes-English-essay-in-phone-text-shorthand.html

Give students time to visit their websites online (high-tech version) or to read the printouts you have given them (no-tech version).

6. Form pairs consisting of one student from Group 1 and one student from Group 2, and get them to report to each other what they found in their research. Then conduct feedback as a whole class (see Activity 5, *Cryptic messages* for additional points you can make about textspeak).

Activity 6 Worksheet A – Summer holidays

My smmr hols wr CWOT. B4, we usd 2 go 2 NY 2C my bro, his GF & thr 3 :-@ kds FTF. ILNY, its gr8. Bt my Ps wr so {:-/ BC o 9/11 tht they dcdd 2 stay in SCO & spnd 2wks up N. Up N, WUCIWUG – 0. I ws vvv brd in MON. 0 bt baas & ^^^^^. AAR8, my Ps wr :-) – they sd ICBW, & tht they wr ha-p 4 the pc&qt... IDTS!! I wntd 2 go hm ASAP, 2C my M8s again. 2day, I cam bk 2 skool. I feel v O:-) BC I hv dn all my hm wrk. Now its BAU...

Activity 6 Worksheet B – Cracking the code

English textspeak	English word or phrase	Word or phrase in your language	Textspeak in your language
smmr	summer		
hols	holidays		

Activity 7: Sports linking

Students produce a short hyperlinked text about a famous sports personality of their choice and add it to a class wiki.

The placing of hyperlinks in an online text can affect both its credibility and readability. This activity aims to raise student awareness of the effects of including too many or too few hyperlinks in a text. It leads to a consideration of what judicious hyperlinking looks like.

Literacy:	**Hypertext literacy** (complexity: **)
Topic:	Sports
Aim:	To raise awareness of the appropriate use of hyperlinks in online texts, and the effects of hyperlinks on reading
Level:	Lower intermediate +
Time:	60 minutes
Tech support:	Wikis:

- General: e-language.wikispaces.com/wikis

- PBworks: usermanual.pbworks.com

- Wikispaces: help.wikispaces.com

Language	
Areas	*Vocabulary:* Sports; biographies *Grammar:* Narrative tenses
Functions	Narrating; discussing
Skills	Reading, speaking, writing

Resources	
High-tech	*Equipment:* Internet-enabled student computers or mobile devices (one per student) *Tools:* Class wiki (e.g. PBworks or Wikispaces) *Documents:* Online worksheet (www.pearsoned.co.uk/hockly)

Low-tech	*Equipment:* One internet-enabled teacher computer and data projector *Documents:* Printed worksheet (follows Activity)
No-tech	*Documents:* Printed Simple English Wikipedia entry; printed worksheet (follows Activity) *Stationery:* Paper

Digital risks

- Like blog services, most wiki services offer different levels of privacy. With young learners, or in contexts where learners reveal their identities, it may be best to make wikis entirely private. With older students and less personally sensitive content, it may be appropriate to make wikis partly or wholly public, so that they can be viewed by others and may even receive feedback. (For other, similar discussions of privacy settings, see Activity 4, *Extreme weather* on blogs, Activity 34, *Online me* on Glogster and Activity 44, *Vox pop* on vodcasts.)

- Teachers should ensure students do not plagiarise text or use copyright images without permission (see Box 1.12; Activity 10, *Copycat*).

Procedure

Before class

- Print one copy of the Bobby Robson text from Simple English Wikipedia (simple.wikipedia.org/wiki/Bobby_Robson) for each student, for use in Step 4 (no-tech version).

- Create a class wiki and invite students to join; this will be used in Step 8 (high-tech version).

1. Introduce the topic of sports. What sports do your students play? What sporting events do they attend or watch on television? Who are the most famous sporting personalities at the moment, and which sports do these personalities play?

2. Tell students they are going to take a sports quiz. Can they match the sporting personality with the nationality and sport? Ask students to refer to **Activity 7 Worksheet – Sports linking** and to complete Task 1 in pairs (see Appendix: Answer keys).

3. Give feedback. What else do they know about these sportsmen and sportswomen? Focus on Bobby Robson – what do they know about him? (They probably won't know much, if anything, which is ideal for the purposes of this task.)

4. Tell students that individually they have 2 minutes to read a short online text about Robson. Point students to the Simple English Wikipedia website entry about Bobby Robson (as described above) and ask them to follow as many hyperlinks as possible in the 2 minutes (high-tech version). Otherwise, display the entry on a screen at the front of the room (low-tech version) or have a printed copy of the Robson text for each student (no-tech version); in the latter cases, ask students to make notes on what they find out.

Variation

Give stronger classes 1 minute to read the text. For higher levels, use the full Wikipedia entry, which has more complex language (en.wikipedia.org/wiki/Bobby_Robson). Time and stop the group.

5. Ask students what they have found out about Robson.

6. Ask students to discuss the questions in Task 2 on the worksheet in small groups, or as a whole class. (Even if students have followed the low-tech or no-tech versions here, many of them will have had the experience of reading online hyperlinked texts.) In feedback on this discussion, elicit or make the following points:

- Factual online texts with no hyperlinks can look as if they have not been fully researched, or are not based sufficiently on fact.

- Including hyperlinks in a text can make it look more factual. However, we need to consider what is hyperlinked, and how it adds to the text. Some of the hyperlinks in the Robson text may not be particularly helpful or useful.

- Including too many hyperlinks in a text can make it difficult to read, because we constantly need to decide whether to follow the link or not. This can slow down our reading and make us understand and remember less. It can be especially challenging when reading in a foreign language. And if we do follow hyperlinks, we can easily lose the thread of the narrative or argument.

- More information is given earlier in this text (see Chapter 1: *First focus: Language, Hypertext literacy*).

7. Now ask students to read the text about Venus Williams in Task 3 on the worksheet. Give them 30 seconds to read it individually. Time this, and then invite them to discuss the two questions below the text, in the same groups as before. In your feedback, elicit or make the following points:

   - Reading offline (or on paper) can help us ignore the distractions of hyperlinks, as hyperlinks simply won't work offline. Sometimes it may be better for us to read without following hyperlinks, especially if a text is dense or difficult to understand.

   - Hyperlinks in an online text usually take us to factual information that can be proved or disproved, such as facts about an event, person or product.

8. As a final writing task, ask students to work in pairs to choose a sports personality and write a paragraph of around the same length as the Simple English Wikipedia text about that person. They should do so on a class wiki, which can be set up free of cost with a service such as PBworks or Wikispaces, and they should include hyperlinks to information within Simple English Wikipedia itself or to other factual online sources (high-tech version). Alternatively, students can write texts on paper and underline any words they would hyperlink, adding footnotes to explain what sort of information each would link to (low-tech and no-tech versions).

9. Ask the pairs to evaluate each other's use of hyperlinking by viewing the texts on the class wiki and making comments using the 'discussion' tab on each wiki page (high-tech version), or by exchanging handwritten texts and writing comments at the bottom of each page (low-tech or no-tech versions). You can provide a final round of feedback on the appropriate and less appropriate use of hyperlinks in the student-produced texts.

Extension 1

Ask students to search Simple English Wikipedia to see if there is an entry about their chosen sports personality, and to review the use of hyperlinking in the article. Students can sign up for a Simple English Wikipedia account, and then edit the article to improve the hyperlinking by adding or removing links. If there is no entry for their chosen personality, they can submit their own entry (high-tech version).

Extension 2

Encourage students to add hyperlinks from their e-portfolios to their class wiki texts, and any texts they have edited on Simple English Wikipedia (see Chapter 3: *Assessing digital work*, *Assessing through e-portfolios*) (high-tech version).

Activity 7 Worksheet – Sports linking

1. Sports

Look at these sporting personalities. Match the two columns.

1	Venus Williams	a	English football player
2	Diego Maradona	b	Spanish Formula 1 driver
3	Bobby Robson	c	American golfer
4	Marion Jones	d	Swiss tennis player
5	Martina Hingis	e	British athlete
6	Michelle Wei	f	Pakistani cricket player
7	Fernando Alonso	g	American tennis player
8	Imran Khan	h	Argentinian football player
9	Suzuki Ichirō	i	Filipino boxer
10	Manny Pacquiao	j	Japanese baseball player

2. Online texts

Discuss these questions:

- While you were reading the Simple English Wikipedia text about Bobby Robson, did you click on any of the hyperlinks? Why/why not? (If you were reading it on the projector screen, or on paper, which links would you have liked to follow? Why?)

- Do you find it easy to read an online text with many hyperlinks? Why/why not?

- Do you think there were too many/not enough hyperlinks in the Robson text?

- Exactly what information in the Robson text was hyperlinked? Are these hyperlinks a good choice? What hyperlinks would you include or leave out if this was *your* online text?

- What is the effect of including hyperlinks in an online text?

3. Venus Williams

Read this text in 30 seconds:

Venus Ebony Starr Williams (born June 17, 1980 in Lynwood, California, United States) is a former World No. 1 ranked female tennis player and Olympic gold medalist who has won 13 Grand Slam titles, including 5 singles, 6 women's doubles, and 2 mixed doubles titles. Williams is the older sister of fellow former World No. 1 tennis player Serena Williams. The Williams sisters are noted for their power games, and Venus holds the record for the fastest serve ever recorded by a female player in a main draw match (128.8 mph). Venus Williams played against French player Marion Bartoli in the Wimbledon final on July 7. Williams won her fourth Wimbledon final on July 7, 2007.
[From Simple English Wikipedia: simple.wikipedia.org/wiki/Venus_Williams;
accessed 14/01/2012]

Discuss:

- Was the experience of reading this text different? If so, how and why was it different?

- Imagine that you wrote this text about Williams for Simple English Wikipedia. Circle the words you would hyperlink. What kinds of sites would you hyperlink to? Compare with a partner, and explain your hyperlink choices. Then look at the original Simple English Wikipedia entry online and compare.

Activity 8: Building links

Students create online resource libraries to support a point of view.

This activity shows students how the judicious choice of links can influence a reader's opinion on a topic. Students are encouraged to consider how this affects their learning and understanding of the world. You may want to do Activity 25, *Search race*, before attempting this activity, to ensure that your students have the search skills they need.

Literacy:	**Hypertext literacy**, **Search literacy** and **Information literacy** (complexity: ***)
Topic:	Controversies (see suggestions below)
Aim:	To find supporting evidence for a point of view, and to raise awareness of the role hyperlinked materials play in learning
Level:	Upper intermediate +
Time:	90 minutes
Tech support:	Blogs:

- General: e-language.wikispaces.com/blogs
- Blogger: support.google.com/blogger/?hl=en
- Edublogs: help.edublogs.org

Presentation software:

- Keynote: support.apple.com/manuals/#iwork
- PowerPoint: goo.gl/vfLwD
- Prezi: prezi.com/learn/getting-started/

Wikis:

- General: e-language.wikispaces.com/wikis
- PBworks: usermanual.pbworks.com
- Wikispaces: help.wikispaces.com

Word-processing software:

- Apple Pages: support.apple.com/manuals/#iwork
- Microsoft Word: goo.gl/KXnLe

Language	
Areas	*Vocabulary:* Controversial topics
Functions	Expressing agreement and disagreement; expressing opinions
Skills	Reading, speaking

Resources	
High-tech	*Equipment:* One internet-enabled teacher computer and data projector; internet-enabled student computers or mobile devices (one per pair) *Tools:* Wiki(s) (e.g. PBworks or Wikispaces) *or* blog(s) (e.g. Blogger or Edublogs) *or* presentation software (e.g. Keynote, PowerPoint or Prezi) *or* word-processing software (e.g. Apple Pages or Microsoft Word)
Low-tech	Not available for this activity
No-tech	Not available for this activity

Procedure

Before class

- Choose one of the topics from Hermione_111's '33 Controversial Topics and How to Teach Them' at Busy Teacher (goo.gl/pOKoQ), or choose a topic of your own that you know will work with your students. The aim is to choose a subject that will generate some disagreement in the class (e.g. 'Movie piracy is not a crime and doesn't harm anybody'), for use in Step 2.

- *(Optional)* Bookmark useful links for use in Step 3.

1. Introduce the theme, either through personal anecdote or some visuals from Google Images, and get reactions from your students.

2. Display a cline on the projector screen or draw one on the board (see the example below) and get students to write their names where they feel they fit in with the statement.

Movie piracy is not a crime and doesn't harm anybody

disagree   ‹ 5 ------ 4 ------ 3 ------ 2 ------ 1 ------ 0 ------ 1 ------ 2 ------ 3 ------ 4 ------ 5 ›   agree

As a whole group, brainstorm points both in favour of and against the statement, and write them on the screen or board.

3. Split the class into two groups on either side of the '0' on the cline and tell them that they have 30 minutes to find as much evidence as possible to support their side of the argument (either for – or against – the statement). Within their groups, students can work in pairs on gathering this evidence. They can use any search engines they prefer (see Box 1.5 and Activity 25, *Search race* for ideas), and they must come up with a set of links to supporting websites at the end of the 30 minutes. Monitor and help where needed during the data collection phase. You may want to have a set of links already bookmarked to get them started or help out if they get stuck.

4. As they find resources, students should add them to an online platform such as a wiki or blog or else list them on a presentation slide (e.g. in Keynote, PowerPoint or Prezi) or in a word-processed document (e.g. Apple Pages or Microsoft Word), ensuring that the links are active for later use.

5. Now swap the groups over and give them time to follow the links for the other side of the argument, again asking students to work in pairs within their groups. Once they have had time to read about the other side of the argument each student should write their name on the cline again to show how they feel about the statement now (use a different colour!).

6. Go through the sites together as a whole group, examining how reputable each is (see Activity 27, *Tree octopus* for more on assessing websites). Conclude with a short discussion:

   • How does the person or organisation creating the website affect the content and viewpoint taken?

   • How easily did students alter their opinion from a small sample of websites?

   • What implication does this have for their online study habits?

Extension

Encourage students to upload their lists of links to their e-portfolios, or to add hyperlinks from their e-portfolios to their wiki or blog lists (see Chapter 3: *Assessing digital works, Assessing through e-portfolios*).

Activity 9: Food boards

Students create multimedia notice boards about their favourite local foods.

This activity encourages students to explore an online multimedia notice board site (Pinterest) and create their own boards. They can also take part in the Pinterest community outside the classroom by following, liking and/or commenting on other users' boards.

Literacy: **Multimedia literacy** (complexity: ***)

Topic: Foods and recipes

Aim: To create online multimedia boards

Level: Elementary +

Time: 60 minutes

Tech support: Photosharing:

- General: e-language.wikispaces.com/social-sharing#Photosharing

- Pinterest: pinterest.com/about/help/

Language	
Areas	*Vocabulary:* Foods; recipes *Grammar:* Sequencing adverbs (e.g. first, then, finally)
Functions	Describing a process (recipes)
Skills	Writing, speaking, reading

Resources	
High-tech	*Equipment:* One internet-enabled teacher computer and data projector; internet-enabled student computers or mobile devices (one per pair) *Tools:* Pinterest *Tools (optional):* Pinterest app

Low-tech	*Equipment:* One internet-enabled teacher computer and data projector *Tools:* Pinterest *Tools (optional):* Pinterest app *Documents:* Printed Pinterest Help page
No-tech	*Documents:* Printed Pinterest boards; printed Pinterest Help page *Stationery:* Poster-sized paper, coloured pens and magazines (for images)

Digital risks

Creating a Pinterest account is not an immediate process and can take several days. We suggest that the teacher should set up a Pinterest account well in advance, and then give these account details to students for them to create individual Pinterest boards in the same account. Note that Pinterest account holders need to be aged 13 or more, so creating a single teacher account also enables teachers to use Pinterest with younger learners, if this is deemed appropriate.

Procedure

Before class

- Ask students to bring images of their favourite local dishes to class, either in digital format (e.g. on their mobile phones – high-tech version) or in hard copy (low-tech and no-tech versions), for use in Step 1.

- Check that you are familiar with the foods in Step 2 by looking up 'Around the World in 80 Dishes' on the *Epicurious* blog at www.epicurious.com/articlesguides/blogs/80dishes.

- Print out Pinterest boards for use in Step 3 (no-tech version).

- Print out the Pinterest Help page for use in Step 5 (low-tech and no-tech versions).

1. Ask students about their favourite foods. Elicit a few examples and add them to the board (e.g. chocolate, ice cream, pizza, noodles). Students could show the pictures of local foods they have brought to class with them and the names could be added to the board. Try to elicit both international foods *and* local foods.

2. Add the local dishes below to the board. Ask students if they know which country each dish comes from, and what it consists of. (You can check these yourself in advance, as noted above.)

   feijoada (Brazil); lumpia (Philippines); masala dosa (India); nasi goreng (Indonesia); bobotie (South Africa); moussaka (Greece); pierogies (Poland); tempura (Japan); bouillabaisse (France)

3. Ask students whether they know of Pinterest (pinterest.com). It's a free community multimedia noticeboard site on the web. You create your own 'board' and add pictures and videos (and some text) about your favourite things. Typical Pinterest boards show hobbies and interests, travel, pets, sports . . . and food, especially recipes. Show the class a few Pinterest boards related to food, either on the projector screen (high-tech and low-tech versions) or in the form of printouts (no-tech version). Include examples of Pinterest boards with international foods (e.g. chocolate cake, pizza), and examples of Pinterest boards with local dishes (e.g. from Step 1 above).

4. Ask students to work in pairs to search Pinterest for pictures of any of the dishes in Step 2 they haven't seen before (high-tech version). Alternatively, search Pinterest for unknown dishes as a whole class using the teacher computer and projector screen (low-tech version), or show printouts of Pinterest boards for each of the local foods in Step 2 (no-tech version). Check that students now know what each food looks like, and what the main ingredients are, by conducting whole class feedback.

5. Tell students they are going to create Pinterest boards (high-tech and low-tech versions) or posters (no-tech version). They first need to understand how Pinterest works. Present students with the following questions, either on the board or on a handout. Ask them to work in pairs to search the Pinterest Help page (pinterest.com/about/help/) for the answers, either online (high-tech version) or as a printout (low-tech and no-tech versions):

   • What are the behaviour rules (etiquette) for using Pinterest?
   • What is a pin?
   • What is a 'Pin it' button?
   • What is the difference between a pin and a board?
   • What is 'following'?
   • What is a 'repin'?
   • How do you create a new board?

6. Now students are ready to create their own Pinterest boards. Ask them to create a Pinterest board in pairs for one of their favourite local foods; for multinational groups, students can create individual boards showcasing a local food from their country (high-tech version). Alternatively, create several Pinterest boards with different foods as a whole class activity (low-tech version), or ask students to work in pairs or individually to create boards on poster paper using pictures from magazines (no-tech version). Depending on the level of the class, ask students simply to list the main ingredients of their chosen dish(es) on their Pinterest board(s) (lower levels), or ask them to include complete recipes (higher levels). Point out to students that they can link to images or videos on their boards, or they can use their own digital photos or videos, for example from their mobile phones (high-tech and low-tech versions). Students who are creating posters can use their own hard copy photos in a similar way (no-tech version).

7. Once the boards are finished, encourage students to visit each other's boards, and to like or comment on them (high-tech version). If the class has created boards as a group activity, choose one or two of the other foods from Step 1 and visit boards about those foods, liking and/or commenting as a class (low-tech version). If your students have produced paper posters, put these up on the walls of the classroom, and encourage students to walk around with post-it notes, leaving comments on the posters (no-tech version).

Extension 1

If your students have access to mobile devices out of class and are over 13 years of age, encourage them to download the Pinterest app (available for Android, Apple iOS, BlackBerry and Windows devices) and create their own accounts. They can then use the app to visit other Pinterest boards and leave comments, and/or to create their own boards, uploading pictures and videos directly from their mobile devices.

Extension 2

Encourage students to add hyperlinks from their e-portfolios to their Pinterest board or boards (see Chapter 3: *Assessing digital work, Assessing through e-portfolios*) (high-tech version).

Activity 10: Copycat

Students learn to search for Creative Commons images. They write a blog entry about an animal, accompanied by images.

Knowing how to make appropriate use of digital images produced by others is a key multimedia literacy (especially 'visual literacy') skill. This activity helps students understand the difference between restricted copyright images and Creative Commons images, and how they can be used.

Literacy:	**Multimedia literacy** and **Search literacy** (complexity: ***)
Topic:	Animals
Aim:	To raise awareness of copyright and the appropriate use of digital images
Level:	Beginners +
Time:	45 minutes
Tech support:	Blogs:

Blogs:

- General: e-language.wikispaces.com/blogs
- Blogger: support.google.com/blogger/?hl=en
- Edublogs: help.edublogs.org

Word-processing software:

- Apple Pages: support.apple.com/manuals/#iwork
- Microsoft Word: goo.gl/KXnLe

Language	
Areas	*Vocabulary:* Animals (or any lexical set that can be clearly represented in images) *Grammar:* Can/can't; present simple tense
Functions	Describing (animals)
Skills	Listening, writing

Resources	
High-tech	*Equipment:* One internet-enabled teacher computer and data projector; internet-enabled student computers or mobile devices (one per student) *Tools:* Class blog (e.g. Blogger or Edublogs); word-processing software (e.g. Apple Pages or Microsoft Word) *Tools (optional):* ImageCodr *Documents:* Animal name cards
Low-tech	*Equipment:* One internet-enabled teacher computer and data projector *Tools:* Word-processing software (e.g. Apple Pages or Microsoft Word) *Documents:* Animal name cards
No-tech	*Documents:* Animal name cards; printed images of a tiger and other animals

Digital risks

- Teachers should inform themselves about Creative Commons licences as well as the availability of other copyright-free materials, such as those in the public domain (see Box 1.12). They should guide students on how to find CC or copyright-free materials and ensure that students do not use copyright images without permission.

- Teachers should ensure that the SafeSearch function of Google Images (www.google.com/preferences?hl=en) is set at least to 'Moderate' or, depending on the context, to 'Strict', before students begin to use it.

Procedure

Before class

- Review Creative Commons copyright licences (see Box 1.12).

- Prepare 10–15 cards with the names of animals to play Pictionary in Step 1.

- Search for and print out 8–10 colour images of animals, including some copyright images and some Creative Commons-licensed images, for use in Step 2 (no-tech version).

- Find a copyright-protected image of, e.g. a tiger (with © on the image) via a Google Images search. Bookmark the page (high-tech and low-tech versions) or print out the image (low-tech version) for use in Step 3.

1. Review animal vocabulary by playing Pictionary. In advance, prepare a set of cards with the names of animals. Divide your students into two teams (A and B) and draw a line down the middle of the board, dividing it into one half for Team A and one half for Team B. Take one student from each team, and show both of them one of the animal cards. Each student then needs to draw a picture of the animal on their team's half of the board, as quickly as possible. The first team to correctly guess (and pronounce) the name of the animal gets a point. Choose another student from each team and repeat the process. Continue until the cards are finished. To round off the activity, ask students to work in pairs to list as many of the animals as they can remember. Provide students with a handout listing all the animals so that they can check their spelling.

2. Choose one of the animals you have reviewed, e.g. a tiger. Ask students to individually search for pictures of tigers in Google Images (www.google.com/imghp) and to choose two images that they especially like (high-tech version). Students should then compare their choice of pictures with a partner, and explain why they like each one. If you have one computer in the classroom, use it to search while connected to a projector, and ask the class to decide as a group on two pictures they like (low-tech version). Otherwise, bring in printed colour images of animals and get the class to choose the two they like most (no-tech version).

3. Using the projector screen, show students your image of a tiger and explain why you like it (high-tech and low-tech versions). Otherwise show your printed image of a tiger (no-tech version). Make sure that you have chosen the image in advance (as described above) and that it is restricted by copyright with a © symbol on the image itself. Point out to students that they cannot use a copyright-protected image in their work. Ask them to look again at their two chosen images – do they have copyright symbols? If not, they should click on each image and visit the website where it is hosted (high-tech version); or you should do this on the projector screen while the class watches (low-tech version); or you should hand out printouts of the relevant websites (no-tech version). The aim is to find out whether there is further information about copyright on each site. However, it is often not clear whether an image is available for reuse or not. If it is not clear, students should not use the image. If they have done this activity individually (high-tech version), ask for a show of hands on

how many copyright-protected (or copyright-unclear) images they have chosen as compared to images that can be reused freely.

4. How can students find images that are available to use in their work? Tell students about Creative Commons (CC) licences (creativecommons.org). Indicate that although they can use many CC images in their work, they still need to check the conditions on each licence. Then demonstrate two ways to find CC images (high-tech and low-tech versions). (Note that the no-tech version of the activity ends at this point, with an explanation of the existence and nature of CC images.)

Google Images search

Demonstrate the following steps on the projector screen:

- Go to Google Images (www.google.com/imghp), and click on **Advanced Image Search** (under the tools sign in the top right corner of the screen).

- In **Find results – related to all of the words**, type 'tiger'. In **Usage Rights – Return images that are**, choose **labeled for reuse** from the drop-down menu. Remember to use 'Moderate' or 'Strict' SafeSearch settings, as indicated in the *Digital risks* box.

- Click the **Search images** button (on the bottom right of the screen).

Some of the results returned will be from the Flickr photosharing website (you can see the web address where the picture is hosted by moving your cursor over it), which you can introduce to students.

Flickr search

Ask students if they know about or use the Flickr photosharing site (www.flickr.com), which contains more than 100 million CC photos (see Box 1.12). Searching in Flickr may produce more reusable images than searching in Google Images.

Demonstrate the following steps on the projector screen:

- Go to the Flickr search page (www.flickr.com/search) and click on **Advanced Search** (to the right of the search box).

- In **Search for – All of these words**, type 'tiger'. Towards the bottom of the page, in the Creative Commons section, click on **Only search within Creative Commons-licensed content**.

- Click the blue **Search** button at the bottom of the page.

- A page of images will appear. Click on one of the images, and you will be taken to the Flickr page where the image is hosted. Basic information about the person who uploaded the photo, such as their username, will appear on the right. Further down on the right, you will see additional information about the licence for the photo.

- Click on the information under **License** (in this case, click on **Some rights reserved**), and you will be taken to a page which clearly and simply describes under exactly what conditions the image may be reused. Talk this through with students.

- Many Creative Commons licences require attribution – that is, the creator of the image must be acknowledged when the image is reused. Show students that the best way to do this is to include the photographer's name (or Flickr username), along with the web address of the image, underneath the image itself.

Tell students that when they search for images to illustrate written work in word-processed documents, blog posts, wiki entries, etc., they can filter their search results to show only reusable images, in both Google Images and in Flickr.

For more sources of readily reusable images – whether CC, public domain or otherwise copyright-free – see the 'E-tools' page of the E-language wiki at: e-language.wikispaces.com/e-tools#Creative Commons.

6. Ask students individually to choose an animal and to prepare a short paragraph about it in a word-processed document (high-tech version), or ask the class to choose an animal together and to collaboratively write a paragraph about it in a word-processed document shown on the projector screen (low-tech version). Students must illustrate their paragraph with two Creative Commons images and acknowledge the sources. (They can do this manually or using the ImageCodr service described below.) For lower level students, the paragraph could be a series of sentences outlining what the animal can (or can't) do, where it lives and what it looks like. If possible, students should then add their paragraphs as posts to a class blog, which can be set up free of cost with a service such as Blogger or Edublogs. By encouraging students to share their work and chosen images in a blog post, it is much clearer *why* they should choose reusable images, especially if the blog is in the public domain.

7. In subsequent classes and in any digital work that students produce, encourage them to search for and use Creative Commons-licensed images and to acknowledge sources.

Extension 1

Ask students to paste or type the URL of a CC image they have found on Flickr into the ImageCodr service (www.imagecodr.org/get.php) (high-tech version). In this way, they can generate an image with the CC licence automatically attached to it. Using the code supplied, they can insert this image into a webpage, blog or wiki. You can also demonstrate this to the whole class on the projector screen (low-tech version).

Extension 2

Encourage students to add hyperlinks from their e-portfolios to their blog posts (see Chapter 3: *Assessing digital work, Assessing through e-portfolios*) (high-tech version).

Activity 11: Envisioning the facts

Students interpret and design infographics.

Infographics, which display facts and figures in easily accessible formats, now figure widely both online and in print journalism. In this activity students view and interpret an infographic before producing one themselves. This activity goes well with Activity 2, *Being digitally literate*.

Literacy:	**Multimedia literacy** (complexity: ***)
Topic:	Information overload
Aim:	To produce an infographic about technology use
Level:	Intermediate +
Time:	90 minutes (+ homework)
Tech support:	Infographics:

- General: e-language.wikispaces.com/data-visualisation
- Easel.ly: goo.gl/ojmrh
- Piktochart: http://piktochart.com/faq/

Polling:

- General: e-language.wikispaces.com/polling
- SurveyMonkey: help.surveymonkey.com

Presentation software:

- Keynote: support.apple.com/manuals/#iwork
- PowerPoint: goo.gl/vfLwD
- Prezi: prezi.com/learn/getting-started/

Word-processing software:

- Apple Pages: support.apple.com/manuals/#iwork
- Microsoft Word: goo.gl/KXnLe

Language	
Areas	*Vocabulary:* Information, facts and figures *Grammar:* Present simple tense (for facts); question forms
Functions	Presenting factual information
Skills	Reading, writing

Resources	
High-tech	*Equipment:* One internet-enabled teacher computer and data projector; internet-enabled student computers or mobile devices (one per student) *Tools:* Infographics software (e.g. Easel.ly or Piktochart) *or* presentation software (e.g. Keynote, PowerPoint or Prezi) *or* word-processing software (e.g. Apple Pages or Microsoft Word) *Tools (optional):* Polling software (e.g. SurveyMonkey) *Documents:* Online worksheet (www.pearsoned.co.uk/hockly)
Low-tech	*Equipment:* One internet-enabled teacher computer and data projector *Documents:* Printed worksheet (follows Activity)
No-tech	*Documents:* Printed infographics; printed worksheet (follows Activity) *Stationery:* Paper, coloured pens and magazines (for images)

Digital risks
Some infographics may contain inappropriate content. Review the ones you plan to use beforehand, and – where possible – give students direct links to the infographics within the sites you choose.

Procedure

Before class

- Print out copies of the infographics from Steps 2 and 4 for each student in the class (no-tech version).

1. Start with a personal anecdote about information overload in your life: it always helps to situate this kind of discussion in your and your students' realities. You may focus attention on how much time you spend online, how distracted you are on the net, etc. Put students into pairs and have them compare anecdotes about their browsing and tech use habits, then conduct feedback as a whole group.

2. Put the word 'sharepocalypse' on the board and ask students what they think it means. You may have to help them with hints:

   • it's connected to online content;
   • it's about how much we share;
   • 'pocalypse' is short for 'apocalypse'.

   If your students are struggling to make sense of the word, ask them to go to the Sharepocalypse infographic (summify.com/static/infographic/social-sharing.png) (high-tech version), show it on the projector screen (low-tech version), or give out printouts (no-tech version). This infographic was produced in 2011 by Summify, using data from Facebook, Hubspot, Mashable, Nielsen and TechCrunch.

3. Elicit reactions from students. How much 'content' do they view on a daily basis, and how much do they share with others? Do they have time each day to keep up with what's going on in their digital lives?

4. Refer students to **Activity 11 Worksheet – Sixty seconds online** and ask them to complete it individually. Put them into pairs to compare their answers (see Appendix: Answer keys), then direct them to GO-Globe's In 60 Seconds infographic (goo.gl/nTfRB) to find the correct answers (high-tech version); alternatively, show it on the projector screen (low-tech version) or give out printouts (no-tech version). Conduct feedback as a whole group. Was anyone surprised by any of the facts and figures?

5. Tell students that what they're looking at is called an 'infographic' – a combination of 'information' and 'graphic'. An infographic is a graphic (visual) representation of information or data (see Chapter 1: *First focus: Language, Multimedia literacy*). They are going to make an infographic about the class use of technologies.

6. Divide the class into four groups and give each group one of the following topics:

   • mobile phone use
   • computer games

- internet use
- music and movies

Give each group ten minutes to brainstorm questions they want to ask in their topic area, then conduct feedback as a whole group. Once the questions are decided, they can prepare their survey – this can be done as an online survey using a polling service like SurveyMonkey (www.surveymonkey.com) (high-tech version) or on paper (low-tech and no-tech versions).

7. Each student should answer each of the four surveys. This can be done either in class or at home, whether the surveys have been prepared online (high-tech version) or composed on paper and photocopied (low-tech and no-tech versions). Once the data has been collected, students can move on to making the final infographic.

8. There are some free tools for making infographics, including Easel.ly (www.easel.ly) and Piktochart (piktochart.com) (for more options, see Angela Ancorn's 2010 blog post '10 Awesome Free Tools to Make Infographics' at MakeUseOf.com: www.makeuseof.com/tag/awesome-free-tools-infographics/); otherwise, your students could make them using presentation software (e.g. Keynote, PowerPoint or Prezi) or word-processing software (e.g. Apple Pages or Microsoft Word). In either case, students can make use of Creative Commons images (for more on CC images, see Activity 10, *Copycat*) (high-tech version). Alternatively, students can make their infographics on paper, perhaps using images cut out from magazines (low-tech and no-tech versions). Each group should prepare their part of the infographic with the data they've gathered and the images they've chosen. Once all four sections are in place they can be combined into one single graphic.

9. The completed infographic should provide plenty to discuss in the next class. A discussion about technology use and overreliance on technology fits well with Activity 31, *My digital life*.

Extension

Encourage students to add their infographics to, or to link to them from, their e-portfolios (see Chapter 3: *Assessing digital work, Assessing through e-portfolios*) (high-tech version).

Activity 11 Worksheet – Sixty seconds online

Match the two columns

Every sixty seconds on the internet:

60+	videos are added to YouTube
6,600+	emails are sent
1,700+	new blogs are created
600+	iPhone apps are downloaded
694,445	images are uploaded to Flickr
13,000+	downloads of Firefox are made
168,000,000	tweets are written
98,000+	searches are done on Google
70+	wall posts are made on Facebook
79,364	domains are registered

Activity 12: Sales techniques

Students produce a targeted advertisement for a product.

This activity examines multimedia literacy (especially, 'media literacy') from the advertising angle – what goes into an advert for a particular product, and what that says about the product and the target audience.

Literacy:	**Multimedia literacy** (complexity: ***)
Topic:	Advertising
Aim:	To produce an advertisement in the form of a vodcast
Level:	Intermediate +
Time:	120 minutes
Tech support:	Vodcasting/video editing:

- General: e-language.wikispaces.com/vodcasting
- iMovie: www.apple.com/findouthow/movies/
- Movie Maker: goo.gl/S6O2r

Vodcasting/videosharing:

- Vimeo: vimeo.com/help
- YouTube: support.google.com/youtube/?hl=en

Language	
Areas	*Vocabulary:* Advertisements
Functions	Describing objects and functions
Skills	Speaking, writing

Resources	
High-tech	*Equipment:* One internet-enabled teacher computer and data projector; internet-enabled student computers or mobile devices (one per group); student mobile phones with cameras, or digital cameras (one per group) *Tools:* Video-editing software (e.g. iMovie or Movie Maker) *Tools (optional):* Videosharing site (e.g. Vimeo or YouTube) *Documents:* Online worksheet (www.pearsoned.co.uk/hockly)
Low-tech	Not available for this activity
No-tech	Not available for this activity

Digital risks
Some of the content of websites featuring TV advertisements may be culturally inappropriate for your teaching context. Always check online resources before using them.

Procedure

Before class

- *(Optional)* Find a suitable advert on the Thinkbox website (www.thinkbox.tv) as a warmer for use in Step 1.

1. Start by asking about a current advertisement on television in the country where you teach. Try to pick one that has generated some controversy, or is universally popular. Ask who has seen it and what they think of it. Alternatively, you might like to start with a pre-selected advert (as described above).

2. Ask students to name some favourite advertisements and discuss the following as a whole class:

   - What makes a good TV advertisement?
   - How important is a good 'story'?
   - Do you like advertisements that develop a story in episodes?
   - What do you think of the roles of women and men in adverts?
   - Have you ever bought anything as a direct result of a TV advert?

3. Divide students into five small groups and tell them they are going to make an advertisement for a new mobile phone. They will need to map out a storyboard for their advertisement before making and editing the video. Refer groups to **Activity 12 Worksheet – Design your advert** and assign

them one of the target audiences (but ensure that each group keeps their target audience secret at this stage):

- businesspeople
- adult men
- stay-at-home parents
- teenagers
- pensioners

4. Help out as needed with the storyboarding process. Depending on how quick your students are, this process – and the resultant photo-taking and video-recording – may require up to an hour.

5. Groups will need to edit the videos and images as well as adding title credits, captions and some music using Apple's iMovie or Microsoft's Movie Maker (or similar software). Students can find Creative Commons music for their adverts at the CCMixter site (ccmixter.org) or other sources listed on the 'E-tools' page of the E-language wiki (e-language. wikispaces.com/e-tools#Creative%20Commons).

6. Finished videos can be uploaded to a class YouTube channel (www.youtube. com) or another videosharing site like Vimeo (vimeo.com), or simply viewed in class. Each group should present their advert (without saying who their target audience is) and get feedback from the rest of the class. Students viewing the videos should try to identify the target audience and say why the advertisement is (or isn't) effective for that audience:

- What elements in the advertisement reveal the target audience?
- Do these elements play on stereotypes of that audience?
- What messages do you get about the target audience?
- Which advertisement is the most effective?

Extension 1

Higher level students may delve further into gender stereotyping by exploring the Lynx campaign (see the Lynx YouTube channel at www.youtube.com/user/ thelynxeffect) or the Old Spice campaign (see the Old Spice YouTube channel at www.youtube.com/user/OldSpice). Further controversial advertising campaigns can be seen on the Benetton Media and Press website (www. benettongroup.com/media-press/image-gallery).

Extension 2

Encourage students to add their videos to, or to link to them on YouTube or Vimeo from, their e-portfolios (see Chapter 3: *Assessing digital work, Assessing through e-portfolios*).

Activity 12 Worksheet – Design your advert

Your group is going to create and edit a video advertisement for a mobile phone for a particular target audience. Your teacher will tell you which target audience your advertisement is aimed at. **Important: Your target audience is a secret! Don't share this information with other groups.**

Before you create and edit your video, you will need to collect the following media elements:

- Some photographs of your product (use a phone you have in your group).
- Some video footage of your product (again, use a phone you have in your group).
- Some music from CCMixter (ccmixter.org) or a similar site to use in the advertisement.

1. Think about your target audience:
   - What would make the phone attractive to them?
   - What kind of image of themselves would they like to see in the advert?
   - What would they want to do with the phone?
   - Why should they buy it?

2. Map out your storyboard:
   - How does the advert start?
   - What's the 'story' for the advertisement?
   - What information does your audience need at the end?

3. Gather your media:
   - Take any photos you need.
   - Shoot the video.
   - Find some suitable music.
   - Write any other parts of the script (voiceover, captions, etc.).

4. Now make your video! Use the video-editing software provided by your teacher.

Activity 13: Showcasing hobbies

Students produce a slideshow, with audio, about a hobby or interest.

The ability to combine media into a finished and polished document or arte-fact is part of the digital literacies portfolio. In this activity, students view an audio slideshow and then create one of their own.

Literacy: **Multimedia literacy** (complexity: ***)

Topic: Hobbies

Aim: To produce an audio-visual slideshow

Level: Elementary +

Time: 90 minutes + homework

Tech support: Multimedia sharing:

- General: e-language.wikispaces.com/social-sharing#multimedia-sharing

- VoiceThread: voicethread.com/?#c28

Presentation software:

- Keynote: support.apple.com/manuals/#iwork

- PowerPoint: goo.gl/vfLwD

- Prezi: prezi.com/learn/getting-started/

Language	
Areas	*Grammar:* Present simple tense
Functions	Describing objects and actions; giving opinions; giving instructions
Skills	Listening, speaking, reading, writing

Resources	
High-tech	*Equipment:* One internet-enabled teacher computer and data projector; internet-enabled student computers or mobile devices (one per student) *Equipment (optional):* Mobile phones with cameras, or digital cameras *Tools:* VoiceThread *Tools (optional):* Presentation software (e.g. Keynote, PowerPoint or Prezi); VoiceThread app
Low-tech	*Equipment:* One internet-enabled teacher computer and data projector *Tools:* VoiceThread *Tools (optional):* Presentation software (e.g. Keynote, PowerPoint or Prezi); VoiceThread app
No-tech	Not available for this activity

Digital risks

Ensure that your students are aware of the privacy settings on VoiceThread so that they can decide who can view their presentations. As with other activities using creative websites, ensure they are familiar with copyright for any images they use (see Activity 10, *Copycat*).

Procedure

Before class

- Prepare your Keynote, PowerPoint or Prezi presentation and/or gather your realia for use in Step 1.

- Prepare your VoiceThread presentation for use in Step 2.

1. Introduce the theme by talking about a hobby of your own. You could use a Keynote, PowerPoint or Prezi presentation, along with some realia, to make your talk visually appealing, interesting and multi-sensory. Encourage your students to ask you questions when you have finished your presentation.

2. Now show them an online presentation on your chosen hobby, using VoiceThread with photos and audio commentary. Get students to compare

the two presentations. Which one did they think was better? What are the advantages and disadvantages of one format over the other? Possible suggestions:

Face-to-face presentation	Online presentation
• audience can ask questions • audience can handle realia • presenter can get instant feedback • pressure to perform • . . . • . . .	• bigger potential audience • may get comments from a global audience • may bring contact with other enthusiasts • may bring contact with experts in the field • must be more polished • possibility of anonymous negative feedback • . . . • . . .

3. Tell students that they are going to create an online presentation about one of their hobbies or interests. In the remaining class time they will prepare the content and gather together the photographs they'll need for the VoiceThread presentation.

4. Get students to interview each other in pairs about their chosen hobby. The interviewer should take notes. They need to listen carefully and make a clear record of what they learn. This record should then be returned to the interviewee for checking, after which the interviewee can use it as the basis for their VoiceThread presentation audio.

5. Once each student has their content, encourage them to map out a storyboard. This can be done using PowerPoint or similar software (high-tech version) or on paper (low-tech version).

6. Once the content from their interview is in place they should think about the photos they'll need to illustrate their talk – these can be taken using their own mobile phones or digital cameras if available, or sourced from Google Images or Flickr (see Activity 10, *Copycat* for guidelines on finding Creative Commons-licensed images) (high-tech version). Alternatively, help each student to take one or two photos using the teacher's mobile phone or digital camera, or to search for one or two

relevant images using the teacher computer connected to the internet (low-tech version).

7. Show students how to create an account with VoiceThread and how to get started with a presentation: you will need to show them how to upload or choose their images, record a commentary and save their presentation. Note that students tend to spend a lot of time practising and editing when recording their own voices for public sites, so the actual production is best done for homework, when they will have the time and the privacy to produce a result they will be happy sharing. Once they have produced their VoiceThread presentation, they should share the address with you and their classmates – this can be done in a follow-up class or by email (high-tech version). Alternatively, produce one whole class slideshow: this means that each person will have some input into the final product, but you will need to do the recording and uploading in class using your own mobile phone or digital camera and the teacher computer (low-tech version).

8. VoiceThread allows viewers to leave comments. Ensure that you visit each of the slideshows and give some general feedback; try to encourage students to visit each other's and do the same (high-tech version). Otherwise, students can make verbal comments about the final version of the group presentation shown on the projector screen (low-tech version).

Variation

There is a VoiceThread app available for Apple iOS devices. You may want to investigate using this with your students if you have access to Apple devices.

Extension

Encourage students to embed their VoiceThread presentations in, or link to them from, their e-portfolios (see Chapter 3: *Assessing digital work, Assessing through e-portfolios*) (high-tech version).

Activity 14: Selling English

Students create a film collage of examples of English advertising in their environment.

This activity encourages students to collect digital photos and/or videos of examples of English they see around them being used to advertise products. These examples are collated into short films or 'vodcasts'. The activity helps students develop critical awareness of how English is used to 'sell' things, and it also develops their recording, editing and film-making skills. The activity runs over two classes – a preparatory class (Class 1), and a class in which students produce film collages (Class 2).

Literacy:	**Multimedia literacy** (overall complexity: ***)
Topic:	Advertising
Aim:	To create an advertising collage in the form of a vodcast
Level:	Elementary +
Time:	30 minutes (Class 1) + 60 minutes (Class 2) + homework
Tech support:	Vodcasting/video editing:

- General: e-language.wikispaces.com/vodcasting
- iMovie: www.apple.com/findouthow/movies/
- Movie Maker: goo.gl/S6O2r

Vodcasting/videosharing:

- Vimeo: vimeo.com/help
- YouTube: support.google.com/youtube/?hl=en

Language	
Areas	*Vocabulary:* Advertising; filming *Grammar:* Comparative and superlative adjectives
Functions	Discussing
Skills	Reading, speaking, writing

Resources	
High-tech	*Equipment:* One internet-enabled teacher computer and data projector; internet-enabled student computers or mobile devices (one per pair); mobile phones with cameras, or digital cameras (one per pair) *Tools:* Video-editing software (e.g. iMovie or Movie Maker) *Tools (optional):* Videosharing site (e.g. Vimeo or YouTube)
Low-tech	*Equipment:* One internet-enabled teacher computer and data projector; one mobile phone with camera, or digital camera *Tools:* Video-editing software (e.g. iMovie or Movie Maker) *Tools (optional):* Videosharing site (e.g. Vimeo or YouTube)
No-tech	Not available for this activity

Procedure

Before class

- To prepare for Class 1, search the internet for a few examples of English used for advertising in public spaces (e.g. billboards, posters and shop signs), or take your own digital photographs. If you find images online, make sure they are under Creative Commons licences or in the public domain. Bookmark the relevant webpages or set up a folder of your digital photos on your computer. Note that if you are teaching in an English-speaking environment, it will be relatively easy to find examples of English used for advertising in public spaces. However, even in non-English speaking environments, you may be able to find some examples to photograph.

- To prepare for Class 2, create a short film using a tool such as Apple's iMovie or Microsoft's Movie Maker. Include a soundtrack using Creative Commons music (e.g. from CCMixter at ccmixter.org), your own com-position, or simply a voiceover. Consider building in short subtitles saying where each image is from.

Class 1: English in advertising

1. Introduce the idea of English advertising in the environment around us by asking students to think back over the past week, and to note down any examples of English advertising or slogans they have seen outside of their English class (e.g. in magazine, newspaper and TV advertisements,

and on billboards, posters and shop signs). If students are in an English-speaking environment, they will have seen plenty of examples of these, so ask them to think about any examples of advertising which particularly struck them. Get feedback. Show students the examples you have collected.

2. Ask students to consider the effect of using English in advertisements. In small groups, students should discuss some or all of the following questions:

- (For students in an English-speaking environment) Do advertisements in public spaces in your country sometimes include English? Can you share any examples you remember?

- What effect do advertisers want to create by including English?

- Do you think a product looks 'cooler' or 'better' because it includes English in the advertisement?

- Are you more or less likely to buy a product because English is used in the advertisement?

- Imagine you are an advertising executive in your country. Would you include English in an advertisement for any of the following products: a watch, a car, cat food, a hotel, a bank, photography equipment, clothes, frozen food? Why/why not?

3. Tell students that they are going to work in pairs to create a collage in the form of a short film, or vodcast, showing examples of English advertising in their environment. Each pair of students should try to collect at least two examples of English being used in each of the following:

- a magazine or newspaper advertisement
- a public billboard or poster
- a shop sign
- a restaurant/café menu
- any other places using English in advertisements

If possible, students should collect these examples in digital format. There are two main ways they can do this: if students have access to a digital camera or mobile phone with a camera they can take digital photos of real-world objects, or they can simply search the internet for Creative Commons-licensed images (see Activity 10, *Copycat*) (high-tech version). Alternatively, they can cut out and collect advertisements from magazines, newspapers, etc. (low-tech version).

Give students a clear timeframe in which to collect their examples, e.g. one week. Students must bring their examples to class after the deadline, in digital format (high-tech version) or in hard copy (low-tech version).

Class 2: Creating films

1. Show students your film collage (alternatively, you can do this after students produce their own films).

2. Pairs should share their digital photos and videos, and work together on computers to create a short film, or vodcast, using iMovie or Movie Maker; encourage them to add a soundtrack and subtitles for each example image (high-tech version). Alternatively, do this as a whole class activity: students can contribute one or two images each, which can be photographed by the teacher using a digital camera or a mobile phone with a camera, and added to the film created by the whole group using the teacher computer and projector screen (low-tech version).

3. Show the completed films one by one to the class (high-tech version), or show the whole group film from the beginning (low-tech version). After each film, ask the class which advertisements/images they remember most from the film. Ask students what the effect of using English in these advertisements is. Ask them if they think they are more or less likely to buy the product because it includes English in the advertisement – have they changed their minds at all? Point out to students that language can be used by advertisers to manipulate our opinions, and to persuade us to buy products that we may not really need.

Extension

As long as they have used their own digital images in their films, or chosen Creative Commons-licensed images (attributed as necessary), encourage students to add them to their e-portfolios (see Chapter 3: *Assessing digital work, Assessing through e-portfolios*) (high-tech version). The films can also be shared with a wider audience (e.g. other classes, parents) if they are uploaded to a videosharing site such as YouTube (www.youtube.com) or Vimeo (vimeo.com).

Activity 15: Transmedia stories

Students interact with a multimedia story online and create one of their own.

This activity encourages students to reimagine traditional writing and produce a transmedia text of their own, based on a popular online series.

Acknowledgement: Parts of this activity are reproduced with permission from the Inanimate Alice website *Starter Activities Booklet* and are specifically aimed at a younger audience, though adults may also enjoy the story and production values.

Literacy:	**Multimedia literacy** (complexity: ***)
Topic:	Adventure stories
Aim:	To produce a transmedia episode of a popular online story
Level:	Intermediate +
Time:	180 minutes +
Tech support:	Multimedia sharing:

- General: e-language.wikispaces.com/social-sharing#Multimedia%20sharing
- VoiceThread: voicethread.com/?#c28

Presentation software:

- Keynote: support.apple.com/manuals/#iwork
- PowerPoint: goo.gl/vfLwD
- Prezi: prezi.com/learn/getting-started/

Vodcasting/video editing:

- General: e-language.wikispaces.com/vodcasting
- iMovie: www.apple.com/findouthow/movies/
- Movie Maker: goo.gl/S6O2r

Language	
Areas	*Grammar:* Narrative (present and past) tenses
Functions	Narrating
Skills	Reading, speaking, writing

Resources	
High-tech	*Equipment:* One internet-enabled teacher computer and data projector; internet-enabled student computers or mobile devices (one per group) *Tools:* Multimedia sharing site (e.g. VoiceThread) *or* video-editing software (e.g. iMovie or Movie Maker) *or* presentation software (e.g. Keynote, PowerPoint or Prezi)
Low-tech	Not available for this activity
No-tech	Not available for this activity

Procedure

1. Introduce the topic by discussing the kinds of texts your students generally read. Do they prefer comic books, classic novels, novels written for their particular age group, or do they only read shorter texts such as the news or blog posts?

2. Tell them they are going to start 'reading' a story online. Play the first part of Episode #1 – 'China' from the Inanimate Alice website (inanimatealice.com) on the projector screen. Let the story run until you reach the third section (the photographs), then review what the students have learnt about Alice so far. Answers should include:

   - She is 8 years old.
   - She is in Northern China.
   - She stays with her mum at a base camp.
   - Her father is looking for oil.
   - He left two days ago and should have been home by now.

3. Now ask what they would like to know about Alice, and what they think is going to happen next in the story. Get them to look closely at the photographs on the projector screen and ask the following questions:

- What do the photographs tell you about the place where Alice is living?
- What do they tell you about the people her dad is working for?
- Who do you think the people in the photographs are?
- How do you think the photographs were taken?
- What do the moving images of the jeep tell you about the landscape?
- What do the colours in the moving images suggest to you?

4. Play the rest of the story on the projector screen, then ask the following questions and invite students to speculate:

- What do you think actually happened to Alice's dad?
- How does Alice feel about her way of life?
- Will they stay in China after this incident?
- Will Alice get her dog at last?
- What is causing the humming sound in the sky?
- Why don't we ever see Alice?

5. Freeze the narrative on the final screenshot. Ask students to describe in detail what they see, paying particular attention to:

- Objects in the frame
- Colour
- Tone (this will need some explanation)
- Symbols (map, no food signs, etc.)
- Movement

Ask them what it reminds them of: Film? TV? Games? Tell them that this is a version of a *transmedia story* – a text where a story is told using different media platforms (see Chapter 1: *First focus: Language, Multimedia literacy*; note that a true transmedia story would require students to navigate across multiple platforms, so this is a simplified version of the concept). Ask them to help you complete the following table on the board:

Transmedia text	Printed story
Music	**Images**
• Adds atmosphere	• Provide visual context
• Creates suspense	• ...
• ...	• ...

Try to tease out the use of various media in the first episode. Examine the roles of the images, the text, the soundtrack (music, voices, etc.), the use of video, the colours chosen, opportunities for interaction, etc. Do they prefer this kind of text to more traditional books?

6. Tell students that they are going to make a transmedia version of Episode #2 of Inanimate Alice. In the story Alice goes to Italy with her parents on a skiing holiday and something terrible happens up on the snowy mountains. Work together to map out the story based on their suggestions, then divide the students into groups with the following roles:

- **Group A – Video**
  They should collect suitable video material through a Google Advanced Search (www.google.com/advanced_search).

- **Group B – Images**
  They should collect suitable images through Google Images or Flickr (see Activity 10, *Copycat* for further details). Alternatively they may find images at Creative Commons sources such as ELTPics (www.flickr.com/photos/eltpics/sets/).

- **Group C – Audio**
  They should collect background music from a site such as CCMixter (ccmixter.org) and sound effects from a site such as PacDV (www.pacdv.com/sounds/index.html).

- **Group D – Text**
  They will need to write the text for each screen of the story.

Note that in all cases, students should ensure that the media artefacts they collect are under Creative Commons licences, in the public domain, or copyright-free (see Box 1.12 and Activity 10, *Copycat* for further details). Further sources of reusable artefacts may be found on the 'E-tools' page of the E-language wiki (e-language.wikispaces.com/e-tools#Creative%20Commons).

7. Once all the media artefacts have been sourced, bring the class back together to discuss what they have found and where it fits in the story. Then move on to create it.

8. The final story can be created using VoiceThread (see Activity 13, *Showcasing hobbies*), or video-editing software such as iMovie or Movie Maker (see Activity 12, *Sales techniques*), or presentation software such as Keynote, PowerPoint or Prezi. This can be done either in small groups or as a whole class activity.

9. When students finish their story or stories, watch it/them together. Then watch Episode #2 of Inanimate Alice. How did their story or stories compare to the original? Whose was closest? Which did they prefer?

Activity 16: Avatars

Students create online avatars.

Many virtual worlds and games require you to create an 'avatar', or online character. This activity encourages students to create avatars, and then to discuss the significance of the images we choose for our online identities.

Literacy: **Gaming literacy** and **Personal literacy** (overall complexity: ****)

Topic: Appearance and personality

Aim: To raise awareness of online identity and virtual worlds/ games

Level: Elementary +

Time: 60 minutes

Tech support: Gaming:

- General: e-language.wikispaces.com/gaming
- Club Penguin: support.clubpenguin.com/help/
- Habbo: help.habbo.com/categories/118-habbo-support
- Moshi Monsters: www.moshimonsters.com/help
- The Sims: help.ea.com/en/the-sims?sso_redirect=1
- World of Warcraft: us.battle.net/wow/en/game/guide/

Presentation software:

- PowerPoint: goo.gl/vfLwD

Virtual worlds:

- General: e-language.wikispaces.com/virtual-worlds
- Second Life: wiki.secondlife.com/wiki/Help_Portal

Word-processing software:

- Apple Pages: support.apple.com/manuals/#iwork
- Microsoft Word: goo.gl/KXnLe

Language	
Areas	*Vocabulary:* Appearance and body; personality and identity *Grammar:* Is; has/have got
Functions	Describing people
Skills	Speaking, reading, writing, listening

Resources	
High-tech	*Equipment:* One internet-enabled teacher computer and data projector; internet-enabled student computers or mobile devices (one per student or pair) *Tools:* PowerPoint; avatar creation site (e.g. Meez, Build Your Wild Self or CYOS); word-processing software (e.g. Apple Pages or Microsoft Word)
Low-tech	*Equipment:* One internet-enabled teacher computer and data projector *Tools:* PowerPoint; avatar creation site (e.g. Meez, Build Your Wild Self or CYOS)
No-tech	*Documents:* Printed images of avatars from virtual worlds/games

Digital risks
Most virtual worlds are aimed at adults only. Virtual worlds aimed at younger learners, such as Club Penguin (www.clubpenguin.com) or Habbo Hotel (www.habbo.com), usually require parental permission. The current activity recommends websites where students can create avatars, rather than navigate around virtual worlds or gaming environments (see Box 1.3).

Procedure

Before class

- Search the web for Creative Commons-licensed images of avatars from virtual worlds like Second Life, or gaming environments like World of

Warcraft (see Activity 10, *Copycat* for how to find Creative Commons-licensed pictures). Choose a range of 6–8 interesting-looking avatars, including animals and unusual objects. Collate your chosen images into a PowerPoint slideshow (high-tech and low-tech versions) or print them out (no-tech version), for use in Step 1.

- *(Optional for high-tech version)* Find and bookmark example avatars from each of the virtual worlds/games in Step 2 below (high-tech and low-tech versions) or print them out (no-tech version).

- Decide which avatar creation site you will use for Step 3 below, and create your own avatar. Bookmark the webpage where you have created it, or copy the image onto a PowerPoint slide (high-tech and low-tech versions); alternatively, print it out (no-tech version).

1. Show your students a number of avatars, either collated into a PowerPoint slideshow (high-tech and low-tech versions) or printed out (no-tech versions). Ask students what they think these avatars show – what qualities or traits are the avatar owners trying to project?

2. Put the following on the board: *Second Life, World of Warcraft, The Sims, Habbo (Hotel), Club Penguin, Moshi Monsters*. Ask students what they know about these. Have they used any of these virtual worlds/games?

   Put students into small groups and give each group the name of one of these worlds on a card, and ask them to find out as much as possible about it in 2 minutes by searching online (high-tech version). They could then report their findings back to the class. Lower level classes could research their assigned virtual world or game in Simple English Wikipedia (simple.wikipedia.org/wiki).

   Alternatively, show pictures of avatars from each of the following virtual worlds/games on the projector screen (high-tech and low-tech versions) or print out pictures of the avatars (no-tech version) and ask students to guess which virtual world/game each comes from:

   - *Second Life:* a MUVE (Multi-User Virtual Environment), or virtual world, for adults. For more information, see the Wikipedia article on Second Life (en.wikipedia.org/wiki/Second_life).

   - *World of Warcraft:* a MMORPG (Massively Multiplayer Online Role-Playing Game) in which players band together to overcome challenges and fulfil quests. For more information, see the Wikipedia article on World of Warcraft (en.wikipedia.org/wiki/World_of_Warcraft).

- *The Sims:* a game in which players create and look after virtual people. For more information, see the Wikipedia article on The Sims (en.wikipedia.org/wiki/The_Sims).
- *Habbo:* a MMORPG for teenagers in which avatars interact in a hotel setting. It was originally called Habbo Hotel. For more information, see the Wikipedia article on Habbo (en.wikipedia.org/wiki/Habbo_hotel).
- *Club Penguin:* a MMORPG for younger children in which the avatars are penguins. For more information, see the Wikipedia article on Club Penguin (en.wikipedia.org/wiki/Club_penguin).
- *Moshi Monsters:* a game aimed at children aged 7–12 in which they adopt a virtual monster and look after it. For more information, see in the Wikipedia article on Moshi Monsters (en.wikipedia.org/wiki/Moshi_Monsters).

Point out that all of these environments are different, but most of them allow users to interact or network with each other. This gives them some similarity with social networking sites (see Box 1.3). World of Warcraft, for example, depends on players collaborating in order to fulfil quests.

Point out that some of the virtual worlds/games above allocate users a standardised avatar (e.g. Club Penguin). Others allow users to create a personalised avatar from templates. Second Life is arguably the world that allows the most variety in terms of avatars – you can choose to be an object, an animal, a mythical being or a real person! If students are familiar with any online games or immersive worlds, what avatars do they have? Ask them to describe their avatars, and how they chose their characteristics.

3. Introduce Meez (www.meez.com/create-avatar.dm) and ask if any students already know or use it. This site is aimed at teenagers and older students and can be used free of cost. Ask students to work individually or in pairs to create a 3D online avatar on the Meez site (high-tech version). Alternatively, students can draw an avatar on paper, based on one they already know or own, or based on the examples you showed in Steps 1 and 2 (low-tech and no-tech versions).

Students can email you the images so you can collate them into a PowerPoint slideshow for Step 6 below, and they may also wish to print out copies (high-tech version). Alternatively, they can post paper versions around the classroom walls for others to see (low-tech and no-tech versions).

Variation

For younger students (aged 6–12), choose one of these sites to create avatars (high-tech version):

- Build Your Wild Self: www.buildyourwildself.com
- CYOS (Create Your Own Superhero): marvel.com/games/cyos

4. Show students the avatar you created before class. Elicit a physical description of your avatar, including adjectives to describe general traits, including personality. If necessary, put key structures and vocabulary on the board (*she's got dark spiky hair and green eyes, she looks weird, she looks powerful*, etc.), or build up an entire paragraph of description on the board for lower level students. You can skip this step with higher level students.

5. Ask students to write a paragraph describing their avatar in a word-processing program (high-tech version) or on paper (low-tech and no-tech versions). Monitor and help them with language as necessary.

6. Show the collated PowerPoint images on the projector screen for the class to see (high-tech version) or ask students to circulate and look at classmates' avatar images on the classroom walls (low-tech and no-tech versions). Students can read out their written descriptions, and the class should try to identify which description matches which avatar.

7. Put students into groups of three or four, or work with the whole class, to discuss online identity. Use the discussion points below if necessary. The older and more proficient your students, the more you will be able to explore this topic.

- Explain why you chose certain features for your avatar. What qualities were you trying to project?

- Meez avatars are in human form, but some virtual environments (such as Second Life or World of Warcraft) allow avatars to take non-human form. Imagine choosing the following avatars: an animal, a mythical or fantastical creature (fairy, gnome, dragon, alien, etc.), or an object. What non-human avatar would you choose, and why?

- James Paul Gee, a gaming expert, suggests that we have a 'projective identity' (2007b). This is the way we would like to be, and it falls somewhere between our real-world identity and our virtual identity/identities (see Chapter 1: *First focus: Language, Gaming literacy*). What qualities or traits of your avatar reflect this projective identity? Are there any qualities your avatar has that you would like to have in real life? Rather than physical qualities, think of personality traits or general attributes such as strength of character or humour.

- Does your avatar have any negative qualities, and if so, why did you include them?

- Even if you don't have an avatar in a virtual world, you may have a Facebook, Twitter or LinkedIn account. What is your profile picture (which is sometimes also called an avatar) like? What sort of image do you try to project through your choice of profile picture?

Extension

Encourage students to add their avatars, along with their descriptive paragraphs, to their e-portfolios (see Chapter 3: *Assessing digital work, Assessing through e-portfolios*) (high-tech version).

Activity 17: Choose your own adventure

Students prepare a 'choose your own adventure' game.

With games playing an increasing role in education, this is a chance for students to see exactly what goes into creating even a simple game using text and images. This activity is open-ended in terms of time, so can be either a short class activity or a longer-term project.

Acknowledgement: We first saw a version of this activity on a free course run by Graham Stanley on the SEETA platform (www.seeta.eu).

Literacy:	**Gaming literacy** (complexity: ****)
Topic:	Adventure games
Aim:	To raise awareness of and implement basic game design
Level:	Intermediate +
Time:	90 minutes +
Tech support:	Gaming:

- General: e-language.wikispaces.com/gaming

- Pick a Path: en.wikipedia.org/wiki/Choose_Your_
Own_Adventure

Presentation software:

- PowerPoint: goo.gl/vfLwD

Language	
Areas	*Vocabulary:* Mystery, adventure and crime *Grammar:* Present simple tense; narrative tenses
Functions	Narrating
Skills	Writing, reading, speaking

Resources	
High-tech	*Equipment:* One internet-enabled teacher computer and data projector; internet-enabled student computers or mobile devices (one per group) *Tools:* PowerPoint *Documents:* Online worksheet (www.pearsoned.co.uk/hockly)
Low-tech	*Equipment:* One internet-enabled teacher computer and data projector *Tools:* PowerPoint *Documents:* Printed worksheet (follows Activity)
No-tech	Not available for this activity

Digital risks
Some content on some of the sites recommended for this activity may not be suitable in certain contexts. Choose example adventure games in advance and link directly to them for your students.

Procedure

Before class

- Before you do this activity you will need to create a simple adventure using PowerPoint, for use in Step 2. You can find more details on the 'Choose your own adventure' page of the Go Go Gidgits site (www.learningplace.com.au/deliver/content.asp?pid=40754).

- Select an example of a 'Pick a path' adventure for use in Step 3. You will find examples on the Choose Your Own Adventure wiki (editthis.info/choose_your_own_adventure/Main_Page), or, for more basic examples, try Larry Ferlazzo's *The Best Places to Read and Write 'Choose Your Own Adventure' Stories* (goo.gl/9r4Nj).

1. Introduce the theme of games using **Activity 17 Worksheet – Games and me**. Conduct feedback as a whole group and pick up on any interesting topics or revelations.

2. Introduce the theme of 'Pick a Path' adventures using your own example created in PowerPoint. Go through the adventure on the projector screen

with the students. Ask students to vote on the choices and work your way through the short story as a whole class.

3. Now show students the other example adventure you selected (as described above). Work through it with them in the same way.

4. Tell students they are going to write a 'Pick a Path' adventure. How would they start writing an adventure game: story, synopsis, storyboard, flowchart . . . ?

5. The writing stage is best done in small groups. For a simple approach to this activity, students can use PowerPoint (high-tech version) or paper (low-tech version) to produce the final adventures (see Variation, below, for ideas on more complex approaches involving richer production tools). In their groups students should follow these steps:

   • choose a theme for their adventure;

   • decide on the main character;

   • map out the possible endings;

   • chart the route to these endings (see S.M. Ragan's *Choose Your Own Adventure Game as Directed Graph* at www.seanmichaelragan.com/img/chimneyrockoutline.png for further ideas).

6. This is a rather open-ended writing project that may take one or two classes, or may run for longer if your students are enjoying and learning from it. Once the adventures are complete, they can be shared with – and played by – other groups.

Variation 1

There are lots of possible variations on this activity. For example, you could try using a wiki for students to make their adventures (see the Choose Your Own Adventure wiki as a good example of this approach); or you could use Flickr (see David Muir's *You Are in a Maze of Long Straight Passages, All Alike,* at www.flickr.com/photos/daviddmuir/1924752950/); or you could even use YouTube (for examples, see Greg Kulowiec's *Choose Your Own Adventures: Tutorial* at: goo.gl/u5Rfk) (high-tech version).

Variation 2

The Choose Your Own Adventure wiki encourages multiple authors and edits from visitors, so you may want to open up the stories in progress to other groups: this may take the form of story editing or refining, but might also involve a process of peer review of writing and language, as groups move through the editing process (high-tech version).

Extension

Encourage students to upload their completed PowerPoint games to their e-portfolios (see Chapter 3: *Assessing digital work, Assessing through e-portfolios*) (high-tech version).

Activity 17 Worksheet – Games and me

Talk to your partner about the games you play:

- What games machines do you have (Xbox, Wii, etc.)?
- What sorts of games do you like to play?
- How many hours per week do you spend playing games?
- What was the last game you played?
- Do you prefer single or multiplayer games?
- Do you ever play games online?
- Do you ever play games on your mobile phone?
- Have you ever thought of developing a game?

Activity 18: History hunt

Students create multimedia local history quizzes on mobile devices.

This activity gets the students creating multimedia 'clues' in an app for a mobile handheld device, such as a smartphone or tablet. These are becoming the convergence devices of choice in both low- and high-tech contexts (see Box 1.1). Becoming familiar with the multimedia possibilities of smartphones and other handheld devices is an important literacy in our increasingly mobile world. This activity is a mini-project and will take at least three 1-hour classes to complete.

Acknowledgement: Thanks to Anne Fox for this activity (see also the note at the end of the activity).

Literacy:	**Mobile literacy**, **Multimedia literacy** and **Gaming literacy** (complexity: ****)
Topic:	Local history
Aim:	To create a local history quiz in the form of a multimedia mobile app
Level:	Elementary +
Time:	60 minutes (Class 1) + 60 minutes (Class 2) + 60 minutes (Class 3) + homework
Tech support:	Blogs:

- General: e-language.wikispaces.com/blogs
- Blogger: support.google.com/blogger/?hl=en
- Edublogs: help.edublogs.org

Mapping:

- Google Maps: earth.google.com/outreach/ tutorial_mymaps.html

Mobile learning:

- General: e-language.wikispaces.com/m-learning
- Apps: e-language.wikispaces.com/apps
- Foursquare: support.foursquare.com
- Quizlet: quizlet.com/faqs/

- SCVNGR: support.scvngr.com/home
- Wikitude: www.wikitude.com/faq

Multimedia sharing:

- General: e-language.wikispaces.com/social-sharing#multimedia-sharing
- Glogster: www.youtube.com/watch?v=hvQX5LeQ-zg

Wikis:

- General: e-language.wikispaces.com/wikis
- PBworks: usermanual.pbworks.com
- Wikispaces: help.wikispaces.com

Language	
Areas	*Vocabulary:* Buildings; historical events *Grammar:* Passive voice; past simple tense; question forms
Skills	Reading, writing, speaking, listening

Resources	
High-tech	*Equipment:* One internet-enabled teacher computer and data projector; internet-enabled student computers (one per group); internet-enabled student mobile devices running the Android operating system or the Apple iOS (one per group) *Tools:* SCVNGR; Google Maps *Tools (optional):* Glogster; class blog (e.g. Blogger or Edublogs) *or* class wiki (e.g. PBworks or Wikispaces); Foursquare app
Low-tech	*Equipment:* One internet-enabled teacher computer and data projector; one mobile device running the Android operating system or the Apple iOS *Tools:* SCVNGR *Tools (optional):* Foursquare app
No-tech	Not available for this activity

Digital risks

- Using mobile phones – particularly internet data plans – can be expensive. Ensure that students are aware of what their contract entitles them to: a certain amount of data is often included in a phone contract, but in other cases downloading data (images, video, text) may be expensive. (In this activity, the mobile phones used need to have a data plan in order to download SCVNGR 'challenges' in situ.)

- You may need to clear this activity with the management of your institution to fit in with the policy for mobile phone use (if there is one). In addition, ensure that the institution cannot be held responsible for any expenditure by students using mobile phone data plans.

- For young learners, parental permission must be sought if students are to leave the school in order to complete the treasure hunt in local history spots.

Procedure

Before class

- Ensure you have access to a mobile phone running the Android operating system or the Apple iOS.

- Plan to put students into small groups of three or four, ensuring that each group has one Android or Apple iOS mobile device to work with (high-tech version). These could be a class set of tablet computers (such as iPads), digital media players (such as iPod Touches), or mobile phones (such as iPhones or Android phones), or you can group students so that one student per group already owns one of these devices. For student-owned devices, check data plans in advance (see Digital risks). You will need to do all of this well in advance of the class.

- Sign up for an account with SCVNGR (www.scvngr.com) or a similar service for building multimedia quiz apps. Note that the SCVNGR app allows five free 'challenges' (quiz questions) per account. The minimum age to set up an account is 13. Teachers with young learners under 13 need to use their own SCVNGR accounts, but can write to SCVNGR requesting additional 'challenges' if necessary, so as to ensure enough for each group of students. Adults can sign up for their own SCVNGR accounts. Alternative multimedia mobile quiz apps include Quizlet (quizlet.com) and Wikitude (www.wikitude.com).

- Read through the class procedure below, and then create four questions about local history sites or events, for use in Class 1, Step 4. These should include:

  - one text question;
  - one question with an image (photographed by you, e.g. on a mobile phone);
  - one question with a short audio file (recorded by you, e.g. on a mobile phone);
  - one question with a short video file (filmed by you, e.g. on a mobile phone).

  Upload them to SCVGR via a computer, and test your questions on your mobile phone. Remember that questions in SCVNGR are called 'challenges', and a series of challenges forms a 'trek'.

Class 1: Research

1. Introduce the topic of local history. Put the names of the four sites or events (i.e. those linked to the four questions you created in the 'Before class' stage) on the board. Ask students what they know about these. Elicit a few key historical facts related to them (e.g. *The oldest building in town is XX, built in XX. XX happened in the town square in the XX century. The statue in XX street is of XX, who did XX*, etc.).

2. Use Google Maps (maps.google.com) or a paper map of the town to show the route between your chosen sites/events, as an example. Tell students they will work in small groups to produce their own route as a history 'treasure hunt', with questions that can be viewed on mobile devices. Elicit more historical points of interest/events in your town. If your town is small enough, you could even take your students out of class for a reconnaissance walk to identify important locations, instead of using a map (see Digital risks above if you work with younger learners).

3. Put students into groups (as described under Before class). Ask them to explore a list of 4–5 websites which contain information about local history (high-tech version), or bring in printed historical material such as tourist office leaflets, maps, books or encyclopaedias (low-tech version). Each group should create their own route of 5–10 key local

historical sites/events and mark them on a Google Map (high-tech version) or a map from the tourist office, or even a hand-drawn map (low-tech version). The locations should be numbered in order to create a route. This is to help students prepare the order of their questions (see Step 4).

4. Students now need to decide on a question for each location. The question can consist of:

   - text (e.g. *'What is the date above the town hall entrance?'*), or
   - text with an image (e.g. *'What is this building?'* with a picture of the town hall), or
   - a short audio file (e.g. the first text question above recorded by a student), or
   - a short video file (e.g. a clip of the town hall with an audio voiceover question, filmed by a student on a mobile phone).

   Each question must include a very short text for a wrong answer (e.g. *'Not correct – try again!'*), and a text for a correct answer which includes information on where to go for the next question (e.g. *'That's right! Now go to the train station'*). The correct answer could also include an instruction (e.g. *'Take a photo of the statue outside the town hall'*).

   On the projector screen, show students your own SCVNGR history questions as examples – and see if they know the answers! They can research any questions they don't know for homework, or by visiting the sites after school. Ideally, try to ensure that your own chosen sites/events would require students to actually *visit* the relevant places to find the answers. Highlight the different media used in each of your example questions (text, image, audio, video), and point out how each correct answer leads to the next question.

5. Give students time to revise their planned questions, and choice of media, in light of the examples you have shown them.

6. Ask them to collect photos or short video clips for their chosen questions on their mobile phones outside class. They should bring these images or video clips to the next class (high-tech version).

Classes 2 and 3: The history 'treasure hunt'

1. Log into your SCVNGR account online, and review your own SCVNGR questions with the class using the projector screen. Check the answers. Draw attention again to the different media used in each question.

2. Allow students time to finish preparing their questions in their groups, if they haven't done so in the previous class. They may want to produce audio questions by recording these on their group's mobile device, for example (high-tech version).

3. On the projector screen, show students how to upload multimedia questions to the SCVNGR app, using your own examples prepared in the Before class stage. Student groups can then upload their questions to their SCVGR accounts (high-tech version). Alternatively, upload a selection of questions from different groups to the teacher's SCVNGR account as a whole class activity, using the internet-enabled teacher computer and projector screen (low-tech version).

4. Tell students to test their own quiz, or the class quiz, on a mobile device.

5. In their groups, students should then try at least one other group's treasure hunt, or preferably more; ideally, they should visit local historical landmarks to do so, downloading each question when they reach the landmark (high-tech version). If it is not feasible for students to leave the school, the treasure hunts can be carried out in class, with students searching for the information on the web in their groups. Alternatively, this can be carried out as a whole class activity, with the treasure hunt answers being marked on a Google Map or a printed map (low-tech version).

6. Conduct a review/feedback stage once the treasure hunt(s) has/have been completed. How successfully was it/were they completed? What kinds of questions were included in the treasure hunt(s) (e.g. taking a photo, recording a comment, etc.)? Allow students to compare and share what they have learned. Discuss any challenges thrown up by the project, and what students enjoyed/didn't enjoy about it.

Extension 1

Ask students to produce a multimedia online poster, e.g. in Glogster (www. glogster.com), including five of the most important or interesting local history facts they have learned through the treasure hunts (high-tech version). Embed the posters in, or link to them from, a class blog or wiki, or encourage students to add them to their e-portfolios (see Chapter 3: *Assessing digital work, Assessing through e-portfolios*).

Extension 2

Students with mobile phones could use the Foursquare app (available for Android, Apple iOS, BlackBerry and Windows devices) to take photos at key locations in the local area – ranging from famous historical sites and public buildings to shops and restaurants – and upload them, with commentary, for other visitors to those sites to view on their mobile devices.

Note: See Anne Fox's account of this project, carried out with young learners in Denmark:

- The History Game – Will it Work? (annefox.eu/2011/08/19/the-history-game-%E2%80%93-will-it-work/)

- The History Game – Part 2 (annefox.eu/2011/11/21/the-history-game-part-2/)

Activity 19: A picture a day

Students document their lives on a mobile image site.

This activity covers a variety of literacies. It encourages people to think about what they share, when and with whom.

Literacy:	**Mobile literacy**, **multimedia literacy** and **personal literacy** (complexity: ****)
Topic:	Daily life
Aim:	To document daily life through a series of photos
Level:	Elementary +
Time:	90 minutes + homework
Tech support:	Photosharing:

- General: e-language.wikispaces.com/social-sharing#Photosharing

- Instagram: help.instagram.com

- Posterous Spaces: posterous.uservoice.com/knowledgebase

- Posterous Spaces sample: travelgavin.posterous.com

- Smilebox: www.smilebox.com/collages.html

Language	
Areas	*Vocabulary:* Any, or an area specifically chosen for recycling by the teacher *Grammar:* Any, or an area specifically chosen for recycling by the teacher
Functions	Discussing daily routines, habits and customs
Skills	Speaking, writing

Resources	
High-tech	*Equipment:* One internet-enabled teacher computer and data projector; internet-enabled student computers (one per student); student mobile phones with cameras, or digital cameras (one per student) *Tools:* Posterous Spaces *Tools (optional):* Smilebox; Instagram app
Low-tech	*Equipment:* One internet-enabled teacher computer and projector; student mobile phones with cameras, or digital cameras (as available) *Tools:* Posterous Spaces *Tools (optional):* Smilebox; Instagram app
No-tech	Not available for this activity

Digital risks

- This activity is only appropriate for students who have access to smartphones with cameras in their everyday lives. Before you decide to do this activity, check on this. Be wary of reinforcing the digital divide if only some students have such access (see Box 1.4; Activity 29, *News in my networks* for more details).

- As with all media uploading sites, ensure that your students are aware they should only be uploading their own photographs.

- Ensure that students are familiar with the privacy settings of Posterous Spaces. Encourage them to use private (member) spaces for sharing their photos.

Procedure

Before class

- Ensure all students have a mobile phone with a camera (high-tech version), or can borrow one (low-tech version).

- Set up your own Posterous Spaces account (posterous.com) and upload a few images and descriptions of the four or five days leading up to the class, for use in Step 2. You may wish to take a look at 'The Teacher's Guide to Using Posterous Spaces' on the Edudemic website (goo.gl/R4teT).

- Make a collage of the photos from your own Posterous Spaces account from the past week – a good site for making collages is Smilebox (www.smilebox.com/collages.html) – for use in Step 1.

1. Show your collage on the projector screen. Invite your students to guess what you've been doing for the past week, where you've been, when, etc. As they guess the significance of the photos, give them some more information about each of them.

2. Show students your Posterous Spaces account and the postings they've seen. Tell them they are going to keep a photographic record of one week in their lives. As they go about their daily lives, they will be taking at least one photograph per day using a mobile phone or digital camera, uploading it to their Posterous account, and adding a short paragraph describing it. Get them to think back to the past week and make some notes about what they did each day.

3. In pairs, get students to tell each other about each day in the past week. Encourage pairs to ask questions and get more information. If you want them to use a particular lexical set then you may want to limit this activity, e.g. 'describe the clothes you were wearing each day', or 'describe what you did in the evenings', etc.

4. For Steps 4–6, students can work on individual computers or internet-enabled mobile devices (high-tech version), or else they can use the teacher computer and take turns (low-tech version). Walk them through setting up a Posterous Spaces account on the projector screen. Next, ensure that each student has a space set up and that they know how to add a new post. Alternatively, if you wish to simplify the whole activity, consider setting up one space for the whole class and having all the students as contributors; this will cut down on the time needed.

5. Get each student to add a post with the notes they made from Step 3, above. This will be a simple text-only post unless they wish to include a Creative Commons image from the web (see Activity 10, *Copycat*). This can be done in class or for homework if they have the equipment.

6. Once each student has added their first post, show them how to make their space private and invite their classmates to subscribe, ensuring that they also invite you to subscribe so that you can monitor and give feedback. Alternatively, each student can simply add their post to the group space.

Extension 1

This is an open-ended activity that may become a regular interest for some of your students. Part of the students' homework for the following week could be to continue to document their lives in their Posterous Space(s), adding photos from their mobile phones or digital cameras, as well as short paragraphs explaining where each photo was taken and what they were doing. Ensure that you give some feedback to each student and encourage their classmates to leave comments as well.

Extension 2

Students with mobile phones may wish to use the Instagram app (available for both Android and Apple iOS devices) to document different aspects of their lives and share them with the Instagram community. Because Instagram photos attract comments, there is plenty of opportunity to practice informal conversational language. Another possibility is to have students photograph uses of English that they see in the environment around them (see Activity 14, *Selling English* for ideas).

Extension 3

Encourage students to add hyperlinks from their e-portfolios to their Posterous Space(s) (see Chapter 3: *Assessing digital work, Assessing through e-portfolios*) (high-tech version).

Activity 20: Mobile rules

Students negotiate a set of class rules for acceptable mobile device usage.

With the near-ubiquity of mobile handheld devices, including mobile phones and tablets, students expect to be able to use them throughout the day. This activity encourages them to think about how these devices may help them in their learning.

Note: In low-tech environments (and even some no-tech environments) students are increasingly likely to have mobile devices to hand, so it is worth considering how these may become part of your classroom practice (see Chapter 3: *Teaching in technology-limited environments*).

Literacy:	**Mobile literacy** (complexity: ****)
Topic:	Mobile phone rules
Aim:	To raise awareness of the impact of mobile devices on learning, and to negotiate a fair use policy for class
Level:	Intermediate +
Time:	60 minutes (+ homework)
Tech support:	Wikis:

- General: e-language.wikispaces.com/wikis
- PBworks: usermanual.pbworks.com
- Wikispaces: help.wikispaces.com

Language	
Areas	*Vocabulary:* Mobile devices; learning; habits *Grammar:* Modal verbs (for permission and obligation)
Functions	Giving opinions; expressing agreement and disagreement; discussing rules
Skills	Speaking, writing, reading

Resources	
High-tech	*Equipment:* One internet-enabled teacher computer and data projector; internet-enabled student computers or mobile devices (one per group); mobile phones (as available) *Tools (optional):* Class wiki (e.g. PBworks or Wikispaces)
Low-tech	*Equipment:* One internet-enabled teacher computer and data projector; mobile phones (as available)
No-tech	*Documents (optional):* Printed websites

Digital risks
See Activity 18, *History hunt* for digital risks in using mobile phone data plans.

Procedure

1. Tell students about your phone (or tablet computer): what make and model it is, what it can do, and what you actually do with it every day. Try to include a mixture of social, entertainment and learning uses for your chosen device. Now put students into pairs and ask them to do the same for mobile handheld devices they may own (if there are not enough mobile devices in the class you may need to make small groups for this stage). Conduct feedback using these three columns on the board (see examples below):

Social uses	Entertainment	Learning
• Texting	• Games	• Dictionaries
• Facebook	• Films	• Exercises
• …	• …	• …
• …	• …	• …

There will probably be very few entries in the 'learning' column – this may be because mobile devices are banned in class, or because your students have never considered their use in terms of learning, either in class or out of class.

2. Tell students you are going to be concentrating on how their mobile devices can help them in class. Elicit common features of the mobile devices students regularly bring to class, such as:

- digital camera
- video camera
- microphone
- note-taking app
- internet access

Once you have a list of common features on the available devices, put the students into small groups to brainstorm possible uses of these features in class. Give them the example below to get them started, and then have them come up with lists along the same lines:

- microphone: speaking practice
pronunciation practice
interviews

You may need a stimulus to help them with this stage of the class. A good place to start is Alom Shaha's blog post 'Don't ban mobiles in school, let students use them' in *The Independent* (goo.gl/h58Mk). Give students time to browse the article (high-tech version), read through it with them on the projector screen (low-tech version), or distribute printed copies (no-tech version). Again, conduct feedback as a whole class.

3. Now brainstorm possible disadvantages of using mobile devices in class. Again, it may be difficult for students to start this conversation, so give a couple of examples:

- students may check Facebook during lesson time;
- students may text each other answers to quizzes.

Conduct feedback as a whole class.

4. Tell students they are going to establish a set of rules for the use of mobile devices in your class. Ask them to look back at their uses in Step 1 of this activity and identify those that they think are acceptable in class, and those that are not. At this stage students may need to justify their choices, particularly with regard to sending texts, checking social networking sites, etc. This will work well as a whole class discussion. As the discussion progresses, keep notes on the screen (high-tech and low-tech versions) or on the board (no-tech version).

5. Students should use the notes to produce a final contract for mobile use in class. You can find out more about class contracts, and see an example, in 'Establishing the ground rules' on the British Council's Teaching English website (goo.gl/bP5Ze).

Variation

You may want to use a wiki for the writing and editing process, either in class or for homework. This will allow students to modify and add to each other's ideas (high-tech version).

Activity 21: HTML basics

Students learn some of the basics of HTML.

Knowing how to recognise and change elements in coding languages allows us to escape the constraints of templates, and gives us greater control over the format and appearance of some online communication. A basic familiarity with the common coding language HTML (HyperText Markup Language), which underpins most webpages, including blogs, wikis, etc., is a good place to start.

Literacy: **Code literacy** (complexity: *****)

Topic: Animals

Aim: To raise awareness of HTML and how it works

Level: Elementary +

Time: 60 minutes

Tech support: HTML guides:

- HTML Dog: htmldog.com/guides/htmlbeginner/
- Quackit: www.quackit.com/html/tutorial/

Word-processing software:

- Apple Pages: support.apple.com/manuals/#iwork
- Microsoft Word: goo.gl/KXnLe

Language	
Areas	*Vocabulary:* Animals; formatting of documents
Skills	Reading, writing

Resources	
High-tech	*Equipment:* One internet-enabled teacher computer and data projector; internet-enabled student computers or mobile devices (one per student or pair) *Tools:* HTML generator (e.g. Easy HTML Tag Generator, Online HTML Code Generator or Quackit); word-processing software (e.g. Apple Pages or Microsoft Word) *Documents:* Online worksheets (www.pearsoned.co.uk/hockly)
Low-tech	*Equipment:* One internet-enabled teacher computer and data projector *Tools:* HTML generator (e.g. Easy HTML Tag Generator, Online HTML Code Generator or Quackit) *Documents:* Printed worksheets (follows Activity)
No-tech	Not available for this activity

Digital risks

Students may initially feel overwhelmed by the appearance of HTML code. Reassure them that with a few quick pointers they will be able to read it easily, and this will help them to understand and change the formatting of webpages, blogs, wikis and so on.

Procedure

Before class

- Read and follow all of the lesson steps below to ensure that you are familiar with the basics of HTML coding. We suggest that you use the Easy HTML Tag Generator (www.spiderweblogic.com/HTML-Tag-Generator.aspx), but other free HTML generator sites include Online HTML Code Generator (htmlcode.discoveryvip.com) and Quackit (www.quackit.com/html/html_generators/html_code_generator.cfm).

- Prepare the elephant text on the Easy HTML Tag Generator for use in Steps 6–7.

1. Introduce the topic of animals. Then show students this piece of formatted text from **Activity 21 Worksheet – Exploring HTML** on the projector screen. Ask them to guess the animal. It will take students only a few seconds to identify the animal described (*elephant*).

<u>*What am I?*</u>

I am a huge grey animal with big ears. I live in **India** *and* **Africa**.

2. Focus on the formatting, and ensure students understand these basic formatting terms: *text, font, font size, bold, italics, colour, underline, paragraph, alignment (centre/left/right)*. You can check this by asking:

   - What two words are in a different size font? (*huge, big*)
   - What words are in bold? (title, *India, Africa*)
   - What words are in italics? (title, *and*)
   - What word is in colour? (*grey*)
   - What words are underlined? (title)
   - How many paragraphs are there? (one)
   - How is the text aligned? (the title is centred; the sentence is aligned left)

3. Show students the HTML version of the text below on the projector screen, and ask them what it is. Help them see it is the same text from Step 1, but in 'code' (HTML). Explain that on a webpage formatting features are created in a code known as HTML (HyperText Markup Language). Every webpage is underpinned by a page written in code that looks similar to this.

   ```
   <p style="text-align: center;"><span style="text-decoration: underline;"><em><strong>What am I?</strong></em></span></p>

   <p>I am a <span style="font-size: xx-large;">huge</span> <span style="color: #808080;">grey</span> animal with <span style="font-size: large;">big</span> ears. I live in <strong>India</strong> <em>and</em> <strong>Africa</strong>.</p>
   ```

   On the projector screen, highlight a few HTML tags, e.g.:

   - bold is <strong> (or <b>)
   - italics is <em> (or <i>)
   - paragraph is <p>

4. Refer students to Worksheet A, and ask them to identify the tags in pairs. Conduct feedback. On the board, point out that HTML tags are placed in < > brackets. Tags are then placed around a word or phrase, e.g.:

   ```
   <strong>What am I?</strong>
   ```

This shows that 'What am I?' should be in bold. The forward slash / shows where the bold should end. <b> and </b> could also be used in this case.

By simply typing over a tag, it can be changed, e.g.

<em>What am I?</em>

The HTML tags now show that 'What am I?' should be in italics. <i> and </i> could also be used in this case.

5. Ask students to work individually or in pairs to write a two-line text describing an animal, including information about its size, colour and where it lives, but not the name of the animal. Ask students to type the text in a word-processing program (high-tech version), or to write it on paper (low-tech version).

6. Ask students to work with an online HTML generator, individually or in pairs (high-tech version). Alternatively, conduct this and the steps below as a whole class exercise, showing the content on the projector screen, and using one student text as an example (low-tech version).

   • Students should type their descriptions into the text box in the Easy HTML Tag Generator (www.spiderweblogic.com/HTML-Tag-Generator. aspx). At the same time, show the elephant text from Worksheet A on the projector screen so students can see it.

   • Students should format their texts using the text editing toolbar. This is also called a WYSIWYG (What You See Is What You Get) editor. Students should include bold, italics, underlined words and coloured words in their texts. Format the elephant text on the class computer as an example.

   • Students should show a nearby individual or pair their formatted text. Can they guess the animal?

7. Students will now change the HTML in their descriptions to reformat their texts. First, show them how to do this on the projector screen, still using the elephant text from Worksheet A as an example, and following the tasks on **Activity 21 Worksheet B – Practising HTML**.

   • Click on the HTML icon to show the HTML source code (see Worksheet B).

   • Make the following changes in the code, by typing over it:

- Click 'Update' at the bottom of the HTML Source Editor to go back to the text and see the changes. Here is how the text now looks:

What am I?
I am a huge grey animal with big ears. I live in **India** *and* **Africa**.

8. Refer students to Worksheet B. Students should follow the steps to edit the HTML of their own texts (high-tech version) or do this as a whole class activity with the internet-enabled teacher computer and projector, using the previous example student text from Step 6 (low-tech version). Save a copy of the elephant text if you intend to go on to do Activity 22, *HTML advanced* with students in the future.

9. Ask students why understanding the basics of HTML can be useful (see Chapter 1: *First focus: Language, Code literacy*). Conduct a discussion around this, in the first language if students are less proficient in English. Highlight the following points:

   - A very basic level of code literacy helps you understand how webpages work. By learning a few key terms and symbols, you can read the code that underpins most webpages.

   - Most free web tools (webpages, blogs, wikis) come with pre-packaged templates, which give them set looks and features. Knowing how to read and modify the code allows you to make personalised changes.

   - It's very easy to learn the basics of HTML, at least enough to make changes to the format and appearance of webpages.

   - Imagine that you upload a video or image to a sidebar in your blog (see Activity 35, *Personal blogging*), but it is far too large. How can you change it? Going into the HTML source code means you can manually change the size of the video or image.

   - If you have set up a class blog or wiki, go to the source page so that students can see the HTML code that underpins what they have written there previously.

   - Ask for students' reactions to this quote by Douglas Rushkoff (2010): 'If we don't learn to program, we risk being programmed ourselves' (see Chapter 1: *First focus: Language, Code literacy*).

Activity 21 Worksheet A – Exploring HTML

1. Normal text:

What am I?

I am a huge grey animal with big ears. I live in **India** *and* **Africa**.

2. HTML:

<p style="text-align: center;"><span style="text-decoration: underline;"><em><strong>What am I?</strong></em></span></p>

<p>I am a <span style="font-size: xx-large;">huge</span> <span style="color: #808080;">grey</span> animal with <span style="font-size: large;">big</span> ears. I live in <strong>India</strong> <em>and</em> <strong>Africa</strong>.</p>

3. Match the formatting effect with the HTML tags:

Formatting effect	HTML tag
1. different size fonts	<em>
2. words in **bold**	<p>
3. words in *italics*	<span style="font-size: xx-large;"> <span style="font-size: large;">
4. words in colour	<span style="text-decoration: underline;">
5. underlined words	<strong>
6. a new paragraph	<p style="text-align: center;">
7. centred text	<span style="color: #808080;">

Note: Because the internet was invented in the USA, US spelling is used in HTML code (e.g. 'color' and 'center').

Activity 21 Worksheet B – Practising HTML

1. Type your text into the Easy HTML Tag Generator (www.spiderweblogic. com/HTML-Tag-Generator.aspx). Use the toolbar to format the text.

2. Click on the HTML icon in the editing toolbar:

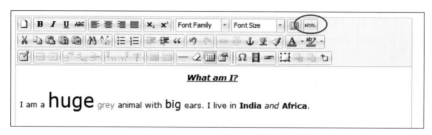

The text appears in a pop-up window in HTML:

Type within the HTML Source Editor box, and make these changes to the tags:

- align the title to the left
- change one bold word to italics
- change any word(s) to a plum colour ("color: #cc99ff;")
- change one large font to small, or vice versa

3. Look at the changes in another student's or pair's text.

Activity 22: HTML advanced

Students learn how to embed images and video in a webpage using HTML tags.

This activity introduces students to more HTML tags and the skills of embedding media in websites. This is a popular request from students when they work with blogs and wikis, and a technique they will use on a regular basis. Ensure that you have done Activity 21, *HTML basics*, as the current activity builds on the HTML tags learnt there.

Literacy:	**Code literacy** and **Multimedia literacy** (complexity: *****)
Topic:	Animals
Aim:	To raise awareness of HTML and media embedding
Level:	Elementary +
Time:	60 minutes

Tech support: Blogs:

- General: e-language.wikispaces.com/blogs
- Blogger: support.google.com/blogger/?hl=en
- Edublogs: help.edublogs.org

HTML guides:

- HTML Dog: htmldog.com/guides/htmlbeginner/
- Quackit: www.quackit.com/html/tutorial/

Language	
Areas	*Vocabulary:* Animals; formatting of documents
Skills	Reading, writing

Resources	
High-tech	*Equipment:* One internet-enabled teacher computer and data projector; internet-enabled student computers or mobile devices (one per student or pair) *Tools (optional):* Individual blogs or class blog (e.g. Blogger or Edublogs)
Low-tech	*Equipment:* One internet-enabled teacher computer and data projector *Tools (optional):* Class blog (e.g. Blogger or Edublogs)
No-tech	Not available for this activity

Digital risks

- Remember that it is perfectly legal for you and your students to embed Creative Commons images in your webpages, blogs or wikis, provided that you follow the licence conditions, which most commonly require attribution (acknowledgement of the creator and source) and non-commercial use. However, it is important to check the licence for each image, since requirements vary (see Activity 10, *Copycat* for more details).

- It is also perfectly legal for you and your students to embed YouTube videos (or those hosted on other videosharing sites, such as Vimeo) in your webpages, blogs or wikis, as long as the 'Embed' code is provided alongside the video (it is usually accessible through a 'Share' button or tab).

Procedure

Before class

- Add an image to the elephant text from Activity 21, *HTML basics,* as described in Step 2.

1. Start by reminding students of the HTML tags they learnt in Activity 21. Show them your original webpage on the projector screen:

<u>*What am I?*</u>

I am a huge grey animal with big ears. I live in **India** *and* **Africa**.

Then show them the HTML that produced it:

```
<p style="text-align: center;"><span style="text-decoration: underline;">
<em><strong>What am I?</strong></em></span></p>

<p>I am a <span style="font-size: xx-large;">huge</span>
<span style="color: #808080;">grey</span> animal with
<span style="font-size: large;">big</span> ears. I live in
<strong>India</strong> <em>and</em>
<strong>Africa</strong>.</p>
```

Conduct whole class revision, eliciting the meaning and function of the HTML tags used in the original text.

2. Tell students they are going to work individually or in pairs to improve the texts they made in Activity 21 by adding a picture and a video to the webpage. They will start by adding an image. On the projector screen, show them your HTML page with an image added:

What am I?

Feeding Elephants by Sandy Millin, eltpics on Flickr – http://www.flickr.com/photos/eltpics/6209145564/

I am a **huge** grey animal with big ears. I live in **India** _and_ **Africa**.

Then show them the corresponding HTML:

```
<p style="text-align: center;"><span style="text-decoration: underline;">
<em><strong>What am I?</strong></em></span></p>
```

```
<p style="text-align: center;"><a href="http://www.flickr.com/
photos/eltpics/6209145564/" title="Feeding elephants by eltpics,
on Flickr"><img src="http://farm7.staticflickr.com/6139/
6209145564_22e62456ae.jpg" width="500" height="375"
alt="Feeding elephants"></a>
```

```
<p style="text-align: center;">Feeding elephants by Sandy Millin, eltpics
on Flickr – http://www.flickr.com/photos/eltpics/6209145564/</p>
```

```
<p style="text-align: center;">I am a <span style="font-size:
xx-large;">huge</span> <span style="color: #808080;">grey</span>
animal with <span style="font-size: large;">big</span> ears. I live in
<strong>India</strong> <em>and</em> <strong>Africa</strong>.</p>
```

Elicit what the following parts of the image code mean:

```
<a href="http://www.flickr.com/photos/eltpics/6209145564/"
title="Feeding elephants by eltpics, on Flickr">
```

(*the link back to the original image, plus the image title*)

```
<img src="http://farm7.staticflickr.com/6139/6209145564_
22e62456ae.jpg" width="500" height="375" alt="Feeding elephants">
```

(*the actual source file of the image, the dimensions and the alternative text description*)

```
</a>
```

(*the end of the image link*)

```
<p style="text-align: center;">Feeding elephants by Sandy Millin,
eltpics on Flickr – http://www.flickr.com/photos/eltpics/
6209145564/</p>
```

(*the Creative Commons attribution for the image*)

Show them how the image can be made bigger or smaller by changing the 'width' and 'height' attributes. Also point out that the text which appears when you hover over the image can be altered by making changes to the 'alt' tag.

3. Ask students to find a Creative Commons image for their animal using Flickr Advanced Search (see Activity 10, *Copycat* for more details). Ensure that they choose the Creative Commons option at the bottom of the Advanced Search page. Once they have found an image they should click on the 'Share' button and grab the HTML code:

Feeding elephants

@sandymillin

They should then paste this code into their original webpage from Activity 21, between the two paragraphs as in your example. Remind them how to do this on the Easy HTML Tag Generator site they used previously (see Activity 21, *HTML basics*). When they have their image in their webpage, encourage them to try resizing it and changing the alternative text.

4. Tell students it's also possible to embed videos in their webpages. Ask them if they can find out how to do this using a YouTube video (the embed code can be found under the 'Share' button):

Note that the video will not show in the Easy HTML Tag Generator, but will play perfectly in a browser if the finished webpage is loaded. Show how the video can also be resized, in exactly the same way as an embedded image.

Extension 1

If you have a class blog, or students have their own blogs (see Activity 35, *Personal blogging*), ask them to add a couple of images and a video to a recent or new post. Ensure that they can resize the media to fit in with the design of the blog. They can work individually on their own blogs or in pairs on the class blog (high-tech version) or as a whole group on the class blog using the teacher computer and the projector screen (low-tech version).

Extension 2

Encourage students to add hyperlinks from their e-portfolios to their blog post(s) (see Chapter 3: *Assessing digital work, Assessing through e-portfolios*) (high-tech version).

Activity 23: Travel clouds

Students learn to navigate and produce word clouds.

Word clouds show the key terms in a text. They are a good introduction to the concept of tag clouds, which are a common way of indexing materials online and will be explored in Activity 24, *Travel tags*.

Acknowledgement: Thank you to Adam Marchant for the extension activity idea.

Literacy:	**Tagging literacy** and **Multimedia literacy** (complexity: ***)
Topic:	Travel
Aim:	To raise awareness of the concept of tag clouds by exploring word clouds, and to investigate how key words in a text can be visually represented in a word cloud
Level:	Elementary +
Time:	60 minutes
Tech support:	Word clouds:

- General: e-language.wikispaces.com/folksonomies#wordclouds
- TagCrowd: tagcrowd.com/faq.html
- Tagxedo: www.tagxedo.com/faq.html
- Wordle: www.wordle.net/faq

Word-processing software:

- Apple Pages: support.apple.com/manuals/#iwork
- Microsoft Word: goo.gl/KXnLe

Language	
Areas	*Vocabulary:* Travel and tourism; cities *Grammar:* Present simple tense (for facts)
Functions	Describing a town or city
Skills	Reading, writing, speaking

Resources	
High-tech	*Equipment:* One internet-enabled teacher computer and data projector; internet-enabled student computers or mobile devices (one per pair) *Tools:* Word cloud sites (e.g. Wordle, TagCrowd or Tagxedo); word-processing software (e.g. Apple Pages or Microsoft Word) *Documents:* Online worksheet
Low-tech	*Equipment:* One internet-enabled teacher computer and data projector *Tools:* Word cloud sites (e.g. Wordle, TagCrowd or Tagxedo); word-processing software (e.g. Apple Pages or Microsoft Word) *Documents:* Printed worksheet (follows Activity)
No-tech	Not available for this activity

Procedure

Before class

- (*Optional*) Create a word cloud from a short online text about a city, using Wordle (www.wordle.net), TagCrowd (tagcrowd.com) or Tagxedo (www.tagxedo.com), for use in Step 1.

1. Show students the first word cloud on **Activity 23 Worksheet – Travel clouds** (or the word cloud you created before class) on the projector screen. Tell students these are the key words from an online text. What is the topic? (*Barcelona – it's an entry on Barcelona from Simple English Wikipedia.*)

   Show students the original text online, or put the text below into a word-processed document or PowerPoint slide to show students:

> *Barcelona is a city in Spain. It is the capital city of Catalonia, which is a section of Spain. Barcelona is on the Mediterranean coast. The city is between the rivers of Llobregat and Besòs, and south of the Pyrenees mountains. Barcelona is the second most populated city in Spain, and the tenth in the European Union.*
> *(From Simple English Wikipedia: simple.wikipedia.org/wiki/Barcelona; accessed 12/01/2012)*

2. Ask students what a word cloud is, and why it's useful. (*Word clouds are visual displays of the frequency of words in a text: the more often a word appears in the text, the bigger it is in the word cloud. Word clouds can show at a glance what the major themes or topics of a text are, and can also show whether some words have been overused. Note that most word cloud services remove extremely common words, including articles, pronouns and common verbs, in order to create the display of key words. For more on the distinction between word clouds and tag clouds, see Chapter 1: Second focus: Information, Tagging literacy.*)

   Tell students they will now produce a word cloud in pairs to try this out.

3. Ask students to work in pairs to create a short text about a town or city in a word-processed document (high-tech version) or do this as a whole class activity using the teacher computer and projector screen (low-tech version). Students can choose a town or city they have visited, or one they would like to visit. Encourage them to search sites like Simple English Wikipedia (simple.wikipedia.org) to find out information about their chosen town or city (high-tech version), but point out that they need to produce texts in their own words. Monitor and correct language as appropriate.

4. Tell students to copy and paste their text into one of the word cloud generators listed below (high-tech version):

   • Wordle: www.wordle.net

   • TagCrowd: tagcrowd.com

   • Tagxedo: www.tagxedo.com

   Alternatively, paste the students' collaboratively generated text into a word cloud generator and show it on the projector screen (low-tech version).

5. If students are working on computers in pairs, they can swap seats with another pair, to look at the other pair's word cloud (high-tech version). Pair A can guess the following from Pair B's word cloud:

- What town/city is the original text about?
- What are the main pieces of information about the town/city, based on the key words in the word cloud?

Pair A can then check their predictions with Pair B, and vice versa.

Alternatively, if you have created one whole class text and word cloud, draw students' attention to the key words in the word cloud and their relative size (frequency) (low-tech version).

Extension

For higher level adult students, show a job advertisement (possibly one related to tourism and travel) and give students a time limit (e.g. 15 minutes) in which to write a short job application letter, either in pairs in a word-processing program (high-tech version), or individually on paper (low-tech version). Choose one of the students' job application letters, and using the internet-enabled teacher computer and projector screen, copy and paste (or type) the text into the same word cloud site you used for Step 4. Generate a word cloud. Ask students to look at the job advertisement again and to identify the key words in the advertisement. Do the key words in the word cloud match the key words in the advertisement? If so, how frequent are they? Point out to students that they can put their own texts into word cloud generator sites to check that they are including necessary keywords, and also to check that they are not overusing just one or two words.

Look at the word cloud. What is the topic?

Activity 24: Travel tags

Students learn to navigate and produce tag clouds.

Tag clouds are a common way of indexing materials online. This activity follows on well from Activity 23, *Travel clouds*, in which students create word clouds. Word clouds are visual displays of word frequency in a text, whereas tag clouds are online indexes created by users.

Literacy:	**Tagging literacy** and **Multimedia literacy** (complexity: ***)
Topic:	Travel
Aim:	To increase familiarity with the concept of tag clouds
Level:	Elementary +
Time:	60 minutes
Tech support:	Blogs:

- General: e-language.wikispaces.com/blogs
- Blogger: support.google.com/blogger/?hl=en
- Edublogs: help.edublogs.org

Photosharing:

- General: e-language.wikispaces.com/social-sharing#Photosharing
- Flickr: www.flickr.com/tour/#section=welcome

Tag clouds:

- General: e-language.wikispaces.com/folksonomies#tagclouds

Word-processing software:

- Apple Pages: support.apple.com/manuals/#iwork
- Microsoft Word: goo.gl/KXnLe

Language	
Areas	*Vocabulary:* Travel and tourism; cities *Grammar:* Present simple tense (for facts); parts of speech
Functions	Describing a town or city
Skills	Reading, speaking, writing

Resources	
High-tech	*Equipment:* One internet-enabled teacher computer and data projector; internet-enabled student computers or mobile devices (one per pair) *Tools:* Word processing software (e.g. Apple Pages or Microsoft Word) *Tools (optional):* Flickr; blog(s) (e.g. Blogger or Edublogs)
Low-tech	*Equipment:* One internet-enabled teacher computer and data projector *Tools:* Word processing software (e.g. Apple Pages or Microsoft Word) *Tools (optional):* Flickr
No-tech	*Documents:* Printed blog posts and tag cloud from the Urban Travel Blog

Procedure

Before class

- Print out the latest blog post, the tag cloud, and several older posts accessible through the tag cloud from the Urban Travel Blog (www.urbantravelblog.com), for use in Steps 2–3 (no-tech version).

1. Introduce the topic of travel blogs. Ask students if they have ever kept a travel blog, or whether they visit travel blogs to find out information about a country or city before they travel.

2. Ask students to work in pairs to visit the Urban Travel Blog and read the latest blog post online (high-tech version). Alternatively, show the blog on the projector screen and read the latest post as a whole class activity (low-tech version), or else give students a printout of the latest blog

post (no-tech version). Ask students to identify which city the blog post is about.

3. Blogs often have clickable 'tag clouds', which make it easy to see at a glance what the main topics are, and then to search for blog posts on a certain topic. On the projector screen, show students the tag cloud in the right-hand column of the Urban Travel Blog (as described above under Before class; high-tech and low-tech versions), or give students a print-out of the tag cloud (no-tech version). Point out how the words in the tag cloud are different sizes – the bigger the word, the more frequently it is used as a tag (i.e. an indexing term). So if a tag like 'London' is larger than others, there will be more blog posts about London than other cities. Click on some of the tags to show how blog posts related to that topic then appear (high-tech and low-tech versions).

4. Ask students what word classes are included in the Urban Travel Blog tag cloud, apart from the names of countries and cities (*the most common are nouns, e.g. water, winter, bikes, tours; with some present participles, e.g. gaming; and some adjectives, e.g. quirky*).

5. Ask students which of the more unusual tags they would like to explore, and click on these to see what posts appear (high-tech and low-tech versions), or give students printouts of some of the posts (no-tech version). Give students 5–10 minutes to read some of the posts. Ask them to report back on the information they find.

6. (Skip this step in a no-tech context.) Tags are also useful for labelling photos. Ask whether anyone in the class has an account on the photosharing service Flickr and whether they have noticed the use of tags there. Show the Flickr photosharing site (www.flickr.com) on the projector screen. Type 'Barcelona' (or the name of another city) into the search box. Click on one of the photos. As a group, look at the tags on the right-hand side. Tags are not always in English, so when tagging a photo in Flickr, users need to decide what language to tag in, as well as what keywords to include. Hold your mouse over a tag, and you can select whether to see more photos with this tag from this Flickr member, or from everyone on Flickr.

7. How do you decide what tags to include with a blog post or photo? This will depend on the content. Tell students they will now produce a tag cloud to try this out. In pairs, ask students to type up a short text of about 150 words about a town or city in a word-processed document (high-tech version), or to write this text on paper (low-tech version). Monitor and correct language as appropriate.

8. Ask students to decide on four or five tags for their texts. Point out that tags are words or labels that can summarise the content/topic, or appear within the text. For example, a text about Barcelona may include information about the city, but not the word 'travel', which is also a key concept, and a word that people are likely to use when researching Barcelona for a trip. Students can create their tag clouds by typing these words (high-tech version) or writing them on paper (low-tech and no-tech versions), in a cloud format (e.g. like the Urban Travel Blog).

9. Pairs can share their typed or handwritten tag clouds. The class should identify what town or city each pair chose for the text, and some of the key information included. The individual texts can be read out or exchanged among pairs to check.

10. Conduct feedback on the tags chosen. Discuss how, if these texts were blog posts, the chosen tags would make each text more or less easy to find in an internet search.

Extension

If you have a class blog, or students have their own blogs (see Activity 35, *Personal blogging*), ask them to add their city texts as blog posts, and to tag their posts with the words they chose in Step 8 above (high-tech version). Ensure that the blog(s) has/have a tag cloud widget included; most blog tools will tell you how to do this on the Help or FAQ pages. Students can then link to their blog posts and/or tag clouds from their e-portfolios (see Chapter 3: *Assessing digital work, Assessing through e-portfolios*).

Activity 25: Search race

Students explore a number of search engines and learn how each can be effective for specific types of search.

Currently, Google is the search engine of choice. However, using only one search engine can limit the range of results returned. Familiarity with a number of types of search engines, and the kinds of results they offer, gives students more choices when searching for information. This task introduces students to a range of search engine types by asking them to research the topic of pollution.

Literacy:	**Search literacy** (complexity: ***)
Topic:	Pollution and environment
Aim:	To explore a variety of search engines
Level:	Intermediate +
Time:	60 minutes (+ homework)
Tech support:	Aggregators:

- Netvibes: help.netvibes.com
- Symbaloo: service.symbaloo.com/index.php?p= help&app=portal

Search:

- General: e-language.wikispaces.com/search

Language	
Areas	*Vocabulary:* Pollution; environment *Grammar:* Present simple tense; passive voice
Functions	Expressing likes and dislikes
Skills	Reading, writing, speaking, listening

Resources	
High-tech	*Equipment:* One internet-enabled teacher computer and data projector; internet-enabled student computers or mobile devices (one per pair) *Tools:* Search engines (see Worksheet A) *Tools (optional):* Aggregator (e.g. Netvibes or Symbaloo) *Documents:* Online worksheet (www.pearsoned.co.uk/hockly)
Low-tech	*Equipment:* One internet-enabled teacher computer and data projector *Tools:* Search engines (see Worksheet A) *Documents:* Printed worksheet (follows Activity)
No-tech	Not available for this activity

Digital risks

Remember to use 'Strict' or 'Moderate' SafeSearch settings on Google, and, where possible, equivalent settings on other search sites (see Activity 10, *Copycat* for more on safe settings).

Procedure

Before class

- Ensure you are familiar with each of the search engines on **Activity 25 Worksheet A – Search engines**, so that you can add important points about each when students give feedback on them.

1. Put the word 'Google' on the board and ask students what it is (*a search engine*). What other search engines do they know? What search engine(s) do they use? You may find your students only use Google, but if they mention any others, ask what differences in results they notice with different search engines. Remember that YouTube, too, is sometimes used as a search engine by students. Point out that Google may not always be the best search engine – depending on what you are looking for (images, blogs, etc.), more specialised search engines can be more effective (see Box 1.5).

2. Ask students to guess how many results a Google search for the word 'pollution' will produce (*hundreds of millions*). Now, Google this word and show the results on the projector screen. Ask students to notice what

sources are near the top. Wikipedia should be in your top few results. Ask students to think about the effects of this. Google primarily returns results that are popular and recent, and very often a single key source of information – Wikipedia – is at or near the top of the list. If we only use one search engine to look for information, we tend to end up always consulting the same sources (see Chapter 1: *Second focus: Information, Search literacy*; Activity 26, *Search me*).

3. Ask students to imagine that they want to find synonyms for the word 'pollution', or images of pollution, or blogs about pollution in the developing world, or graphs about levels of pollution from different countries. They could use Google and add more keywords into the 'pollution' search, but they could also consult specialised search engines.

4. Tell students that in pairs they are going to explore different types of specialised search engines (high-tech version). Ask them to refer to **Activity 25 Worksheet A – Search engines**. If you have more than six pairs of students in the class, assign search tasks to more than one pair. Alternatively, find the answers to Worksheet A as a whole class activity, showing the results on the projector screen; afterwards, skip Steps 5 and 6 below and go straight to Step 7 (low-tech version).

5. Ask each pair to try out their assigned search engines by carrying out their search task. They should note down one thing they like and one thing they dislike about their two search engines, as well as the answer to their search task (high-tech version).

6. Ask pairs to report back to the class on the information they found *and* their assigned search engines. If possible, students should show their search engines (and how they searched) to the class by using the internet-enabled teacher computer and projector screen. Other students should fill in the 'Like'/'Dislike' section for each search engine on the worksheet while they listen, and also note down any interesting information about pollution (high-tech version).

7. Ask students to refer to **Activity 25 Worksheet B – Search race**. In the same pairs as before, they need to find the information using the best search engines from Worksheet A. Each pair should work on one computer and the pair which finishes first must shout 'Stop!' (high-tech version). Alternatively, conduct the search race as a whole class *research* (not race) activity, using the internet-enabled teacher computer and showing the results on the projector screen; in this case, skip Step 8 (low-tech version).

8. Stop the search race as soon as the first pair finishes, and conduct feed-back (high-tech version). Show the URLs found by the winning pair on the projector screen, and also ask the class for their thoughts on each search engine. What do they like/dislike about each?

Extension

Ask students to add 8–10 of the most interesting links about pollution to an aggregator site like Symbaloo (www.symbaloo.com) or Netvibes (www. netvibes.com) (high-tech version). Students can add links to these aggregator sites from their e-portfolios (see Chapter 3: *Assessing digital work, Assessing through e-portfolios*). These resources can also form the basis for a writing task or project about pollution in Canada and China in subsequent classes, or for homework.

Activity 25 Worksheet A – Search engines

Complete the task assigned to your pair using the two suggested search engines. Note down your answer to the search task as well as making notes about what you like and dislike about each search engine.

Pair 1: Visual search engines for words

Search task: Find three words (one adjective, one noun and one verb) that have a similar meaning to 'contaminate'.
Suggested search term(s): contaminate

```
Answer (note down the words):



```

- **Visuwords:** http://www.visuwords.com/

  Like:

  Dislike:

- **Visual Thesaurus:** http://www.visualthesaurus.com/

  Like:

  Dislike:

Pair 2: Image search engines

Search task: Find three images of Beijing: one of the city, one of a famous building and one of Beijing in winter.
Suggested search term(s): Beijing; Beijing building; Beijing winter

```
Answer (note down the URLs of the images):



```

- **Tag Galaxy:** http://taggalaxy.de/

  Like:

  Dislike:

- **Flickr Storm:** http://www.zoo-m.com/flickr-storm/
  Like:
  Dislike:

Pair 3: Blog search engines

Search task: Find three blog posts about pollution issues in China.
Suggested search term(s): pollution China

> Answer (note down the URLs of the blogs):

- **Icerocket:** http://www.icerocket.com/
  Like:
  Dislike:

- **Technorati:** http://technorati.com/
  Like:
  Dislike:

Pair 4: Search engines for graphs and data

Search task: Find information about how much CO_2 (carbon dioxide) is produced by different countries. How much does Canada produce?
Suggested search term(s): CO_2 world

> Answer (note down the key information):

- **Visual Loop:** http://visualoop.tumblr.com/
  Like:
  Dislike:

- **Zanran:** http://zanran.com/
  Like:
  Dislike:

Pair 5: Metasearch engines (search engines that combine the results from several other search engines)

Search task: Find information about the most polluted places in the world, including an image, information from a newspaper article, and a tweet from Twitter or a status update from Facebook (if possible).
Suggested search term(s): world most polluted places

Answer (note down the URLs of these sources):

- **Spezify:** http://spezify.com/
  Like:
  Dislike:

- **Webcrawler:** http://www.webcrawler.com/
  Like:
  Dislike:

Pair 6: Video search engines

Search task: Find three videos about oil sands in Canada.
Suggested search term(s): oil sands Canada

Answer (note down the URLs of the videos):

- **YouTube EDU:** http://www.youtube.com/education
  Like:
  Dislike:

- **Vizband:** http://www.vizband.co.uk/
  Like:
  Dislike:

If YouTube is not accessible in your country, try this video news repository:

- **BBC News:** http://www.bbc.co.uk/news/world_radio_and_tv/

Activity 25 Worksheet B – Search race

Use the best search engine from Worksheet A for each search. When you finish, shout 'Stop!'.

1. Find an infographic (an online poster with key information and images) about how much CO_2 the internet produces.

   URL: _____

2. Find a video showing traffic pollution in Beijing.

   URL: _____

3. Find a blog entry by an environmental group/activist about the Canadian oil sands.

   URL: _____

4. Find two synonyms for 'pollution'.

   URL: _____

5. Find a tweet and a Facebook update about pollution in your country.

   URL: _____

6. Find an image of the Canadian oil sands.

   URL: _____

Activity 26: Search me

Students learn about how search engines personalise search results based on prior search history.

This activity introduces students to the idea of personalised search and helps them understand how their search and browsing habits affect their search results.

Literacy:	**Search literacy** and **Information literacy** (complexity: ***)
Topic:	Personalised search
Aim:	To raise awareness of how search engines filter results for individuals, and how this can impact on their studies/work
Level:	Intermediate +
Time:	60 minutes (+ homework)
Tech support:	Search:

- General: e-language.wikispaces.com/search

- Google: support.google.com/websearch/?hl=en

Language	
Areas	*Grammar:* Modal verbs (for probability)
Functions	Expressing probability
Skills	Speaking, reading, writing

Resources	
High-tech	*Equipment:* Internet-enabled student computers or mobile devices (one per student) *Tools (optional):* TED app *Documents:* Online worksheet (www.pearsoned.co.uk/hockly)
Low-tech	*Tools (optional):* TED app *Documents:* Printed worksheet (follows Activity)
No-tech	*Documents:* Printed worksheet (follows Activity)

Procedure

Before class

- Ask your students to keep a record of what they search for in Google or other search engines over two or three days before class, for use in Step 1. (Of course, they can be selective – it is important to respect their privacy.) If possible, this should take the form of a list of specific search terms. If your students know how to do it, encourage them to keep screenshots of the first page of results they get from each search.

1. Give students a piece of paper and ask them to write down ten of their most recent search terms. These should be anonymous. Collect the pieces of paper and then either stick them on a wall of the classroom or read them out in random order. Students should try to guess which of their classmates made those searches and justify their guesses based on what they know about each person.

2. Refer students to **Activity 26 Worksheet – Search them** and get them to work through it individually, before comparing answers in pairs or small groups. Conduct feedback as a whole class and make sure students understand how 'personalised search' works (see Appendix: Answer keys). Discuss the impact on them as students, professionals, etc.

3. Ask students to discuss the Task 2 questions in pairs. If they have kept screenshots of their own web search results (as described above), encourage them to look through the lists with their partners, discussing what the lists might reveal about each person.

Extension 1

If students have internet access at home, ask them to conduct a Google search using a term or terms agreed upon by the class. Ensure that all students use the local country version of Google to increase comparability. Students should bring a printout of the first page of search results, or a list of the results, to class the next day. Ask volunteers to share their results. How different are they? What might that say about each student?

Extension 2

More details of personal web filtering can be found on Eli Pariser's website, The Filter Bubble (www.thefilterbubble.com/what-is-the-internet-hiding-lets-find-out), and in the video of his 2011 TED talk, *Beware online 'filter bubbles'* (www.ted.com/talks/eli_pariser_beware_online_filter_bubbles.html). Both of these resources can be used to further the discussion. If students have mobile devices they may want to use the TED app (available for Android, Apple iOS and Windows devices) to watch this and similar videos in their spare time.

Activity 26 Worksheet – Search them

1. These four people all used a popular search engine to search for 'Java'. They were using their own laptops, and were in the same class at the same time. What do you think the search results tell you about each person?

Rena	Ahmed
• might be looking for a holiday?	• _____
• _____	• _____
• _____	• _____
• _____	• _____
• _____	• _____
• _____	

About 24,900,000 results (0.19 seconds)

Java - Wikipedia, the free encyclopedia
en.wikipedia.org/wiki/Java
Java (**Indonesian**: Jawa) is an island of Indonesia. With a population of 135 million (excluding the 3.6 million on the island of Madura which is administered as ...
↳ Central Java - Java (disambiguation) - West Java - East Java

All about island of Java Indonesia
www.javaindonesia.org/
all you need to know about **Java Indonesia**, from history of Java island, religion, volcano and earthquake, also **Java Indonesia** culture. All place information also ...

News for java indonesia
Indonesia to face Everton in **Java** cup
Jakarta Post - 7 hours ago
Marouane Fellaini. AP/Tatan SyufianaThe **Indonesian** soccer team will face the English Premier League club, Everton FC, in the inaugural **Java** ...

130 Rescued After Shipwreck South of Indonesia
New York Times - 11 hours ago

Java Travel Information and Travel Guide - Indonesia - Lonely Planet
www.lonelyplanet.com/indonesia/java
16 Jul 2010 - **Java** tourism and travel information such as accommodation, festivals, transport, maps, activities and attractions in **Java, Indonesia** - Lonely ...
↳ Places in Java - Indonesia - Java (Chapter) - Yogyakarta - Java image gallery

Java maps.google.co.uk

About 80,700,000 results (0.28 seconds)

Ads related to java coffee   Why these ads?

Personal Java Coffee Press
£35.00 - millets.co.uk
Waitrose Select Java Coffee
£3.29 - Ocado

Java coffee - Wikipedia, the free encyclopedia
en.wikipedia.org/wiki/Java_coffee
Java coffee is a coffee produced on the island of Java. In the United States the term "Java" by itself is, in general, slang for coffee. The Indonesian phrase Kopi ...

Java Coffee & Tea Co. - Fine Coffee & Tea - Houston, Texas
www.javacoffee.com/
Java Coffee & Tea is a supplier of freshly roasted coffees, world class teas, and unique gifts for coffee & tea lovers.

Java Coffee Break - your free guide to the world of Java ...
www.javacoffeebreak.com/
Java Coffee Break features free Java tutorials and articles. Learn Java now!

Bjava Coffee | Where Espresso Is Art
www.bjavacoffee.com/
This Week At Bjava **Coffee**. Wednesday morning we will be at the Indianapolis City Market Farmers Market on Market St. Come on by the booth from ...

Why is Coffee Called Java? « Broken Secrets
brokensecrets.com/2010/01/20/why-is-coffee-called-java/
20 Jan 2010 - I love **coffee**. I started drinking it in college, like most people, for the caffeine boost. Over time, I got really attached to the flavor. I went through a ...

Images for java coffee - Report images

Olga	Ramón
• _____	• _____
• _____	• _____
• _____	• _____
• _____	• _____
• _____	• _____
• _____	• _____

About 31,400,000 results (0.23 seconds)

Java (programming language) - Wikipedia, the free encyclopedia
en.wikipedia.org/wiki/Java_(programming_language)
Java is a programming **language** originally developed by James Gosling at Sun Microsystems (which has since merged into Oracle Corporation) and released ...
→ History · Practices · Syntax · Examples

The Java Language Specification - Oracle Documentation
docs.oracle.com/javase/specs/
Java Language and Virtual Machine Specifications. Java SE 7. documentation icon The **Java Language** Specification, Java SE 7 Edition. Download PDF ...

Trail: Learning the **Java Language** (The Java™ Tutorials)
docs.oracle.com/javase/tutorial/java/index.html
This beginner **Java** tutorial describes fundamentals of programming in the **Java** programming **language**.

Java Language Basics Article - SitePoint
www.sitepoint.com/java-language-basics/ - United States
11 Apr 2001 - Are the complexities of **Java** and programming in general getting you down? In this article, Kevin brings you up to speed on the basic syntax of ...

The Java(tm) **Language**: An Overview
java.sun.com/docs/overviews/java/java-overview-1.html
Describes how **Java** is a simple, object-oriented, network-savvy, interpreted, robust, secure, architecture neutral, portable, high-performance, multithreaded. ...

The Java Language Environment: Contents
java.sun.com › Java Technology › Reference › White Papers
A White Paper May 1996. James Gosling Henry McGilton. 1. Introduction to Java · 1.1Beginnings of the **Java Language** Project · 1.2Design Goals of Java ...

About 95,000,000 results (0.23 seconds)

Java (band) - Wikipedia, the free encyclopedia
en.wikipedia.org/wiki/Java_(band)
Java is a French rap **group**, formed in 1997 and currently composed of François Xavier Bossard (accordion/keyboard), Erwan Seguillon (singer/songwriter). ...

East Of Java The Rock Band
www.livebandphotos.co.uk/eastofjava/
East Of **Java** The Rock **Band**. ... relevent **bands** that havent had any gigs listed on this site in the last year are automatically deleted off the photo **band** gallery.

East Of **Java Band** Gig List
www.livebandphotos.co.uk/bandgiglist/?East%20Of%20Java
Gigs for the **band** East Of **Java** in pubs on this website. The Gig list database doesn't contain every gig for every **band** and may miss last min cancellations so ...

East of **Java** are simply the best rock
www.eastofjava.org/indexsimple.htm
East of **Java** are simply the best rock/indie/covers **band** in town. You won't find a better collection of musicians delivering powerful guitar based music anywhere ...

The Hot **Java Band** by The Hot **Java Band** - Apple
itunes.apple.com/gb/album/the-hot-java-band/id43953675
Preview songs from The Hot **Java Band** by The Hot **Java Band** on the iTunes Store. Preview, buy and download The Hot **Java Band** for £7.99. Songs start at just ...

iTunes - Music - The Hot **Java Band**
itunes.apple.com/gb/artist/the-hot-java-band/id43953483
Preview and download top songs and albums by The Hot **Java Band** on the iTunes Store. Songs by The Hot **Java Band** start at just £0.79.

java band (from charlotte nc) beach, jazz, top 40 - YouTube
www.youtube.com/watch?v=9EJ0G7J2rhs
23 Jul 2011 - 9 min - Uploaded by javamuzic
Charlotte NC Street Band 2 47. Watch Later Error Charlotte NC.

2. Talk to a partner about the following questions:

- Why do you think the results are different for each person?
- How do you think the search engine determines what to show in the results?
- What does this kind of 'personalised search' mean for you?

Activity 27: Tree octopus

Students analyse spoof (or bogus) websites.

A fundamental part of information literacy is the ability to gauge the reliability of the information found on websites. This activity gives students criteria with which to analyse websites.

Literacy: **Information literacy** (complexity: ***)

Topic: Endangered animals

Aim: To raise awareness of the importance of evaluating information on websites, by visiting a number of spoof websites

Level: Lower intermediate +

Time: 60 minutes

Language	
Areas	*Vocabulary:* Endangered animals and habitats; websites *Grammar:* Present simple tense (for scientific facts)
Functions	Giving opinions
Skills	Reading, speaking

Resources	
High-tech	*Equipment:* One internet-enabled teacher computer and data projector; internet-enabled student computers or mobile devices (one per pair) *Documents:* Online worksheets (www.pearsoned.co.uk/hockly)
Low-tech	*Equipment:* One internet-enabled teacher computer and data projector *Documents:* Printed worksheets (follows Activity)
No-tech	*Documents:* Printed picture of an octopus; printed homepages of spoof websites (listed below); printed worksheets (follows Activity)

Procedure

Before class

- Find a picture of an octopus online (high-tech and low-tech versions) or a printed picture of one (no-tech version), for use in Step 1.
- Print one copy of the homepage of the Pacific Northwest Tree Octopus website (zapatopi.net/treeoctopus) for each student, for use in Step 2 (no-tech version).
- Print the homepages of the websites on **Activity 27 Worksheet C – Real or fake**? for use in Step 5 (low-tech and no-tech versions) and Step 6 (no-tech version only).

1. Show students an image of an octopus and elicit what they know about this creature. Pre-teach vocabulary: *tentacles, habitat, reproductive cycle, predators*. Tell students they are going to learn about one particularly endangered species of octopus – the Pacific Northwest tree octopus. Try to do this as seriously as possible, to convince students that this species really exists.

2. Ask students in pairs to visit the Pacific Northwest Tree Octopus site (as described above), and to find the answers to Task 1 on **Activity 27 Worksheet A – The Pacific Northwest Tree Octopus** (high-tech version). Alternatively, show the homepage on the projector screen, giving students time in their pairs to read and note down the information they find (low-tech version). Otherwise, give a printed copy of the homepage to each pair (no-tech version). Get feedback on the Task 1 questions, and check that everybody found the same information.

3. Ask students whether they think the Pacific Northwest tree octopus really exists. Even if they have realised that the site is a *spoof* or *bogus* one (explain these words), ask students to analyse carefully what makes this site convincing at first. Ask them to discuss the points on **Activity 27 Worksheet B – Analysing a website**.

4. In feedback on this activity, highlight for students how some elements on this website make it more credible (such as links to real websites, or the images and layout), while there are also carefully laid clues that show it to be a spoof. The overall objective of the site is to make people laugh by seeming credible. It doesn't try to completely fool the reader, or to get the reader to donate money, for example.

5. Divide your students into pairs and allocate each pair a number from 1 to 7 (if you have more than 14 students, simply have more than one pair look

at the same sites). Tell students that they are going to look at two web-sites on a particular topic: one of the sites is real, and the other is a spoof. Can they spot which is which? Ask students to refer to **Worksheet C – Real or fake?**. Students should use the checklist on Worksheet B to analyse their allocated sites on the computer (high-tech version). Alternatively, give pairs a printed copy of each of their allocated website homepages to analyse (low-tech and no-tech versions).

Note: The first in each pair of sites on Worksheet C is the spoof site, but some of them are very convincing. (For more spoof websites, see Chapter 1: *Second focus: Information, Information literacy*).

6. Get feedback from each pair on their two sites. If possible, show each of the sites on the projector screen as the pairs tell the class how they decided which was the spoof site and which was real (high-tech and low-tech versions). Otherwise, have more printed copies of the homepages available for students to refer to (no-tech version). Point out that none of these websites intend to exploit or defraud the reader – but there are some that do, so it's important to know how to evaluate the veracity and trustworthiness of a website.

Activity 27 Worksheet A – The Pacific Northwest Tree Octopus

Visit a website about the endangered Pacific Northwest tree octopus (http://zapatopi.net/treeoctopus) to find out more about it. Fill in some notes in the grid below:

Geographical location	
Habitat	
Average size	
Use of tentacles	
Usual skin colour	
Reproductive cycle	
Predators	
Other tree octopus species	
One way to help save the species	

Activity 27 Worksheet B – Analysing a website

Look carefully at the Northwest Pacific Tree Octopus site. It is a good example of a spoof website that is very well designed. Look especially at the following elements, and discuss with your partner how they make the site more or less convincing:

Style and layout:

- the web address (or 'URL' – 'uniform resource locator');
- the title of the homepage;
- the layout, font and colours;
- the images and map;
- the use of hyperlinks;
- the style of the language and vocabulary used.

Content:

- content in the tabs (the sections under the title, e.g. 'FAQs' (Frequently Asked Questions); 'Sightings'; 'Media'; 'Activities');
- the 'scientific' information on the homepage;
- content in the 'News' and 'Blog' entries (in the column on the left);
- links to the webpages of organisations such as the World Conservation Union, the [World] Wildlife Fund, and the UNEP World Conservation Monitoring Centre (all in the last paragraph on the homepage);
- the quotes in the top right corner of the homepage;
- the disclaimer at the bottom of the homepage, and the 'Address concerns to . . .' line at the very bottom right;
- when the website was last updated (usually on the bottom line).

What do you think the overall aim of this site is?

Activity 27 Worksheet C – Real or fake?

In pairs, visit your two sites. Which is the fake site? Use the criteria on Worksheet B to help you decide.

Pair 1: Chemistry

Dihydrogen Monoxide Research Division: http://www.dhmo.org/

Carbon Monoxide: http://www.carbonmonoxidekills.com/

Pair 2: Birth and genetics

Genochoice: http://www.genochoice.com/

Gender Prediction Kits: http://www.babyzone.com/pregnancy/fetal_development/genetics_gender/article/gender-prediction-kits

Pair 3: Food

The Ova Prima Foundation: http://www.ovaprima.org/

NZ Nutrition Foundation: http://www.nutritionfoundation.org.nz/nutrition-facts/nutrition-a-z/Eggs

Pair 4: Water

Dehydrated Water: http://www.buydehydratedwater.com/

International Water Association: http://www.iwahq.org/1nb/home.html

Pair 5: Endangered animals

Save the Guinea Worm: http://www.deadlysins.com/guineaworm/index.htm

Vaquita: http://www.worldwildlife.org/species/finder/vaquita/vaquita.html

Pair 6: Cloning

Clones: http://www.d-b.net/dti/

Cloning Fact Sheet: http://www.ornl.gov/sci/techresources/Human_Genome/elsi/cloning.shtml

Pair 7: Museums

The Museum of Jurassic Technology: http://www.mjt.org/

The Virtual Museum of Bacteria: http://bacteriamuseum.org/cms/

Activity 28: Fun facts

Students search for and evaluate online sources to determine the truth (or otherwise) of 'facts'.

This activity helps students to look at multiple sources and evaluate them in order to check facts on the internet.

Literacy: **Search literacy** and **Information literacy** (complexity: ***)

Topic: Unusual facts

Aim: To raise awareness of how to check online sources

Level: Lower intermediate +

Time: 45 minutes

Tech support: Microblogging:

- General: e-language.wikispaces.com/microblogging

- Twitter: support.twitter.com

Language	
Areas	*Vocabulary:* Animals *Grammar:* Present simple tense (for facts)
Functions	Expressing opinions; discussing facts versus opinions
Skills	Reading, listening, speaking

Resources	
High-tech	*Equipment:* One internet-enabled teacher computer and data projector; internet-enabled student computers or mobile devices (one per pair) *Tools (optional):* Twitter
Low-tech	*Equipment:* One internet-enabled teacher computer and data projector
No-tech	*Documents:* Printed search results (see below)

Procedure

Before class

- Choose three or four 'facts' from the 'Bizarre, Odd, Strange, Unusual Facts!' page on the Mysterytopia website (mysterytopia.com/2008/10/bizarreoddstrangeunusual-facts.html) and conduct web searches to check their veracity. Alternatively, use the 'facts' suggested in Step 1.

- Print out search results, i.e. the top pages of several websites that appear in the search results, for use in Steps 3–4 and 5 (no-tech version).

1. Tell students you are going to share some unusual facts about animals. Use the 'facts' you have chosen (as described above), or use those below. Dictate them and have students write them down as accurately as they can.

   - *Ants don't sleep.*
   - *A pregnant goldfish is called a 'twit'.*
   - *Cows give more milk if they listen to music.*

2. In pairs, students should decide whether or not each of these statements is true. Put the sentences on the board so students can check their dictations, and then check whether students think each statement is true or not.

3. In pairs, students should search the web to check whether each statement is true (high-tech version), or else the whole class can work together using the projector screen (low-tech version) (see Activity 25, *Search race* for ideas on possible search engines to use). Alternatively, hand out the sets of search results you have previously prepared on paper (no-tech version).

   For each statement, students should follow links to various web pages, and evaluate the sources of information in terms of reliability and veracity. In some cases, searches may take students to unofficial question-and-answer forums (the ant or goldfish statement), and in some cases to a newspaper article (the cows statement) (high-tech and low-tech versions).

4. Conduct feedback with the class by carrying out each search again as a whole class (high-tech version) or having students revisit the printed search results (no-tech version). Alternatively, feedback can be conducted in conjunction with the initial whole class search (low-tech version). Evaluate each of the sources found, examining how reputable each is (see Activity 27, *Tree octopus* for more on assessing websites).

- **Ants don't sleep:** *Some informal question-and-answer forums seem to endorse this. However, checking several sources will reveal that some species of ant have 'sleep episodes'.*
- **A pregnant goldfish is called a 'twit':** *Once again, some informal question-and-answer forums seem to endorse this. However, checking several sources will reveal that goldfish carry eggs, so cannot become 'pregnant'. A fish carrying eggs is said to be 'gravid'.*
- **Cows give more milk if they listen to music:** *A search will lead to several reputable newspaper articles endorsing this idea.*

Point out to students that informal question-and-answer forums may contain unreliable information or hearsay. They need to check multiple sources, and evaluate those sources, to ensure that facts really are facts. An article from a reputable newspaper is more likely to contain correct information than a discussion in an unmoderated question-and-answer forum.

5. Show students the 'Bizarre, Odd, Strange, Unusual Facts!' page on the Mysterytopia website (high-tech and low-tech versions). Ask them to work in new pairs to choose six statements they particularly like; each pair must then research their six statements to determine whether they are true or not (high-tech version). Alternatively, choose six statements as a class, and conduct a search with the teacher computer and projector screen (low-tech version). Otherwise, hand out printed search results for six statements you have chosen in advance, and ask students to determine whether the statements are true or not, based on the printouts.

6. Conduct feedback on the statements chosen, and whether each was found to be true or not.

Extension

If your students have Twitter accounts, ask them to tweet some of their favourite 'facts' from the class using a computer or mobile device (high-tech version). Ask them to challenge their Twitter followers – who could be students in another class – to determine whether each statement they tweet is true or not. This is a simple, fun activity that can connect work done in the classroom with students' emerging PLNs (see Activity 30, *Connecting people* and Activity 39, *A class PLN*).

Activity 29: News in my networks

Student follow the news for a week via their social networks and report back in class.

This activity helps raise students' awareness of both formal and informal sources of news, and encourages them to use their own social networks to filter the news as a way of dealing with information overload (see Box 1.7). The activity runs over two classes – a preparatory class (Class 1), and a class in which students report back on their experience of filtering news (Class 2). This activity leads well into Activity 30, *Connecting people.*

Literacy:	**Filtering literacy** and **Network literacy** (complexity: ***)
Topic:	News
Aim:	To develop the ability to filter information, and to discuss news and current affairs
Level:	Upper intermediate +
Time:	30 minutes (Class 1) + 60 minutes (Class 2) + homework
Tech support:	Microblogging:

- General: e-language.wikispaces.com/microblogging

- Twitter: support.twitter.com

Social networking:

- General: e-language.wikispaces.com/social-networking

- Facebook: www.facebook.com/help/

Language	
Areas	*Vocabulary:* News and current affairs *Grammar:* Past tenses; reporting verbs; passive voice
Functions	Discussing current affairs; giving opinions
Skills	Reading, speaking

Resources	
High-tech	*Equipment:* One internet-enabled teacher computer and data projector; internet-enabled student computers or mobile devices (one per student) *Tools:* Twitter; Facebook *Tools (optional):* Flipboard app *Documents:* A recent online newspaper; online worksheet (www.pearsoned.co.uk/hockly)
Low-tech	*Equipment:* One internet-enabled teacher computer and data projector; internet-enabled student computers or mobile devices (as available) *Tools:* Twitter; Facebook *Tools (optional):* Flipboard app *Documents:* A recent online newspaper; printed worksheet (follows Activity)
No-tech	*Documents:* A recent newspaper; printed worksheet (follows Activity)

Digital risks

- Not all students will have the internet-enabled computers or mobile devices necessary to access social media outside the classroom. Before you decide to do this activity, check on students' access to such equipment. It may be preferable not to reinforce elements of the digital divide in situations where only some students have such access (see Box 1.4). In this case, teachers may wish to carry out only the in-class part of the activity without setting the homework assignment (Class 1, Step 4), or leave the homework assignment as an optional extra for those who may be interested in carrying it out by themselves. Class 2 could be omitted.
- Even if they have adequate devices, not all students will have, or will want to set up, an account on a microblogging site such as Twitter or a social networking site such as Facebook. Before you decide to do this activity, check your students' attitudes to social media, and find out whether they are happy to take part in an activity that requires the use of Twitter and Facebook (or similar services).
- If you decide to work with microblogging and, especially, social networking sites, consider giving students pointers on digital safety (see Activity 36, *Setting the scene* for more details and ideas).
- The current activity focuses on news and current events, which is a topic more suited to older teenagers and adults.

Procedure

Before class

- Having checked whether your students have adequate digital equipment and are prepared to work with social media, check whether they already have accounts with services such as Twitter, Facebook, or similar. If not, ensure that each student signs up for at least one of these services, for use in Step 4.

Class 1: Getting the news

1. Introduce the topic of the news by showing the day's newspaper, either in digital format using the projector screen (high-tech and low-tech versions) or in hard copy (no-tech version). Ask students to identify the current stories in the news.

2. Put the students in pairs or small groups and ask them to discuss the following questions:

   • What official media do you use to get the news? (*newspaper, TV, online news sites, news blogs, etc.*)
   • What are the advantages of using official media to get the news? What are the disadvantages?
   • What informal networks do you use to get the news? (*information from work colleagues, neighbours, Twitter, Facebook, etc.*)
   • What are the advantages of using informal networks (e.g. friends and colleagues, or social networking tools) to get the news? What are the disadvantages?

   Conduct feedback with the class, pointing out that there are advantages to using official media (*quality journalism; more impartial reporting of facts*) but there are also disadvantages (*official news channels often take an editorial line, so they are not completely impartial; there are now so many sources of news available, especially online, that we are in danger of information overload*). Similarly, there are advantages to using informal networks (*our friends and colleagues pass on only news they think is relevant or interesting, so we avoid information overload*) but there are also disadvantages (*sources may be untrustworthy; information may get distorted; we may get trapped in 'echo chambers'*; see Box 1.7 for more details). It may be best to go for a mix of sources, obtaining news from both established media and informal networks.

3. Show students each of the sites or services listed below on the projector screen (high-tech and low-tech version) or on printouts (no-tech version), so that they can see some of the news articles, images and videos typically published there.

BBC	Website: www.bbc.co.uk/news/ Twitter: @BBCNews Facebook: www.facebook.com/bbcnews
CNN	Website: edition.cnn.com Twitter: @CNN Facebook: www.facebook.com/cnn
The Huffington Post	Website: www.huffingtonpost.com Twitter: @HuffingtonPost Facebook: www.facebook.com/HuffingtonPost

4. If students have adequate equipment and are prepared to use social media, tell them that they are going to follow the news via their social networks for a week and reflect on the experience. Ask them to 'follow' on Twitter, 'like' on Facebook, and/or add to any similar services, sources such as those above. Explain to students that they can then observe how much news they get directly from official sources; how much news they get indirectly from official sources via friends or contacts; and how much news comes from friends or contacts, without reference to official news sources.

Refer students to **Activity 29 Worksheet – News in my networks**. Ask students to think about the questions and make notes during the week. They will discuss the questions in a week's time.

Class 2: Reporting back

1. Select some of the students to share their chosen news items with the rest of the class. Alternatively, put them into groups of three or four to share their items. Ask if anyone chose the same story to share.

2. Put students in pairs or small groups to discuss the questions on the Worksheet.

3. Conduct open class feedback on the questions to see how students felt about the experience of filtering news through their social network(s). What conclusions can they draw, and will they continue to use social networks as a source of news, or not?

Extension

Draw students' attention to some of the free news apps available for certain mobile phones or tablets (including the news aggregator, Flipboard, which is available for both Android and Apple iOS devices), and ask them to report back periodically in subsequent classes on news items they have read recently. Encourage them to share the items they enjoy via Twitter or Facebook.

Activity 29 Worksheet – News in my networks

Follow the news for one week via your social network(s), e.g. on Twitter, Facebook, and/or similar services. Make notes on the following questions and be prepared to discuss them in class next week:

- How much news are you receiving every day? Is it too much, too little, or about right?

- How often do you follow links back to the original news stories on their respective sites? Often, sometimes, or never?

- Which sources do you find the most interesting/informative/trustworthy?

- Do you pay more/the same amount of/less attention to news from official Facebook or Twitter accounts (like the BBC, CNN or Huffington Post) compared to news shared by friends and acquaintances in your social network(s)?

- Are you receiving news items from other official news sources, which are reposted or retweeted by members of your social network(s)? If so, what are these news items, and where are they from? Are they useful/ interesting items?

- Are you sharing any of the news items you read by reposting or retweeting them to members of your social network(s)? Have members of your social network(s) responded by liking, commenting on, replying to, sharing, reposting or retweeting (etc.) your posts?

- How useful is it to follow news via social networks versus more traditional media such as newspapers or television?

- Choose one news item from this week to tell your classmates about in the next class. Did you find out about it from an official account or from friends or acquaintances? How reliable is the information?

Activity 30: Connecting people

Students think about their face-to-face and digital connections and communications.

This activity focuses on filtering information through social connections. Students identify the experts in their social circles and organise them according to their roles. This follows on neatly from Activity 29, *News in my networks*. It can be followed up by Activity 39, *A class PLN*, where students explore the idea of PLNs (personal learning networks) in more detail.

Literacy:	**Filtering literacy** & **Network literacy** (complexity: ***)
Topic:	Social circles
Aim:	To explore the idea of filtering information through social connections
Level:	Intermediate +
Time:	60 minutes
Tech support:	Social networking:

- General: e-language.wikispaces.com/social-networking
- Edmodo: help.edmodo.com

Word-processing software:

- Apple Pages: support.apple.com/manuals/#iwork
- Microsoft Word: goo.gl/KXnLe

Language	
Areas	*Vocabulary:* Personal skills, interests and hobbies *Grammar:* Present simple tense; can/can't
Functions	Discussing abilities and interests
Skills	Speaking, writing

Resources	
High-tech	*Equipment:* One internet-enabled teacher computer and data projector; internet-enabled student computers or mobile devices (one per student) *Tools:* Word-processing software (e.g. Apple Pages or Microsoft Word) *Tools (optional):* Edmodo *Documents:* Online worksheet (www.pearsoned.co.uk/hockly)
Low-tech	*Equipment:* One internet-enabled teacher computer and data projector *Documents:* Printed worksheet (follows Activity)
No-tech	*Documents:* Printed worksheet (follows Activity)

Procedure

1. Start this activity with a personal anecdote about your PLN (personal learning network; see Box 1.10 and Chapter 4: *Building and maintaining PLNs* for more details). Who do you share with and learn from on a daily basis? Try to include information that will help students complete **Activity 30 Worksheet – My PLN**.

2. Ask students to look at the Worksheet and give them time to think about their responses individually before putting them into small groups to compare their answers. Conduct feedback as a whole group, paying particular attention to how people choose their connections.

3. Now get them to think about their classmates. What do they know about each of them? Ask them to write down the names of each of their classmates and list the skills they know they have, either in a word-processed document (high-tech version) or on paper (low-tech and no-tech versions).

4. As a group, bring all the information together to make small circles of people, as seen below:

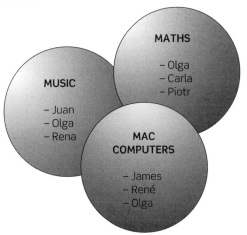

5. Once all the information is collated, ask each person to add any skills or areas of interest they have that the class may not have been aware of. This is a great opportunity for a 'talent audit' in the class, finding out about the skills and interests of everyone.

6. Now take a closer look at the circles. Why do some of the circles overlap? (*Some people are in more than one circle.*) What does this mean in terms of day-to-day communications? (*We can sort our connections into groups and go to specific groups for specific kinds of information or help.*) What does this mean for online communications? (*Joining specific groups on social networking sites such as Facebook means we can use our connections as filters to obtain particular kinds of information or help; similarly, creating lists on services such as Twitter can get us quickly to experts when needed.*)

Extension

Set up an Edmodo account (see Activity 39, *A class PLN*) for the class so that students can stay connected and contact each other if they need to know something in any of the areas of class expertise (high-tech version).

Activity 30 Worksheet – My PLN

Think about the people you interact with each day: face to face, on the phone, by SMS (text message), on Facebook, on Twitter, etc.

1. Fill in the table below about the people who are your main news sources.

Type of news	Source of news
Social news about friends and family	
Social news about what's happening at school or work	
News/information connected to your studies or profession	
National and international news	
News/information about your hobbies and interests	
News about new music and movies	

2. Note down the top five personal connections in your network.

3. Note down the top five school/work connections in your network. Are any of them the same as the top five personal connections? Why/why not?

4. How did you choose these connections? What makes them good?

5. Do you use different social networks for personal and professional reasons?

Activity 31: My digital life

Students reflect on how much time they spend being distracted by technology on a daily basis.

As we gain ever greater access to technologies and online content it's easy to find our entire day wrapped up in digital interactions. This activity helps students break down their daily usage and asks them to focus on how they pay attention. It also encourages them to think about taking some time out. This activity fits well with Activity 2, *Being digitally literate*.

Literacy:	**Filtering literacy** (complexity: ***)
Topic:	Technologies
Aim:	To discuss attention and offer advice on how to improve it
Level:	Intermediate +
Time:	60 minutes
Tech support:	Blogs:

- General: e-language.wikispaces.com/blogs
- Blogger: support.google.com/blogger/?hl=en
- Edublogs: help.edublogs.org

Presentation software:

- Keynote: support.apple.com/manuals/#iwork
- PowerPoint: goo.gl/vfLwD
- Prezi: prezi.com/learn/getting-started/

Wikis:

- General: e-language.wikispaces.com/wikis
- PBworks: usermanual.pbworks.com
- Wikispaces: help.wikispaces.com

Language	
Areas	*Vocabulary:* Technologies; habits and daily routines *Grammar:* Present simple tense
Functions	Describing routines
Skills	Listening, speaking, reading, writing

Resources	
High-tech	*Equipment:* One internet-enabled teacher computer and data projector; internet-enabled student computers or mobile handheld devices (one per pair) *Tools:* Class blog (e.g. Blogger or Edublogs) *or* class wiki (e.g. PBworks or Wikispaces) *Tools (optional):* Presentation software (e.g. Keynote, PowerPoint or Prezi) *Documents:* Online worksheet (www.pearsoned.co.uk/hockly)
Low-tech	*Equipment:* One internet-enabled teacher computer and data projector *Tools:* Presentation software (e.g. Keynote, PowerPoint or Prezi) *Documents:* Printed worksheet (follows Activity)
No-tech	*Documents:* Printed website posts; printed worksheet (follows Activity) *Stationery:* Poster-sized paper, coloured pens and magazines (for images)

Procedure

Before class

- Prepare your presentation and/or gather your realia for use in Step 1.
- Print out a selection of posts for use in Step 3 (no-tech version).

1. Start off with a small presentation about your own daily use of technologies. This is a valuable listening exercise on its own. Tell students about a typical day in your life, the gadgets you use, how often you check your email, etc. You might do this with a Keynote, PowerPoint or Prezi presentation to accompany it (high-tech and low-tech versions) or you might bring in realia – examples of the actual technologies – for visual support (no-tech version). Try to weave in some examples of how you get

distracted and off-topic – how does it happen, and what do you do when it happens?

2. Put students into pairs, and ask them to discuss the points on **Activity 31 Worksheet – Distractions**. Conduct feedback as a whole class. Why do they think these things happen? Do they have too many distractions in their lives? Will this have an effect on their future success?

3. Tell students they are going to read about a school in Norway where computers are used in every class. Ask them to decide what they think the students say about the school, and what their opinions are about using technology in class. Before they read, get them to brainstorm in pairs:

Technology at school	
Advantages	**Disadvantages**
• …	• …
• …	• …

Get some group feedback and display it on the projector screen (high-tech and low-tech versions) or write it on the board (no-tech version). Now have students visit Anne Michaelsen's blog post 'What students say about Facebook and MSN!' on Teaching English using Web 2.0 (goo.gl/ te8kz) and read the advice left by current students for future students at the same school (high-tech version). Alternatively, display relevant posts on the projector screen (low-tech version) or distribute printouts (no-tech version). Ask students to note down the main points and check them against the results of the brainstorming activity.

4. Now the students are going to write similar advice for younger students (though obviously this may be of use to them, too). Put students into pairs and give each pair the following headings:

- using technology in class
- studying at home
- avoiding distractions
- finding a balance

They should try to write at least two pieces of advice for each heading. These may take the form of simple 'dos' and 'don'ts', or could be longer, more personal texts like the blog entries they read in Step 3.

5. Collate students' advice on a class blog or wiki (high-tech version). Alternatively, a whole class Keynote, PowerPoint or Prezi presentation will make a good final product (low-tech version), or else students could create a colourful wall poster (no-tech version).

Extension 1

More advanced groups may take this subject further using the materials found in Matt Richtel's article 'Growing Up Digital, Wired for Distraction' in *The New York Times* (www.nytimes.com/2010/11/21/technology/21brain.html).

Extension 2

With advanced groups, this is an excellent opportunity to discuss study habits and time management. One effective way of managing your time is to use the Pomodoro Technique (www.pomodorotechnique.com). You might want to investigate this with your students and jointly devise a technique for taking breaks at appropriate moments.

Extension 3

Encourage students to add hyperlinks from their e-portfolios to the class blog post or wiki entry (see Chapter 3: *Assessing digital work, Assessing through e-portfolios*) (high-tech version).

Activity 31 Worksheet – Distractions

Respond to these statements with true (T) or false (F):

- I use social networks (e.g. Facebook) at school/college.   (   )
- I often text my friends while I'm in class.   (   )
- I chat to friends online during class.   (   )
- I sometimes look up answers on the web in class.   (   )
- I sometimes miss what my teachers say in class.   (   )
- I'm often online when I should be studying.   (   )
- I sometimes don't do homework because I'm online.   (   )
- I study less and less each year – there are too many distractions! (   )
- I get lost on the net, and spend hours searching and reading.   (   )
- I often have the TV on while I'm online and studying.   (   )

Activity 32: Turn off, tune out

Students learn about switching off digital information and communication channels.

This activity encourages students to think about the effects of their technology-related communications on their daily lives, and introduces the idea of 'switching off' from time to time. It runs over two classes – a planning class (Class 1), and a class in which students report back on their experience of 'switching off' (Class 2).

Literacy:	**Network literacy** and **Filtering literacy** (complexity: ***)
Topic:	Digital communications
Aim:	To raise awareness of how multiple information and communication channels can affect our daily lives, and explore ways of filtering out digital distractions
Level:	Intermediate +
Time:	30 minutes (Class 1) + 30 minutes (Class 2) + homework
Tech support:	Blogs:

- General: e-language.wikispaces.com/blogs
- Blogger: support.google.com/blogger/?hl=en
- Edublogs: help.edublogs.org

Wikis:

- General: e-language.wikispaces.com/wikis
- PBworks: usermanual.pbworks.com
- Wikispaces: help.wikispaces.com

Language	
Areas	*Vocabulary:* Technology, gadgets and the internet *Grammar:* Past tenses
Functions	Discussing
Skills	Writing, speaking

Resources	
High-tech	*Equipment:* One internet-enabled teacher computer and data projector; internet-enabled student computers or mobile devices (one per student) *Tools (optional):* Class blog (e.g. Blogger or Edublogs) *or* class wiki (e.g. PBworks or Wikispaces) *Documents:* Online worksheets (www.pearsoned.co.uk/hockly)
Low-tech	*Documents:* Printed worksheets (follows Activity)
No-tech	*Documents:* Printed worksheets (follows Activity)

Digital risks

This activity is only appropriate for students who have access to internet-enabled computers or mobile devices in their everyday lives. Before you decide to do this activity, check on students' access to such equipment. Be wary of reinforcing the digital divide if only some students have such access (see Box 1.4; Activity 29, *News in my networks* for more details).

Procedure

Class 1: Planning

1. Start with an anecdote connected with 'switching off' in your own life – a time when you chose or were forced to be without internet access, perhaps in the countryside or abroad. Describe the effect it had on you.

2. Refer students to **Activity 32 Worksheet A – Turning off** and ask them to complete it individually before pairing up to compare notes. Give each pair time to talk about their information and communication channels and the order they have put them in before combining pairs into small groups. Conduct feedback as a whole class.

3. Refer students to **Activity 32 Worksheet B – Tuning out**. Tell them they are going to do without one line of communication each day for a week, as an experiment to see how it affects their lives and what they do to cope. Ask them to map out the week and choose a different line of communication for each day. They will note down their thoughts and reactions each day to see how they 'survive', and compare notes with their classmates the following week.

Class 2: Reporting

1. A week later, put students into small groups to compare their experiences. How did filtering out one line of communication change each day for them? What were the good and bad points? Did they learn anything about filtering out information and managing their time more effectively? How do they think they may change their lives in the future, based on their experiments?

Variation

Students could use a class blog or wiki to record their daily reflections for Activity 2 Worksheet, thus encouraging greater reflection and more sharing over the duration of the project (high-tech version).

Extension

Encourage students to upload their completed worksheets to, or link to the class blog or wiki from, their e-portfolios (see Chapter 3: *Assessing digital work, Assessing through e-portfolios*) (high-tech version).

Activity 32 Worksheet A – Turning off

Make a list of all the information and communication channels you use on a daily basis:

- SMS (text messaging)
- instant messaging app or service (e.g. What's App, Viber)
- video calling app or service (e.g. FaceTime, Skype, Tango)
- social networking site (e.g. Facebook)
- . . .
- . . .
- . . .
- . . .

Now put them in order of importance to you, from the one you really couldn't do without (1) to the one you rely on the least.

When you are ready, join a classmate and compare your lists. How do you think you would feel if these tools and gadgets were taken away from you for a week?

Activity 32 Worksheet B – Tuning out

For each day, make a record of which line of communication you chose to go without, and your reactions to that day, e.g.:

Day	Channel	Bad Points	Good Points
(e.g.) Monday	Facebook	Missed chatting to my friends after school. No idea what everyone did in the evening. Felt very left out.	Did my homework on time for once! Had time to go for a walk after dinner.
Monday			
Tuesday			
Wednesday			
Thursday			
Friday			

Activity 33: Faking it

Students create a fake Facebook profile for a fictional or historical character.

Many students, especially adolescents, already have an online presence. This activity encourages students to create an online social networking site profile for a fictional or historical character, in English, which provides not only language practice, but an opportunity to discuss and explore online identity management and our digital footprints.

Literacy:	**Personal literacy** and **Network literacy** (overall complexity: ***)
Topic:	Famous people
Aim:	To raise awareness of social networking profiles, online identity and identity management
Level:	Elementary +
Time:	60 minutes

Tech support: Document sharing:

- General: e-language.wikispaces.com/social-sharing#document-sharing

- Google Docs: support.google.com/docs/?hl=en

Multimedia sharing:

- General: e-language.wikispaces.com/social-sharing#multimedia-sharing

- Glogster: www.youtube.com/watch?v=hvQX5LeQ-zg

Social networking:

- General: e-language.wikispaces.com/social-networking

- Historical Facebook Lesson: goo.gl/Mpen

- LinkedIn: learn.linkedin.com/what-is-linkedin

- My Fake Wall: goo.gl/KtOfP

- The Wall Machine: www.classroom20.com/video/the-wall-machine-demo

Language	
Areas	*Vocabulary:* Famous people and biographies; personal information *Grammar:* Present simple tense
Functions	Giving personal information (name, job, origin, country of residence, etc.); discussing
Skills	Reading, writing, speaking

Resources	
High-tech	*Equipment:* Internet-enabled student computers or mobile devices (one per pair) *Documents:* Online worksheet (www.pearsoned.co.uk/hockly) *Tools:* My Fake Wall *or* The Wall Machine *Tools (optional):* Glogster; LinkedIn
Low-tech	*Equipment:* One internet-enabled teacher computer and data projector *Documents:* Printed Historical Facebook Lesson Google Docs template; printed worksheet (follows Activity) *Tools (optional):* Glogster; LinkedIn
No-tech	*Documents:* Printed Historical Facebook Lesson Google Docs template; printed worksheet (follows Activity) *Documents (optional):* Printed LinkedIn profiles *Stationery (optional):* Poster-sized paper and coloured pens

Digital risks

- Teachers should familiarise themselves with social networking sites such as Facebook, including their privacy settings (see Box 1.9).
- Teachers should be wary of accepting invitations to 'friend' students on social networking sites (see Box 1.3).
- Teachers should provide alternative options to services which require a Facebook profile to log in, as some students may not have or want such a profile. According to Facebook's Terms of Service, students under 13 are not permitted to have a Facebook profile.
- Teachers should choose example profiles carefully, as some of those on public sites may contain language or content which is unsuitable for students, especially young learners.

Procedure

Before class

- Choose or create a profile for a fictional or historical character on a free online service such as My Fake Wall (www.myfakewall.com) or The Wall Machine (thewallmachine.com), both of which are similar to Facebook. Choose a character who will be well known to your students. Fictional characters might include Little Red Riding Hood, Cinderella or Peter Pan; historical characters might include George Washington, Genghis Khan, Marie Curie or Eva Peron. Note that to use My Fake Wall, you and your students will need to create accounts. To use The Wall Machine, you need to sign in with a Facebook account (see Digital risks). Another option is to use the free public Historical Facebook Lesson Google Docs template created by Derrick Waddell (goo.gl/xltgg). None of these sites are real networking sites, and the fake profiles do not connect to each other. Each profile you create is essentially a standalone web page.

- Bookmark the fake profile you have created or chosen (high-tech and low-tech versions) or print out copies for your students (no-tech version), for use in Step 2.

- Print one copy of the Historical Facebook Lesson Google Docs template for each student in the class, for use in Step 3 (low-tech and no-tech versions).

- (Optional) Print a selection of public LinkedIn profiles for Extension 2 (no-tech version).

1. In class, introduce your chosen fictional or historical character and find out what students know about them. Tell students that this character has a Facebook page. Before they view the page, they need to imagine what sort of information the character has included in their profile. Ask students to refer to **Activity 33 Worksheet – Faking it**, and ask them to discuss the points in Task 1.

2. Give students the web address of the fake profile you have chosen or created, and ask them to visit the page in pairs (high-tech version), or show the class the fake profile on the classroom computer (low-tech version), or give out printed copies of the profile (no-tech version). Give students time to read the profile. Ask the class how accurate their predictions were.

3. Tell students that they are going to work in pairs to produce a fake Facebook profile for a fictional or historical character. Allocate characters,

or let students choose one themselves. Point them to your chosen tool (My Fake Wall, The Wall Machine, or the Historical Facebook Lesson Google Docs template). My Fake Wall and The Wall Machine both require the students to work online (high-tech version). The Google Docs template, on the other hand, can be printed out and copied by the teacher before class, and students can create their fake profiles on paper (low-tech and no-tech versions). Students should create one fake profile per pair, including a picture and any other information the profile allows (such as fake friends, comments from friends, etc.). Tell students that during later class feedback they will need to justify the updates, comments and friends they decide to add.

4. When students have created their profiles, ask them to write the URLs on the board, and to visit other pairs' fake profiles (high-tech version). If students have created profiles on paper, these can be put up on the walls of the classroom, and students can walk around and read them (low-tech and no-tech versions).

5. Round off the activity by asking which characters were the most popular, and what sort of information was included in the profiles/status updates/ comments. Ask students to justify the status updates, comments and other elements they chose to include in the fake profiles.

6. Choose one of the pairs' fake profiles, or one that you created, or one of the public profiles from My Fake Wall or The Wall Machine. Tell students to imagine that they are this person's possible future employer. What sort of impression would they get from this profile, from this perspective? Would they give the person a job? Why/why not? What about the perspective of a parent? And if this person was a teacher, what impression would a student get?

7. Ask students to discuss Task 2 on the worksheet in small groups.

8. Conduct open feedback on the questions in Task 2 with the class. Introduce the idea of a *digital footprint* and the need to manage one's online identity (see Box 1.9). Ensure that students are aware of how difficult it is to control who reads your information on social networking sites, and that they realise that even if posts are deleted, they can be traced. For those students who already have social networking profiles, to what extent do they take this into account? What sort of privacy settings do they have on their profiles?

Extension 1

Ask students to contribute to an online class poster in Glogster by adding *one* tip each for managing online identity (high-tech and low-tech versions). Alternatively, students could add one tip each to a large poster on the classroom wall (no-tech version).

Extension 2

With more advanced level classes, show students examples of public profiles from the professional networking site LinkedIn (www.linkedin.com) on the projector screen (high-tech and low-tech versions) or printed out on paper (no-tech version). (Note that it is necessary to sign up to see full profiles.) Ask whether any students already have profiles on this site. Students can work in pairs or groups to consider how LinkedIn users should and shouldn't present themselves online, before feeding back to the whole class. What are the differences between LinkedIn and more social sites like Facebook? Students in Business English or university-level classes might wish to consider setting up their own profiles on LinkedIn.

Extension 3

Encourage students to add hyperlinks from their e-portfolios to their fake profiles and/or to the class glog (Glogster poster) (see Chapter 3: *Assessing digital work, Assessing through e-portfolios*) (high-tech version).

Activity 33 Worksheet – Faking it

Facebook profile for _____

1. What information do you think you will see in this person's Facebook profile? In pairs, discuss and make notes on what will be in each section:

   - Personal information: name, current job, where studied, where lives, where from, date of birth.
   - Photos: who will be in the photos, and where will they be taken? Imagine five photos.
   - Friends: who will be this person's friends? Think of five possible friends.
   - Status updates: what status updates (messages) will this person post? Think of five possible messages.
   - Comments: what comments will friends make on the status updates? Think of two or three comments for some of the status updates.

   Now visit the person's Facebook page and see if you were right!

2. Who reads your profile?

   Look again at the profile you created for a fictional or historical character. Imagine yourself reading this profile from the following perspectives:

   - future employer/boss
   - parent/son/daughter
   - student/teacher

   For each of these readers, what things would you change in the profile? Look especially at the status updates and comments – which ones are not appropriate for each of these readers?

Activity 34: Online me

Students create a multimedia poster about themselves, including digital images and video, using a free online poster tool.

Establishing and managing an online presence is a challenging task, especially when multiple media and even multiple languages may be involved. This activity helps students consider how they should present themselves in a multimedia format to various audiences. It leads well into Activity 35, *Personal blogging*.

Literacy:	**Personal literacy** and **Multimedia literacy** (overall complexity: ***)
Topic:	Personal information
Aim:	To raise awareness of online identity, and how to present yourself online
Level:	Elementary +
Time:	60 minutes (+ homework)
Tech support:	Blogs:

- General: e-language.wikispaces.com/blogs
- Blogger: support.google.com/blogger/?hl=en
- Edublogs: help.edublogs.org

Multimedia sharing:

- General: e-language.wikispaces.com/social-sharing#multimedia-sharing
- Glogster EDU: www.youtube.com/watch?v=80NISdsoouE

Wikis:

- General: e-language.wikispaces.com/wikis
- PBworks: usermanual.pbworks.com
- Wikispaces: help.wikispaces.com

Language	
Areas	*Vocabulary:* Personal information; hobbies and interests *Grammar:* Present simple tense; would
Functions	Talking about yourself; discussing what you would or wouldn't do
Skills	Speaking, writing, reading

Resources	
High-tech	*Equipment:* One internet-enabled teacher computer and data projector; internet-enabled student computers or mobile devices (one per student) *Tools:* Glogster EDU *Tools (optional):* Class blog (e.g. Blogger or Edublogs) or class wiki (e.g. PBworks or Wikispaces) *Documents:* Online worksheet (www.pearsoned.co.uk/hockly)
Low-tech	*Equipment:* One internet-enabled teacher computer and data projector *Tools (optional):* Class blog (e.g. Blogger or Edublogs) or class wiki (e.g. PBworks or Wikispaces) *Documents:* Printed worksheet (follows Activity) *Stationery:* Poster-sized paper, coloured pens and magazines (for images)
No-tech	*Documents:* Printed worksheet (follows Activity) *Stationery:* Poster-sized paper, coloured pens and magazines (for images)

Digital risks

Like many web 2.0 services, Glogster allows you to make your creations public or private. Glogster EDU, on the other hand, is specially designed for teachers and students. There is a free and a premium (paid) version. The free EDU version enables you to create accounts for up to 50 students, and to keep students' glogs (that is, posters created on Glogster) private. While public Glogster creations have the advantage of being easily viewable by friends and family, teachers working with young learners should consider working only with Glogster EDU. This is usually the best option when students are creating work in which aspects of their identities (including, but not limited to, names, locations, or photos and videos which reveal faces or locations) are shown. (For other, similar discussions of privacy settings, see Activity 4, *Extreme weather* on blogs, Activity 7, *Sports linking* on wikis and Activity 44, *Vox pop* on vodcasts.)

Procedure

Before class

- Create an online multimedia poster about yourself with Glogster EDU (edu.glogster.com), for use in Step 3. You could show this to students online (high-tech and low-tech versions), or printed out (no-tech version). You can look at the online poster created by one of the book authors as an example: nickyhockly.glogster.com/nickyglog/.

1. Tell students that they are going to produce one poster each, about themselves, using Glogster EDU (high-tech version) or on paper (low-tech and no-tech versions). Before they start, they need to decide what information to include. Put the following on the board:

   • your family
   • your classmates/work colleagues
   • your boss (or potential future employer)
   • a college or university admissions officer
   • anybody in the world

   Point out that what they include in their poster will depend on the *audience* and *purpose*. Who will see their poster? What message would they like to get across about themselves to each audience? Elicit some of the things that they would/wouldn't include in a poster about themselves. Ask students to refer to **Activity 34 Worksheet – Online me** and decide what photos/pictures, videos and text comments they would add to an online poster, depending on the audience, by filling in the grid. They should then compare their answers with a partner.

2. Ask for feedback. How far do the pairs agree about what to include in their posters? Ask students to consider how presenting a poster online versus on paper would affect their decisions. Discuss how most online tools (like Glogster) allow different levels of privacy – students can choose to make an online poster completely open to the world, and even to allow comments from strangers, or they can make it private, so that only those people with the URL can access it. However, once online, their posters will be there forever, no matter what privacy level they choose, and even if they later delete their work (see Box 1.9). Discuss how this might impact their self-presentation online.

3. If you have created your own glog (i.e. Glogster poster, as described under Before class), show it to the class on the projector screen (high-tech and low-tech versions) or printed out (no-tech version), explaining your decisions about what to include. Then explain that students will create their own posters which could in theory be read by anyone in the world. They can do so online using Glogster EDU (high-tech version) or on paper, using the bank of magazines to find images to illustrate their posters (low-tech and no-tech versions). They could also mark up any photos/ videos they would add to their posters if they were online (and students with access to computers at home could then create their posters in Glogster EDU as homework).

4. As students finish their posters, collect the URLs on the board, and encourage students to visit each other's and make comments while waiting for their classmates to finish (high-tech version). Note that Glogster EDU allows students to keep their glogs private but to still comment on each other's work. If students are creating paper posters, ask them to put them on the classroom walls as they finish, with a blank piece of paper underneath each poster for comments (low-tech and no-tech versions). When everyone has finished their poster, show each student's work to the class on the projector screen (high-tech version) or ask students to point out their own posters on the classroom walls (low-tech and no-tech versions). Each student should explain their poster, saying why they included the particular information they chose.

Extension 1

Embed or add links to all the glogs in a class blog or wiki (high-tech version) or take digital photos of the wall posters and add these images to a class blog or wiki (low-tech version).

Extension 2

Encourage students to add hyperlinks from their e-portfolios to their glogs (see Chapter 3: *Assessing digital work*, *Assessing through e-portfolios*) (high-tech version).

Activity 34 Worksheet – Online me

My poster

What information would you include in an *online* poster about yourself, for these audiences:

- your family
- your classmates/work colleagues
- your boss (or potential future employer)
- a college or university admissions officer
- anybody in the world

Complete this grid. Then compare with a partner.

Audience	Personal information	Photos/ images	Videos	Text/ comments
Family				
Classmates/ work colleagues				
Boss/future employer				
College/uni admissions officer				
World				

Activity 35: Personal blogging

Students create a personal blog around an interest of theirs.

Whilst many students worldwide have some online presence in the form of an account on a social networking site, few engage in extensive writing in the form of a blog. In this activity they will start a blog, and consider appropriate content and behaviour for blogging.

Literacy:	**Personal literacy**, **Print literacy** and **Multimedia literacy** (complexity: ***)
Topic:	Hobbies and interests
Aim:	To raise awareness of the value of blogging
Level:	Lower intermediate +
Time:	90 minutes + homework
Tech support:	Blogs:

- General: e-language.wikispaces.com/blogs

- Blogging for ELT: www.teachingenglish.org.uk/articles/ blogging-elt

- Edublogs: help.edublogs.org

Language	
Areas	*Vocabulary:* Hobbies and interests *Grammar:* Present simple tense; adverbs of frequency; question forms
Functions	Describing hobbies and interests
Skills	Writing, reading, speaking, listening

Resources	
High-tech	*Equipment:* One internet-enabled teacher computer and data projector; internet-enabled student computers or mobile devices (one per student) *Tools:* Edublogs *Documents:* Online worksheets (www.pearsoned.co.uk/hockly)
Low-tech	*Equipment:* One internet-enabled teacher computer and data projector *Tools:* Edublogs *Documents:* Printed worksheets (follows Activity)
No-tech	*Documents:* Printed sample Edublogs blog; printed worksheets (follows Activity)

Digital risks

Students need to be aware of how to manage their online identity when they set up a blog (see Box 1.9; Activity 34, *Online me*).

Procedure

Before class

- You will need to have your own sample blog for one of your hobbies set up beforehand, for use in Step 2. Use the free option at Edublogs (edublogs.org). Ensure you have two or three entries written. You can show the blog on the projector screen (high-tech and low-tech versions) or make printouts (no-tech version).

1. Introduce the subject of blogging using **Activity 35 Worksheet A – Blogs and me**. Once students have had time to do the speaking activity, conduct feedback on the blogs they read/write. Share a list of their favourite blogs on the board. If you're sure that your students don't read or write blogs, then start at Step 2.

2. Show students your blog on the projector screen (high-tech and low-tech versions) or distribute printouts (no-tech version). Ask them to note down the following main features:

   - an 'About' page
   - posts in reverse chronological order

- tags
- comments
- photos or videos
- widgets

3. Tell students they are going to individually set up a blog to write regular posts connected to a hobby or interest. Get them to set up accounts at Edublogs and help them customise their blogs with useful widgets (high-tech version). You may also choose to set up one class blog using the teacher computer and projector screen (low-tech version), or have students create a 'virtual blog' on paper (no-tech version).

4. Get students to look back at your 'About' page and make some notes on the information you've included. You may want to discuss what kind of information is appropriate here:

- avoid personal contact information;
- shield your email address from spambots (software that collects email addresses);
- review the register and content to ensure your material fits with the aim of your blog;
- don't share anything you wouldn't share face to face;
- ensure the content is right for your intended audience.

Students can now move on to creating their own 'About' page: the default page that comes with all new blogs (high-tech version). Alternatively, they can collaboratively create an 'About' page for the class blog (low-tech version) or they can create individual 'About' pages for their 'virtual blogs' (no-tech version).

5. To get students started with their first post, ask them to use **Activity 35 Worksheet B – My hobby** in pairs to gather some basic information that will be the basis of their introductory posts. In each pair, students should make notes for their partner.

6. Encourage students to examine examples of blogs related to their areas of interest – a good place to find these is on the Technorati blog search site (technorati.com). As they visit similar blogs, students should look at the style and content of the posts. You might also encourage them to leave comments on relevant blogs, perhaps sharing the address of their own blog (high-tech version). Alternatively, explore other student blogs as a whole class activity (low-tech version). (Note that this step is not possible in the no-tech version.)

7. Students' first blog posts can be written for homework. If they have the equipment available, they can post their entries directly to their individual blogs or the class blog from home (high-tech and low-tech versions), or else they can do this in the next class (with students taking turns on the teacher computer in the low-tech version). Otherwise students can share their written work on paper with a partner or group in the next class (no-tech version).

Note that some students may want feedback and corrections before making their work public in this way. This is a good chance to practise traditional print literacy skills by taking a process writing approach involving successive drafts of student work (see Chapter 3: *Choosing activities for different levels and contexts, Students' linguistic competence*).

8. Suggest that students enhance their text-based communication by:

   - including hyperlinks to other relevant blogs or sources of information (see Activity 7, *Sports linking*)
   - including public domain or Creative Commons images to illustrate their blogs (see Activity 10, *Copycat*)
   - embedding or linking to videos (see Activity 22, *HTML advanced*)
   - tagging their posts (see Activity 24, *Travel tags*)

   These activities are easiest to realise if students work individually on computers (high-tech version), though they can also be done collaboratively on the teacher computer and projector screen (low-tech version). Otherwise, students might include 'virtual' links, etc., on their paper blogs (no-tech version).

9. Encourage students to write regular posts for their individual blogs (high-tech version) or the class blog (low-tech version). After a couple of posts, spend some time getting feedback from the group:

   - Have students enjoyed blogging so far?
   - Has their knowledge of their hobby advanced?
   - Have they met other bloggers and communicated with them?
   - Has their English improved?
   - Do they intend to continue blogging?

Variation

Blogs also make an ideal reflective journal for students (high-tech version). You may decide that this is a better option in your context. If you decide to follow this route, ensure that blog posts are set regularly as in-class or homework tasks. You will need to guide your students for each post, perhaps with a set of questions along the following lines:

- What have you enjoyed doing this week?
- What have you found difficult this week?
- What areas do you still need improvement in?
- What topics would you like to cover in class?

Extension

Encourage students to add hyperlinks from their e-portfolios to their blogs (see Chapter 3: *Assessing digital work, Assessing through e-portfolios*) (high-tech version).

Activity 35 Worksheet A – Blogs and me

Find out about your partner's blogging habits with this questionnaire:

- What blogs do you read?
  - How often do you read them?
  - How do you keep up with the blogs you read?
  - What do you like about the blogs you read?
  - Do you leave comments or questions on these blogs?
- Do you have your own blog?
  - What is your blog about?
  - How often do you write a new post?
  - Do you have a lot of readers?
  - Do you get a lot of comments?

Activity 35 Worksheet B – My hobbies

Find out about your partner's hobbies with this questionnaire. Make notes about their answers.

- What is your favourite hobby?
- What does it involve?
- How long have you been doing it?
- How much does it cost?
- How much time does it take each week?
- What do you like about it?
- Would you recommend it to others? Why (not)?

Activity 36: Setting the scene

Students consider their digital safety in a number of challenging online scenarios, and come up with ways of dealing with these scenarios.

Many students, especially teenagers, are members of social networking sites. They will potentially come across difficult situations online. Rather than trying to prohibit access, many educators agree that it is far more helpful to teach students the skills to deal with challenging situations. This activity examines a number of online scenarios and helps students consider how to deal with them.

Acknowledgement:	Thank you to Carol Rainbow for the original concept.
Literacy:	**Personal literacy** and **Network literacy** (overall complexity: ***)
Topic:	Digital safety
Aim:	To help students learn to deal with challenging or inappropriate online behaviour
Level:	Lower intermediate +
Time:	60 minutes
Tech support:	Multimedia sharing: • General: e-language.wikispaces.com/ social-sharing#multimedia-sharing • Glogster: www.youtube.com/watch?v=hvQX5LeQ-zg • Glogster EDU: www.youtube.com/ watch?v=80NISdsoouE

Language	
Areas	*Grammar:* Should; second conditional
Functions	Giving advice and making suggestions
Skills	Reading, speaking

Resources	
High-tech	Not available for this activity *Extension tools (optional):* Glogster or Glogster EDU
Low-tech	Not available for this activity
No-tech	*Documents:* Sets of Online Scenarios cards from worksheet (follows Activity) *Stationery (optional):* Poster-sized paper, coloured pens and magazines (for images)

Digital risks

Digital safety is a key area to address, especially with younger learners (see Box 1.9). This topic will also be of interest to adult students, especially those who have children. Not everyone belongs to a social networking site, and some of your students may be reluctant or negative about them (see Box 1.3 on social networks). It's important to listen to these voices, and to acknowledge that some students may not want to use social networking sites or have their children using them.

Procedure

1. Ask students whether they belong to any social networking sites (such as Facebook, Bebo, Cyworld [싸이월드], Mixi [ミクシィ], Orkut, Renren [人人网], VK [ВКонтакте] and so on), and collect a list of these networks on the board. Ask students who are *not* members of a social networking site what their opinion is about these sites. Do they plan to join one? Why/why not?

2. Put students into pairs, and give them a few minutes to brainstorm the pros and cons of belonging to a social networking site. Elicit responses and put them into a grid on the board. Here are some suggestions:

Pros	Cons
• keep in touch with friends and family • meet new people • re-establish contact with people from your past (e.g. primary school) • share web links, photos and videos • share your latest news • contact people with similar interests • practise English or another language • take part in group activities (e.g. chats) • . . . • . . .	• contacts may not really be friends • people post too often • people post photos/videos of you without permission • people post information about you which is not appropriate • misunderstandings can happen easily • cyberbullying • lack of privacy and potential for advertisers to use your information • spam and viruses • . . . • . . .

3. Ask students if they have ever experienced, or know about, uncomfortable situations that can arise on social networking sites. What should you do to protect yourself, and how do you deal with a difficult situation once it has happened? Tell students they will discuss a number of scenarios related to this.

4. Put students into pairs or small groups, and hand out packs of the online scenarios cards from **Activity 36 Worksheet – Setting the scene**, one pack per pair/group. Students should keep these cards face down. They then turn the first card over, discuss it, and note down the card number and a possible way to deal with the situation. You might like to start by discussing one card together with the whole class as an example, and put helpful language on the board if needed (*I would . . .*, *She should . . .*, *If I were her . . .*, etc.). Give students around 20–30 minutes to discuss all the cards in their pairs or groups. While they are talking, monitor and note down common language errors.

5. Conduct feedback with the whole class. Briefly look again at each online scenario and elicit the solutions/suggestions that students came up with. See the key in Appendix: Answer keys for issues to discuss and to make the class aware of. Once you have dealt with the issues, briefly review some of the language errors you heard.

Extension 1

Working in new pairs or groups, students can create a Digital Safety poster, with Ten Top Tips for using social networking sites based on the discussion and feedback in Steps 4 and 5. The posters can be produced using Glogster (www.glogster.com) or Glogster EDU (edu.glogster.com; see Activity 34, *Online me*) (high-tech version) or on paper (no-tech version). Online posters can be shared via the school website (high-tech version). Paper posters can be put up around the classroom or school (no-tech versions).

Extension 2

Encourage students to add hyperlinks from their e-portfolios to their glogs (Glogster posters) (see Chapter 3: *Assessing digital work, Assessing through e-portfolios*) (high-tech version).

Activity 36 Worksheet – Setting the scene

Copy and cut out the cards below, and give one pack of cards to each pair/ group of students. If your students are teenagers, ask them to imagine themselves in each situation and discuss what they would do. If your students are adults, ask them to imagine their own children, or a teenager they know, in each situation. Students should note down the card numbers along with at least one suggestion for how to deal with each scenario.

▶ Card 1 ◀

One of your social networking 'friends', whom you haven't actually met, asks for your address and telephone number so you can meet up in real life.

What do you do?

▶ Card 2 ◀

You have been exchanging private messages on a social networking site with a friend you haven't met. He is the same age as you and has similar interests. He sends you a new photo of himself, and asks you to send him a new photo of yourself.

What do you do?

▶ Card 3 ◀

A real-life friend of yours has hundreds of contacts on her social networking page. She offers to share these friends with you, so that you can have more friends yourself.

What do you do?

▶ Card 4 ◀

A friend posts a message on your page on a social networking site, saying (in your language) : 'Hey, look at this bad stuff people are saying about you!', with a link.

What do you do?

▶ Card 5 ◀

You have created a social networking profile called 'sexygirl1985' (or 'sexyboy1985').
Strangers are now sending you messages which make you feel uncomfortable.

What do you do?

▶ Card 6 ◀

You have been chatting online for several weeks via webcam with somebody you met in a virtual world months ago. One day he asks you to take your shirt off, and says that if you do he will buy you the new jeans you have been talking about.

What do you do?

▶ Card 7 ◀

At a recent party, your friend took some photos of you that you don't like, and he has now put them on his social networking page, tagged with your name.

What do you do?

▶ Card 8 ◀

Your friends are talking about a new website where you can post photos and chat to others. When you go to sign up yourself, you see that the website wants a picture of you, your email address, your home address and your mobile phone number.

What do you do?

▶ Card 9 ◀

Some of your friends have been posting cruel comments about a teacher in your school on their pages on a social networking site. You don't particularly like the teacher, but you don't think he is that bad.

What do you do?

▶ Card 10 ◀

A girl in your class has started sending you nasty mobile phone text messages. She says if you tell anybody, she will make your life hell at school.

What do you do?

▶ Card 11 ◀

Your friend plans to set up an online group called 'Let's burn down the school!' and invite school friends to join it. He thinks it will be a funny joke.

What do you do?

▶ Card 12 ◀

Someone has been posting unpleasant messages to a social networking page with your username. You don't know who it is.

What do you do?

Activity 37: Footprints in the wires

Students consider their digital footprints and what they reveal about them.

Learning how to manage your digital identity is part of becoming digitally literate: managing what you share, and how you share it, is of great importance in an increasingly networked world. This activity looks at possible pitfalls with digital footprints and how to avoid them. The notion of digital footprints is also examined in Activity 33, *Faking it*, and related digital identity issues are covered in Activity 34, *Online me*.

Literacy:	**Personal literacy** and **Network literacy** (complexity: ***)
Topic:	Digital identity
Aim:	To create a poster with advice on managing digital footprints
Level:	Upper intermediate +
Time:	90 minutes
Tech support:	Multimedia sharing:

- General: e-language.wikispaces.com/social-sharing#multimedia-sharing
- Glogster: www.youtube.com/watch?v=hvQX5LeQ-zg
- GlogsterEDU: www.youtube.com/watch?v=80NISdsoouE

Presentation software:

- Keynote: support.apple.com/manuals/#iwork
- PowerPoint: goo.gl/vfLwD
- Prezi: prezi.com/learn/getting-started/

Language	
Areas	*Vocabulary:* Internet scams; technology; online identity *Grammar:* Past simple tense; narrative tenses; should; second conditional
Functions	Giving advice and making suggestions; discussing
Skills	Speaking listening, reading, writing

Resources	
High-tech	*Equipment:* One internet-enabled teacher computer and data projector; internet-enabled student computers or mobile devices (one per pair) *Tools:* Glogster (or Glogster EDU) *or* presentation software (e.g. Keynote, PowerPoint or Prezi) *Documents:* Online worksheet (www.pearsoned.co.uk/hockly)
Low-tech	*Equipment:* Internet-enabled teacher computer and data projector *Documents:* Printed websites; printed worksheet (follows Activity) *Stationery:* Poster-sized paper, coloured pens and magazines (for images)
No-tech	*Documents:* Printed websites; printed worksheet (follows Activity) *Stationery:* Poster-sized paper, coloured pens and magazines (for images)

Digital risks

Some content on the theme of digital footprints may be unsuitable in your context. Be sure to view the suggested websites and supplementary materials before using them in class (see Box 1.9 for more on digital safety, privacy and reputation; Activity 33, *Faking it* for more on digital footprints).

Procedure

Before class

- Print out the characters' webpages from the My Footprint SD website, for use in Step 4 (no-tech version).

1. Ask students to call out a few words and concepts that occur to them when they think of you. What do they really know about you? Display the words and concepts they come up with on the projector screen (high-tech and low-tech versions) or write them on the board (no-tech version).

2. Give students a short presentation about your *digital footprint*, i.e. your online presence as it can be seen by others (see Box 1.9; Activity 33, *Faking it*). Show the networks you are part of and any platforms where

you have a public account or presence (e.g. a blog, Flickr, YouTube). Give your students a quick tour of all this and then ask them to think about the following:

- Have they learnt anything new about you?
- Have they learnt anything surprising about you?
- Would they change their original words now?
- What do they think of your digital footprint?

Conduct feedback as a whole group.

3. Put students into pairs and ask them to look at **Activity 37 Worksheet – My digital footprint**. Give them some time to discuss the questions with their partner, and then invite comments and questions around the discussion points. What sorts of digital footprints do your students have? Do they ever think about what they do online, and how they look to other people?

4. Tell students they are going to read about the digital footprints of some students in America. Divide them into four groups and give each group one of the characters (Beau, Mallory, Anthony, Destiny) on the My Footprint SD website (myfootprintsd.com/index.html). They need to visit the page of their character (high-tech version) or look through the print-outs (low-tech and no-tech versions), and read their character's story (note that the first page for each character has links to two or three other pages they have written – these links, at the bottom of each main page, have the important content). Students need to find out:

- what their character thinks about their own digital footprint;
- what mistakes their character made with managing their digital footprint;
- how their character corrected the mistakes they made;
- what they have learnt from their character.

5. The texts are quite dense in places, and have a lot of slang – give your students enough time to read through them and make some notes. Themes they should discover are:

- phishing problems with a credit card (Beau)
- copyright of online materials (Beau)
- cheating online (Beau)
- inappropriate content (Mallory)

- technology addiction (Mallory)
- identity theft (Mallory)
- sexting (Mallory)
- online bullying (Anthony)
- excessive online gaming (Anthony)
- illegal downloads, viruses (Anthony)
- cyberstalking, picture privacy (Destiny)
- excessive communications, attention issues (Destiny)
- imaginary online identities (Destiny)

6. Create new groups containing one member from each of the original groups and get students to share what they have learnt. They should also find out if anyone in their new group has had any similar experiences to those of the characters they've researched. If so, what did they do?

7. Each group should now make a poster about managing your digital foot-print online. These posters should include anything they learnt from the website, as well as their own experiences and advice. Students may use an online poster service such as Glogster (www.glogster.com) or Glogster EDU (edu.glogster.com) (see Activity 34, *Online me*) or presentation soft-ware such as Keynote, PowerPoint or Prezi (high-tech version). Alternatively they could make a wall poster using paper, coloured pens and images cut out of magazines (low-tech and no-tech versions).

Extension 1

The main My Footprint SD website also has resources for lower levels (myfootprintsd.com/elementary.html) and suggestions for teachers (myfootprintsd.com/teacher.html), where you will find other approaches to using the materials in class.

Extension 2

For more ideas on exploring digital identities with students, see Odin Lab's *This is Me – Digital Identity for Careers* (freely downloadable from www.lulu.com/odinlab).

Extension 3

Encourage students to add hyperlinks from their e-portfolios to their group glogs (Glogster posters) (see Chapter 3: *Assessing digital work, Assessing through e-portfolios*) (high-tech version).

Activity 37 Worksheet – My digital footprint

Discuss these questions with your partner:

- What social networking sites do you use?
- What do you share on your social networking sites?
  - photos?
  - videos?
  - personal information?
  - contact information?
  - likes, interests, hobbies?
  - . . .
  - . . .
- Do you have any other online accounts?
  - Flickr?
  - YouTube?
  - . . .
  - . . .
- How much time do you spend on these sites every day?
- Do you know how to protect your identity online (safety)?
- Do you know how to manage your identity online (privacy)?
- Do you know how to project a positive image online (reputation)?
- Have you had any negative experiences with social networking sites?

Activity 38: Going viral

Students watch a TED talk about viral videos and contribute a description of their own favourite viral videos to a public TED forum.

This activity introduces students to the topic of viral videos through a TED Talk. TED Talk videos are an excellent self-study resource for students, and many have subtitles available in English (as well as other languages). Students discuss the topic of viral videos, and contribute descriptions of their own favourite viral videos to a public TED 'conversation' (forum). As an optional extension activity, students can be encouraged to produce their own short videos – which may potentially go viral!

Literacy:	**Network literacy** and **Multimedia literacy** (complexity: ***)
Topic:	Viral videos
Aim:	To encourage students to explore the phenomenon of viral videos, and to contribute their views to a public forum
Level:	Intermediate +
Time:	60 minutes
Tech support:	Vodcasting/Video editing:

- General: e-language.wikispaces.com/vodcasting
- iMovie: www.apple.com/findouthow/movies/
- Movie Maker: goo.gl/S602r

Vodcasting/Videosharing:

- Vimeo: vimeo.com/help
- YouTube: support.google.com/youtube/?hl=en

Word-processing software:

- Apple Pages: support.apple.com/manuals/#iwork
- Microsoft Word: goo.gl/KXnLe

Language	
Areas	*Vocabulary:* Videos and filming *Grammar:* Present simple tense; verbs of liking and disliking
Functions	Expressing likes and dislikes; giving opinions
Skills	Listening, speaking, writing, reading

Resources	
High-tech	*Equipment:* One internet-enabled teacher computer and data projector; internet-enabled student computers or mobile devices (one per pair) *Equipment (optional):* Digital cameras, or mobile phones with cameras (one per pair or group) *Tools:* Word-processing software (e.g. Apple Pages or Microsoft Word) *Tools (optional):* Video-editing software (e.g. iMovie or Movie Maker); videosharing site (e.g. Vimeo or YouTube); TED app; TEDiSUB app *Documents:* Online worksheet (www.pearsoned.co.uk/hockly)
Low-tech	*Equipment:* One internet-enabled teacher computer and data projector *Tools:* Word-processing software (e.g. Apple Pages or Microsoft Word) *Tools (optional):* Video-editing software (e.g. iMovie or Movie Maker); videosharing site (e.g. Vimeo or YouTube); TED app; TEDiSUB app *Documents:* Printed worksheet (follows Activity)
No-tech	Not available for this activity

Digital risks

Some viral videos, especially those freely selected by students, may contain content which is inappropriate for some educational and cultural contexts or, if viewed online, may be surrounded by inappropriate advertising material. If in doubt, you should preview videos before showing them in Step 6. Similarly, you may wish to offer students guidelines on appropriate videos to choose in Step 8.

Procedure

Before class

- Register an account or accounts to be able to create or contribute to 'conversations' (forums) on the *TED* website (www.ted.com), for use in Step 9. For more information, see the 'About TED' page (www.ted.com/pages/about). Note that if students are going to work in pairs (high-tech version), each pair needs a TED account. If students are going to work as a whole class (low-tech version), the teacher's TED account can be used.

- View Kevin Allocca's talk, *Why Videos Go Viral* (goo.gl/u2U2J). Create a new conversation entitled 'What's your favourite viral video?' or 'The best viral videos' if there is not already an existing conversation open on this topic; this will be used in Step 9.

1. Put the phrase 'viral videos' on the board and ask students what these are (*they are videos that suddenly become popular and attract a very large number of viewers very quickly; they are often posted on YouTube, with embedded versions or links being shared on Facebook and Twitter or by email*). Ask students:

   - Have you ever watched any viral videos?
   - If so, which ones?

   Put a list of any viral videos that students mention on the side of the board, to revisit in Step 6.

2. Tell students they are going to watch a short TED Talk about viral videos, given by Kevin Allocca, YouTube's 'Trends Manager'. Tell students the title of the talk is *Why Videos Go Viral*, and write it on the board. Give students one or two minutes to brainstorm in pairs why they think videos go viral. Elicit their ideas and list them on the board.

3. Refer students to **Activity 38 Worksheet – Viral videos**. Explain that Kevin Allocca mentions three reasons why videos go viral. They will watch the video and note down the three reasons. Reassure them that although he mentions the reasons very quickly in the first few minutes, he revisits them one by one during his talk. He also shows clips from four viral videos during his talk, and students should note the names of these videos as well. Answers are given in Appendix: Answer keys.

4. Show students the video *Why Videos Go Viral* on the projector screen. Depending on the level of your students, you may decide to show the

video with subtitles in English. You can activate subtitles in the dropdown menu beneath the video frame.

5. Encourage students to check their worksheet answers in pairs, and then check with the whole class. Ask students:

   • Did you already know any of the viral videos? Which one(s)?
   • Which viral video from the talk did you like the most? Why?

6. Ask students to vote on one or two videos to watch from the list of viral videos elicited in Step 1 above. Show these videos on the projector screen. (Depending on the students and the context, it may be wise to check the content of the videos before showing them in class; see Digital risks.) Ask students to think about what made each of the videos viral. Conduct feedback.

7. On the projector screen, show students the 'TED Conversations' underneath the Kevin Allocca video window. These are public forums in which viewers who have set up an account (as described above under Before class) can leave comments about specific talks.

8. Tell students that they are going to participate in a conversation about the best viral videos. Ensure that you have set up a new forum conversation if necessary (see Before class). Ask your students to work in pairs to write approximately 100–150 words in a word-processed document (high-tech version), describing their chosen video and ensuring that they have included the title and a link. (Depending on the class, it may be appropriate to offer students guidelines on choosing a suitable video; see 'Digital risks' above.) Alternatively, vote on the class's most popular viral video from Step 1 above, and prepare one text as a class in a word-processed document using the teacher computer and projector screen (low-tech version). Provide feedback on drafts as necessary, so that students have a well-edited and polished version of their text(s) ready to add to the TED conversation.

9. Add the posting(s) to the TED conversation. Encourage your students to visit the forum every few days to see whether others have replied or contributed. Keep an eye on it yourself, and show any new contributions to the forum at the start of subsequent classes.

Extension 1

If your students have access to digital cameras, or mobile phones with cameras, encourage them to work in pairs or small groups to plan, film and edit short sketches (using video-editing software like iMovie or Movie Maker) that they think might go viral. Note that students may need some pointers on digital safety, privacy and reputation (see Box 1.9) before doing so. Depending on their age, you may wish to suggest that they do not reveal their identities or show their faces and locations. Ask students to upload these short films to a video hosting service such as YouTube (www.youtube.com) or Vimeo (vimeo.com), and monitor how many views they get in the coming weeks.

Extension 2

Encourage students to add hyperlinks from their e-portfolios to any videos they create (see Chapter 3: *Assessing digital work, Assessing through e-portfolios*) (high-tech version).

Extension 3

There are TED apps available for Android, Apple iOS and Windows devices, including TEDiSUB for subtitled videos (available for Android and Apple iOS devices). Encourage students with mobile phones or tablets to download the appropriate app and watch TED talks for listening practice; they could watch them with or without subtitles the first time, depending on their level.

Activity 38 Worksheet – Viral videos

You are going to watch a short TED Talk about viral videos, given by Kevin Allocca, YouTube's 'Trends Manager'. Its title is *Why Videos Go Viral*. While watching, answer the questions below.

1. What three reasons does Kevin Allocca give for why videos go viral?

   (a) _____

   (b) _____

   (c) _____

2. What are the titles of the four viral videos Kevin Allocca shows during his talk?

   (a) _____

   (b) _____

   (c) _____

   (d) _____

Activity 39: A class PLN

Students learn about the value of a PLN (personal learning network) as a class sharing and learning tool.

This activity reinforces the value of students maintaining connections with classmates outside the classroom and learning through these connections. It follows on well from Activity 30, *Connecting people*, and encourages a deeper exploration of the ideas first broached there. The activity runs over two classes – a preparatory class (Class 1), and a class in which students reflect on their experience of a PLN (Class 2).

Literacy:	**Network literacy** and **Filtering literacy** (complexity: ***)
Topic:	PLNs
Aim:	To help students understand the value of learning through others in networks outside the classroom
Level:	Intermediate +
Time:	40 minutes (Class 1) + 20 minutes (Class 2) + homework
Tech support:	Social networking:

- General: e-language.wikispaces.com/social-networking
- Edmodo: help.edmodo.com

Language	
Areas	*Vocabulary:* Any, or an area specifically chosen for recycling by the teacher *Grammar:* Any, or an area specifically chosen for recycling by the teacher; question forms
Functions	Expressing likes and dislikes; giving opinions
Skills	Speaking, reading, writing

Resources	
High-tech	*Equipment:* One internet-enabled teacher computer and data projector; internet-enabled student computers or mobile devices (one per student) *Tools:* Edmodo
Low-tech	Not available for this activity
No-tech	Not available for this activity

Procedure

Before class

- Choose a topic you find interesting, research it briefly on the web, and prepare a 140-character summary of the topic, for use in Step 1.

- Create a list of suitable topics for students to research online, for use in Step 2.

- Create a class Edmodo account (www.edmodo.com), for use in Step 3. Ensure that you make a copy of the 'Request to join URL' so you can give it to your students along with the group code.

Class 1: Building a network

1. Show the name of your chosen topic on the projector screen and ask students what they know about it. Conduct feedback as a whole class. Then, show students your 140-character summary and ask them to brainstorm a set of questions they would like to ask you to find out more about the topic. Once they have a set of questions, answer them as a whole group.

2. Now give each student a topic to research individually online (see Activity 25, *Search race* for more on effective searching). Once students have done their research, they should prepare a 140-character summary of their topic.

3. Introduce students to the class Edmodo account and ensure that everyone joins the group. Then post an alert to the group with the 140-character summary of your topic. Get students to do the same. Each alert will show up as a general message to the whole group.

4. Ask students to choose two or three topic alerts that they are interested in. Ask them to think of some follow-up questions to ask the person who

posted the relevant alert. Show them how to send a message to one person, then give them time to message the people whose topics they are interested in.

5. Ask students to make a note of the questions they have been asked. For homework they should answer all the questions they have been asked, conducting online research if necessary. When they have done so, they should look at the answers they have received to their own questions, and post follow-up questions if needed. If not all students have internet access at home or from mobile devices, this step can be done at the start of Class 2.

Class 2: Reflecting on the network

1. In the second class, conduct feedback and get students' reactions to the experience of having these 'learning conversations' on Edmodo. Did they enjoy the process? Did they learn a lot about the topics that interested them? Did other conversations happening in the Edmodo group distract them? How did they deal with those distractions?

2. Ask students to work in groups and reflect on the role of PLNs, considering some or all of the following questions:

    -   What are three advantages of building a personal learning network (made up of classmates) that you can access outside the classroom?
    -   Are there any disadvantages?
    -   How might you use Edmodo to communicate with and learn from classmates in the future?
    -   Are there any other platforms (e.g. Facebook, Twitter) you would use to communicate with and learn from classmates?
    -   What are the advantages and disadvantages of these other platforms compared to Edmodo?
    -   Do you think you will maintain your personal learning network of classmates once you finish this class? Could it be helpful for your future studies or career?
    -   Who else, apart from classmates, could you include in your personal learning network?

Extension

For more ideas on using Edmodo in class, see the official Edmodo blog (blog.edmodo.com).

Activity 40: Our city guide

Students create a guide to their city on a class wiki.

Collaboratively creating online content is an important part of participatory literacy. This activity introduces students to online collaborative work in the form of a class wiki. Ideally this activity should be followed up at a later date with Activity 41, *Our city on Wikipedia*, in which students contribute to a *public* wiki.

Literacy:	**Participatory literacy** and **Print literacy** (complexity: ***)
Topic:	Travel and tourism
Aim:	To encourage students to contribute to a class wiki
Level:	Elementary +
Time:	60 minutes
Tech support:	Wikis:

- General: e-language.wikispaces.com/wikis
- PBworks: usermanual.pbworks.com
- Wikispaces: help.wikispaces.com

Word-processing software:

- Apple Pages: support.apple.com/manuals/#iwork
- Microsoft Word: goo.gl/KXnLe

Language	
Areas	*Vocabulary:* Travel, tourism and cities *Grammar:* Present simple tense; past simple tense (for historical facts)
Functions	Describing city sights, history, food, etc.
Skills	Writing, reading

Resources	
High-tech	*Equipment:* Internet-enabled student computers or mobile devices (one per pair) *Tools:* Class wiki (e.g. PBworks or Wikispaces); word-processing software (e.g. Apple Pages or Microsoft Word) *Documents:* topic cards (see below)
Low-tech	*Documents:* topic cards (see below) *Documents (optional):* Printed Simple English Wikipedia (SEW) Basic English alphabetical wordlist
No-tech	*Documents:* topic cards (see below) *Documents (optional):* Printed Simple English Wikipedia (SEW) Basic English alphabetical wordlist

Digital risks

It is important to consider privacy settings with web 2.0 services like wikis (see Activity 7, *Sports linking* for further information).

Procedure

Before class

- Prepare the topic cards, including a few blank cards, for use in Step 2.

- *(Optional)* Print copies of the Simple English Wikipedia (SEW) Basic English alphabetical wordlist (goo.gl/huimq) for each pair of students, for use in Step 2 (low-tech and no-tech versions).

- Set up a class wiki, with individual pages for pairs of students, for use in Step 3 (high-tech version).

1. Introduce the topic of cities and city guides. When your students travel to a new city (for example, on holiday, or for business) do they buy a guide-book? What sort of information is typically included in a city guidebook? Give students a minute or two to brainstorm this in pairs, and then collate their ideas in a list on the board. Students may suggest some of the following:

- history of the city
- famous monuments
- museums
- art and architecture
- festivals
- transport
- where to eat
- where to stay
- useful language phrases

2. Tell students that as a class they are going to produce a guide for their city or town. (If you teach mixed nationality classes, students can work in pairs or individually to produce a *world* guide, with each student or pair responsible for adding information about their own city or town.) Write the topics from Step 1 above on separate cards, and allocate one card to each pair of students. Have a few blank cards ready, in case students come up with other topics or something particularly suited to their city or town – you can then add those topics on the spot!

   Ask students to work in pairs to write a short text about their topic in a word-processed document (high-tech version) or on paper (low-tech and no-tech versions). These texts, which will form part of a class guide, are a good chance for students to practise traditional print literacy skills. In particular, it is a good chance to take a process writing approach in Steps 3–5 below (see Chapter 3: *Choosing activities for different levels and contexts, Students' linguistic competence*).

   Give students an approximate word limit for their texts (around 100–150 words for lower levels, and around 400–500 words for higher levels). For lower levels, refer students to the 850-word SEW Basic English alphabetical wordlist online (high-tech version) or printed out (low-tech and no-tech versions). Encourage students to use these words if they want to. Monitor and help the students with language as they prepare their texts.

3. If students have created word-processed documents, ask them to copy and paste the first drafts of their texts into their dedicated wiki pages on the class wiki which you prepared earlier (as described above under 'Before class'; high-tech version). The front page of your guide wiki can look something like the one below, with a title and introduction to the guide, an image, and individually linked pages for each pair/topic. Instead of Student A, Student B, etc., use the real names of your pairs of students.

Encourage students to search for Creative Commons images to include with their texts on the wiki (see Activity 10, *Copycat*). Then ask each pair to visit the next pair's wiki page (e.g. Students A+B visit Students C+D's page; Students C+D visit Students E+F's page, etc.) (high-tech version). Students should edit and correct any language mistakes they see, and improve the texts if they can. Ensure that you continue to monitor and help with language at this stage.

If students have created their texts on paper, they can exchange papers to edit and correct each other's work (low-tech and no-tech versions).

4. After this first round of peer correction, students should look again at their own original texts, focusing particularly on any corrections that have been made. To do this, students can click on the 'History' tab for their individual wiki pages, and then compare their original drafts with the corrected versions, which will clearly show up any changes (high-tech version). Otherwise, students can examine the marked up paper copies of their work and create new, improved drafts (low-tech and no-tech versions). Continue to monitor, and help students to spot any erroneous 'corrections' made by classmates. Students can ask you to confirm any corrections they are unsure about. Encourage students to make any further changes they wish to their texts.

5. Once students are happy with the final drafts of their texts, ask them to visit all the other wiki pages in the guide. For each page they visit, they should leave a comment under the 'Discussion' tab. Their comments can consist of additional information or travel tips for the location. In the case of a world guide created by a multinational class, classmates could leave questions they would like to have answered (high-tech version). Texts created on paper can be put up on the classroom walls, with a blank piece of paper added below each for written comments (low-tech and no-tech versions). Students can walk around the class reading the texts and adding comments on the paper.

Finally, let the students return to their original texts and read the comments and/or questions that their classmates have left for them. Students should further modify their texts to incorporate some of their classmates' suggestions and ideas, or to respond to their questions.

6. To round off the activity, discuss with students the concept of multiple authorship. For example, do they think that having several people working together on a text can improve it, both in terms of language and content? Is there a limit to the number of people that can help improve a text?

Extension 1

Discuss with students what sort of privacy settings they would like to apply to the class wiki (see Digital risks in Activity 7, *Sports linking*) (high-tech version). Depending on their decision, the wiki could be shared with other teachers and classes in the school, for example, and these readers could also post comments or questions on the guide entries. Your students could then make further additions or modifications to their texts. With younger learners, parents could be given the URL of the class wiki and encouraged to visit and comment (in the L1). The wiki could also be shared with a wider audience, for example by adding a link to it on the school website, or by listing it as a public wiki. Whatever level of access is decided on, we recommend that comment moderation stays *on* to avoid spam, and that you as the teacher are responsible for moderating all comments received.

Extension 2

Encourage students to add hyperlinks from their e-portfolios to their class wiki texts (see Chapter 3: *Assessing digital work*, *Assessing through e-portfolios*) (high-tech version).

Activity 41: Our city on Wikipedia

Students create an entry for Simple English Wikipedia.

Students are able to explore further participatory literacy in this collaborative activity. Ideally this activity should follow Activity 40, *Our city guide*, in which students contribute to a class wiki, which may be made private or public. In this activity students contribute to a *public* wiki.

Literacy: **Participatory literacy** and **Print literacy** (complexity: ***)

Topic: Travel and tourism

Aim: To show students how to contribute to a public wiki

Level: Elementary +

Time: 60 minutes

Tech support: Wikis:

- General: e-language.wikispaces.com/wikis

- Simple English Wikipedia: simple.wikipedia.org/wiki/ Help:Contents

Word-processing software:

- Apple Pages: support.apple.com/manuals/#iwork

- Microsoft Word: goo.gl/KXnLe

Language	
Areas	*Vocabulary:* Travel, tourism and cities *Grammar:* Present simple tense; past simple tense (for historical facts)
Functions	Stating facts
Skills	Writing, reading

Resources	
High-tech	*Equipment:* One internet-enabled teacher computer and data projector; internet-enabled student computers or mobile devices (one per pair) *Tools:* Simple English Wikipedia; word-processing software (e.g. Apple Pages or Microsoft Word)
Low-tech	*Equipment:* One internet-enabled teacher computer and data projector *Documents:* Printed Simple English Wikipedia pages, including contributor guidelines and the Basic English alphabetical wordlist (see below)
No-tech	*Documents:* Printed Simple English Wikipedia pages, including contributor guidelines and the Basic English alphabetical wordlist (see below)

Digital risks
Students may find it challenging to have their work publicly viewed – and perhaps publicly critiqued or altered on a wiki. Teachers can prepare students for this possibility by reminding them of the advantages of collaborative authorship (see Activity 40, *Our city guide*) as well as discussing its challenges.

Procedure

Before class

- Find the Simple English Wikipedia (SEW) (simple.wikipedia.org) article about the country you are teaching in, and note down the URL (high-tech version) or bookmark it (low-tech version), or alternatively print out one copy per student (no-tech version); this will be used in Step 2.

- Print out the SEW contributor guidelines (goo.gl/EEcvT) and the SEW Basic English alphabetical wordlist online (goo.gl/huimq), for use in Step 3 (low-tech and no-tech versions).

- Create a SEW account for yourself, for use in Step 6.

1. Tell your students about Simple English Wikipedia (SEW) (see Box 1.6). They are going to read the SEW article describing the country in which the

class is taking place. What sort of information do they expect to see in the SEW article? Put their suggestions on the board (e.g. capital city, population, geography, history and monuments, etc.). Ask students how the information in a Wikipedia article will be different from information contained in a tourist guidebook about the country. (Refer to Activity 40, *Our city guide*, if you have previously done that activity with the class.) Point out that Wikipedia information should be strictly factual, with no recommendations or opinions.

2. Give the students the URL of the SEW article about the country to visit in pairs on a computer (high-tech version), or show the article to the class online (low-tech version), or give students a printed copy (no-tech version). Give students a few minutes to read the article, and then ask:

   - Were their predictions about the topics in the article correct?
   - Is all the information strictly factual?
   - How are hyperlinks in the article used? What do they link to? How many hyperlinks are there – too few, enough, too many? (For these questions refer back to Activity 7, *Sports linking*, if you have previously done that activity with the class.)

   Help students with any difficult or unknown vocabulary in the article, ensuring that everyone understands it fully. Then ask students:

   - What do they think of the content?
   - Is it all accurate?
   - Is there information about the country that could be added (and if so, what)?
   - Who wrote this article?

   Point out that anyone can contribute to a Wikipedia article, but that there are certain *guidelines* to follow. Tell students that they are going to create an article for SEW about their city or town (either the city or town where you are teaching the class, or the students' home city or town if they all come from the same place). If the article already exists, then they need to create a paragraph with new information for the already existing article.

3. Put students into pairs, and ask each pair to prepare an article (or extra paragraph) about their city or town for SEW. Students should write their texts in a word-processed document (high-tech version), or on paper (low-tech and no-tech versions). This is another chance for students to practise traditional print literacy skills, and to take a process writing approach in Steps 4–6 below (see Chapter 3: *Choosing activities for different levels and contexts, Students' linguistic competence*).

Refer students to the SEW contributor guidelines and the Basic English alphabetical wordlist online (as described under Before class; high-tech version) or printed out on paper (low-tech and no-tech versions). Students should try to include some of the words in the latter document, where relevant. Monitor and provide help with language.

4. When the students have the first drafts of their texts ready, they can copy and paste them into new pages on a class wiki (high-tech version). This could be the class wiki you created for Activity 40, *Our city guide*, if you did this activity with your students; they can then follow the same wiki peer review process outlined in that activity (Steps 3–5). If you don't have a class wiki, pairs can change places at the computers and read another pair's word-processed text on screen. Students should edit or correct any language mistakes they see, and improve each other's texts if they can. Tell students to track changes for their edits – this mimics the 'History' function on a wiki and enables the reader to see exactly what changes have been made. Ensure that you continue to monitor and help with language at this stage.

   If students are writing their texts on paper, they can exchange papers to edit and mark up each other's work (low-tech and no-tech versions).

5. After this first round of peer correction, students should look again at their own original texts, and focus particularly on any corrections that have been made. Encourage students to review carefully the changes, and make any further changes they wish to their texts. Continue to monitor and help them with language. Correct any erroneous 'corrections' you see. Students can ask you to confirm any corrections they are unsure about.

6. You now have several articles or paragraphs, each one created by a pair of students, about their city/town. As a class, they can vote on the best text, which will be contributed to SEW. Allow students to read all of the texts by displaying them one by one on the projector screen (high-tech and low-tech versions), or by putting paper versions on the classroom walls and letting students walk around to look at them (no-tech version). Conduct the vote. Then look again as a group at the chosen text – either on the projector screen (high-tech and low-tech versions) or photocopied on paper (no-tech version) – and see whether any final edits and improvements can be made. Help and suggest language improvements.

   Once the final version is ready, contribute it yourself to SEW, either by doing this live in class and showing the process on the projector screen (high-tech and low-tech versions) or by doing it later at home (no-tech version). Ensure that you already have a SEW account (as described above under 'Before class'). The text will not instantly appear in SEW, but you will be able to track its progress, including any corrections or discussions about it, from your account. Once it is published, you can show it to students in a subsequent class on the projector screen (high-tech and low-tech versions) or printed out (no-tech version)

7. To round off the activity, discuss with students how they feel about contributing in English to a public wiki, and the fact that a global audience now has access to their work.

Extension 1

You could return to the article a few weeks or months later to see whether there have been any additions or changes made by other Wikipedia users, and then ask the class how they feel about their work being modified. Do they want to make any further changes?

Extension 2

If students are confident enough, you could set up a project in which pairs of students choose a topic of interest to research, create an article, and then contribute the article themselves to SEW (they first need to create a SEW account) (high-tech version).

Extension 3

Encourage students to add links to any SEW articles they have created from their e-portfolios (see Chapter 3: *Assessing digital work, Assessing through e-portfolios*).

Activity 42: Flickr vocabulary book

Students create a growing vocabulary resource on Flickr.

Creating and sharing content online are among the most useful skills we can help students develop. In this activity students collaborate over a period of time to produce a class vocabulary book on the photosharing site Flickr.

Literacy:	**Participatory literacy** and **Multimedia literacy** (complexity: ***)
Topic:	General
Aim:	To produce an online vocabulary resource
Level:	Elementary +
Time:	90 minutes + (+ homework)
Tech support:	Photosharing:

- General: e-language.wikispaces.com/social-sharing#Photosharing
- ELT Pics: http://eltpics.com/indexeltpics.html
- Flickr: www.flickr.com/tour/#section=welcome

Language	
Areas	*Vocabulary:* Any, or an area specifically chosen for recycling by the teacher *Grammar:* Any, or an area specifically chosen for recycling by the teacher
Skills	Writing

Resources	
High-tech	*Equipment:* One internet-enabled teacher computer and data projector; internet-enabled student computers or mobile devices (one per pair); student mobile phones with cameras, or digital cameras (one per pair) *Tools:* Flickr
Low-tech	*Equipment:* One internet-enabled teacher computer and data projector; at least one mobile phone with camera, or digital camera *Tools:* Flickr
No-tech	Not available for this activity

Digital risks

As with all media sharing sites, ensure that your students are only uploading photos they have personally taken and own the copyright for.

Procedure

Before class

- Find a suitable activity for your students on the ELTPics Blog (takeaphotoand.wordpress.com), for use in Step 1.

- Set up a Flickr account and, within the account, set up a group to add your students to, for use in Step 2.

- Upload a couple of sample photographs with descriptions and tags to your Flickr account, as described in Step 3.

1. Ask your students to do the ELTPics Blog activity you have chosen (as described above), either in pairs online (high-tech version) or as a whole class using the projector screen (low-tech version). This is a good way of demonstrating to your students both the value of images and the value of a resource like Flickr. Ensure that your students get the opportunity to explore the ELTPics Flickr sets (www.flickr.com/photos/eltpics/sets/), either in pairs (high-tech version) or as a whole class (low-tech version). Explain what Flickr is for, pointing out these key features:

   - *Purpose:* to share photos online.
   - *Accounts:* free to set up.

- *Sets:* photos can be grouped into collections around a theme.
- *Tags:* photos can be described using keywords or 'tags' (see Activity 24, *Travel tags*).
- *Map:* photos can be located on a world map (if data is available).

Tell your students that they are going to prepare a similar resource for their own studies as a revision tool for vocabulary and grammar. However, because it is publicly viewable, it can also be seen and used by other students and their teachers, so they are in fact creating a public resource. Help them understand the value of this kind of participatory literacy (see Chapter 1: Third focus: Connections, *Participatory literacy*).

2. Show students your Flickr account and group on the projector screen, and send out invitations to each of your students; this kind of administration work is best done at least once in class so that you can be sure everyone has followed along. Ensure that everyone can check their email and accept the invitation (high-tech version) or allow students to do this one by one on the teacher computer (low-tech version); alternatively, set this activity for homework if students have the equipment at home. Once students have accepted the invitation, you can make them 'Moderators' so they can upload pictures.

3. Brainstorm recent lexical and grammatical areas you have covered in class:

- For an example of a lexical area (*beverages*), see: www.flickr.com/photos/eltpics/sets/72157625503458235/
- For an example of a grammar area (*-ing*), see: www.flickr.com/photos/eltpics/sets/72157627035061929/

Once you have enough lexical and grammatical sets listed, assign one to each pair of students (high-tech version) or choose one for the whole class (low-tech version). The idea is to begin the set with a minimum of four images. Give students an example from the class Flickr set you have already created – a picture within one of the lexical sets with the following information added:

- title
- definition
- sample sentence or text using the word
- translation (if appropriate)
- tags

4. Students should work in pairs and use their mobile phones with cameras, or digital cameras, to take pictures. They should then upload them and add sample texts as per your example(s), either during class or for home-work (high-tech version). Alternatively, if you only have one mobile phone with a camera, or one digital camera, you could do this as a whole class activity using the chosen lexical or grammatical set (low-tech version).

5. In the next class, give each pair the opportunity to show the work they have done and allow others to ask questions (high-tech version). Otherwise, review the class set created in the previous lesson (low-tech version). Tell students that this is an ongoing resource that they should add to each week, either in pairs (high-tech version) or as a whole class (low-tech version).

Extension 1

Revisit the Flickr album on a regular basis and use the images that have been uploaded for revision or extension activities. This will ensure that your students appreciate the value of the resource and are encouraged to continue developing it. You could also suggest that they develop quizzes and activities based around the images for their own study, or for their classmates to practise on.

Extension 2

Encourage students to add hyperlinks from their e-portfolios to their Flickr set(s), or to embed the Flickr photos within their e-portfolios (see Chapter 3: *Assessing digital work, Assessing through e-portfolios*) (high-tech version).

Activity 43: A good cause

Students explore the world of online campaigning and think about 'slacktivism'.

This activity introduces students to the idea of campaigning for issues online, and the concept of 'slacktivism'. Having explored various online campaigns, they will produce a campaign which is relevant to their lives. It may be best to run this activity over two classes in the no-tech version.

Literacy:	**Participatory literacy** and **Multimedia literacy** (complexity: ***)
Topic:	Global and local issues
Aim:	To encourage students to explore the world of online campaigning and transpose it to their own context
Level:	Upper intermediate +
Time:	60 minutes
Tech support:	Digital storytelling:

Digital storytelling:

- General: e-language.wikispaces.com/digital-storytelling
- Capzles: www.youtube.com/watch?v=hR_21MeVeqQ
- Tiki-Toki: http://www.tiki-toki.com/faqs/

Multimedia sharing:

- General: e-language.wikispaces.com/social-sharing#multimedia-sharing
- Glogster: www.youtube.com/watch?v=hvQX5LeQ-zg
- VoiceThread: voicethread.com/?#c28

Podcasting/Audio editing:

- General: e-language.wikispaces.com/podcasting
- Audacity: audacity.sourceforge.net/manual-1.2/tutorials.html
- GarageBand: www.apple.com/support/garageband/

Vodcasting/Video editing:

- General: e-language.wikispaces.com/vodcasting
- iMovie: www.apple.com/findouthow/movies/
- Movie Maker: goo.gl/S6O2r

Language	
Areas	*Vocabulary:* Global and local issues; current affairs *Grammar:* Present simple tense; comparative and superlative adjectives (for ranking)
Functions	Discussing current affairs and issues; expressing opinions
Skills	Speaking, listening, reading, writing

Resources	
High-tech	*Equipment:* One internet-enabled teacher computer and data projector; internet-enabled student computers or mobile devices (one per group) *Tools:* Digital storytelling software (e.g. Capzles or Tiki-Toki) *or* multimedia sharing software (e.g. Glogster or VoiceThread) *or* audio-editing software (e.g. Audacity or GarageBand) *or* video-editing software (e.g. iMovie or Movie Maker)
Low-tech	*Equipment:* One internet-enabled teacher computer and data projector *Tools:* Digital storytelling software (e.g. Capzles or Tiki-Toki) *or* multimedia sharing software (e.g. Glogster or VoiceThread) *or* audio-editing software (e.g. Audacity or GarageBand) *or* video-editing software (e.g. iMovie or Movie Maker)
No-tech	*Documents:* Printed Avaaz images and pages (see below) *Stationery:* Poster-sized paper, coloured pens and magazines (for images)

Digital risks

Depending on your political, cultural and educational context, as well as your students' ages and interests, you should carefully consider which online campaigns to show students, and how much freedom to give them in choosing issues to address in their own work (see Chapter 1: *Third focus: Connections, Participatory literacy*). Certain local issues or very broad global issues – such as environmental concerns – may be appropriate.

Procedure

Before class

- Collect together images from selected current campaigns on the Avaaz site (www.avaaz.org/en), storing them in a folder on your computer (high-tech and low-tech versions) or printing them out (no-tech version), for use in Step 1.

- Print out a selection of key pages from the Avaaz site, for use in Step 3 (no-tech version).

- Print out the students' chosen 'Take action now' page, for use in Step 4 (no-tech version).

1. Show students a series of images depicting global issues which are currently being addressed on the Avaaz website, either on the projector screen (high-tech and low-tech versions) or printed out (no-tech version). Ask students to identify the main issue in each photograph, and to name at least one country that is affected by it. Help with ideas and vocabulary as needed.

2. Put students into small groups and get them to rank the issues in the images in order of importance. Once they have ranked them, pair up groups and ask them to explain their rankings to each other and negotiate a new joint ranking. Keep combining groups until you have come together as a whole class with a final ranked list.

3. Have students visit the Avaaz website in groups (high-tech version), show it to them as a class on the projector screen (low-tech version) or provide printouts of key pages (no-tech version). Give them a chance to look at the various campaigns.

4. Ask students to click the 'Take action now' link associated with the class's top-ranked issue (high-tech version), show it to them on the projector screen (low-tech version), or provide printouts (no-tech version; note that because the students' choice is not known in advance, it may be easiest for a teacher using the no-tech version to stop the class at this point, print out copies of the relevant page after class, and continue the activity in a subsequent class).

   Give students a chance to look at the content and answer the following questions:

   - What is the exact issue?
   - What is the proposed solution?
   - How can a visitor to the site 'take action'?

5. The answer to the third question is by sending an email. Tell students this kind of action is often called 'slacktivism' – a combination of 'slacker' and 'activism'. What do they think this means? Is it a good thing or a bad thing? Do they think this kind of action is useful? Have they ever been involved in any online campaigns? Note that a good definition of 'slacktivism' is available on Wikipedia (en.wikipedia.org/wiki/Slacktivism).

6. Tell students they are going to start a campaign related to an issue in their town/city/region (or alternatively they may wish to address a more global environmental issue). Brainstorm local issues and discuss which is the most important (see Step 2 above). The campaign may involve digital storytelling (e.g. using Capzles at www.capzles.com or Tiki-Toki at www.tiki-toki.com), multimedia sharing (e.g. using Glogster at www.glogster.com or VoiceThread at voicethread.com), podcasting (e.g. using Audacity or GarageBand), vodcasting (e.g. using iMovie or Movie Maker), or the creation of other kinds of digital artefacts. Students can work in groups (high-tech version) or as a whole class using the teacher computer and projector screen (low-tech version). Alternatively, they can work in groups to make paper-based posters (no-tech version).

    If your groups are happy working autonomously, try to encourage the creation of a variety of different media artefacts, one from each group (high-tech version). If you have access to tablet computers, students may wish to use the inbuilt video and audio-recording capabilities and create presentations optimised for mobile apps (for example, Capzles and VoiceThread have mobile apps available).

7. Campaign artefacts may be shared using the relevant web services and/or apps (high-tech and low-tech versions) or displayed on the walls of the class (no-tech version). Encourage people to visit, view and comment where appropriate.

Extension

Encourage students to add hyperlinks from their e-portfolios to any online media artefacts they have created (see Chapter 3: *Assessing digital work*, *Assessing through e-portfolios*) (high-tech version).

Activity 44: Vox pop

Students create short 'vox pop' vodcasts describing certain aspects of their culture.

When introducing the topic of stereotypes, it is helpful for students to start with an examination of their own culture and the stereotypes that are associated with it. This can make them more sensitive to other cultural stereotyping. This activity encourages students to examine stereotypes, and then to produce a short vodcast giving their views on their own culture from the perspective of cultural insiders.

Literacy:	**Intercultural literacy** and **Multimedia literacy** (overall complexity: ****)
Topic:	Culture
Aim:	To make a vodcast about culture
Level:	Elementary +
Time:	60 minutes
Tech support:	Vodcasting/Videosharing:

- General: e-language.wikispaces.com/vodcasting
- Vimeo: vimeo.com/help
- YouTube: support.google.com/youtube/?hl=en

Language	
Areas	*Vocabulary:* Food; weather; music; entertainment; physical appearances *Grammar:* Present simple tense
Functions	Making suggestions; discussing
Skills	Listening, speaking, writing

Resources	
High-tech	*Equipment:* Mobile phones with cameras, or digital cameras (one per group) *Tools:* Videosharing site (e.g. YouTube or Vimeo)
Low-tech	*Equipment:* One mobile phone with camera, or digital camera *Tools:* Videosharing site (e.g. YouTube or Vimeo)
No-tech	*Stationery:* Poster-sized paper, coloured pens and magazines (for images)

Digital risks

If students upload their vox pop vodcasts to a videosharing site such as YouTube or Vimeo, privacy settings will first need to be discussed. For young learners, you may want to make the videos completely private. Adults, once they have discussed and understood the risks, may choose to make their videos public, which will allow them to share them more easily with family and friends and to receive feedback. (For other, similar discussions of privacy settings, see Activity 4, *Extreme weather* on blogs, Activity 7, *Sports linking* on wikis and Activity 34, *Online me* on Glogster.)

Procedure

Note: If you are unable to access the YouTube video for Steps 1–4 below, start the class from Step 5 (no-tech version).

1. Write 'American culture' on the board and ask students to brainstorm words they associate with it. Add their words to the board.

2. Show the first two minutes (until 02:00) of *What is American Culture?* from YouTube (www.youtube.com/watch?v=pg87sSaTZSc). The video was made by three US college students studying in the Philippines. Ask your students to pay particular attention to whether any of their brainstormed words appear. Conduct feedback.

3. Put the grid below on the board. In small groups, students should discuss what they think Americans eat, what the weather is like in America, what sort of music Americans enjoy listening to, what Americans do for

fun, and what a typical American looks like. Pairs should note down key words for each of the categories.

Food	
Weather	
Music	
Fun/entertainment	
Looks/physical appearance	

4. Show more of the video (from 02:00 – 08:06 min) and let students see whether their predictions were correct. Conduct feedback. Ask students what they think the message of this video is.

5. Play students the last two minutes of the video (from 08:07 to the end), in which the message of the video is delivered. The American students who made this video want to show that people's ideas about 'American culture' may not always be accurate. In other words, this video looks at stereotypical perceptions, and how the reality can be different or at least more complex.

6. Put '[students' national] culture' on the board (e.g. 'Spanish culture'/ 'Brazilian culture') and ask students to work in small groups to brainstorm words they associate with their own culture. If you teach a multilingual class, choose one or two cultures from among the students present. It may be best to ask students to volunteer to have their cultures discussed in this way.

7. Ask students for feedback. Add the brainstormed words to the board, asking why students chose each word. This should generate some discussion about whether the chosen words really reflect the students' culture(s), or whether they are just stereotypical perceptions associated with the country or countries.

8. Point out that outsiders' and insiders' views of a culture often differ. Put the grid below on the board. Ask students to work in small groups to discuss stereotypical perceptions of their culture ('What people think of us') and to add key words to the first column of the grid. Ask them to also discuss the reality ('What we are really like') according to their own experiences as cultural insiders, and to add key words to the second column of the grid.

	What people think of us	What we are really like
Food		
Weather		
Music		
Fun/entertainment		
Looks/physical appearance		

Conduct feedback by asking groups of students to share their key words from each column, explaining their choices. If you teach a multi-lingual class, you will be able to get feedback about a variety of cultures from students. If you teach a monolingual class, you will get feedback about one culture, but there may be a range of opinions reflected in the key words chosen by different groups.

9. Put students into groups of three. Ensure that each group has access to a mobile phone or digital camera with video-recording capability (high-tech version); if there is only one mobile phone or digital camera with video-recording capability, give groups access to it in turn (low-tech version). Ask students to record short 'vox pop' opinions on each of the categories in Step 8 above. The aim is to produce a short vodcast, which gives an insiders' account of the students' culture, by explaining what food they eat, what the weather is like in the country, what music they typically listen to, what they do for fun/entertainment, and how people in their

country typically look (physical appearance). If possible, use the *What is American Culture?* YouTube video in Step 2 as a model. Ask students to film each other within their group, giving their opinions on these topics.

If you teach a multilingual class, group students so that all three members are from different cultures, and each student can talk about their own culture. If you teach a monolingual class, students can divide up the topics between them and each student can express their opinion on a different topic (food, weather, music, etc.). Students should first plan a storyboard of who is going to say what, and rehearse. Then the spoken clips can be recorded one after the other (by recording and stopping, repeatedly), without having to edit the videos.

Alternatively, get students to create vox pop posters including the categories in Step 8. They can use drawings and images from magazines to illustrate their posters (no-tech version).

10. Ask students to share their videos by passing around the mobile phone(s) or digital camera(s) between groups (high-tech and low-tech versions). Students' vodcasts can also be uploaded to a video-hosting site such as You Tube (www.youtube.com) or Vimeo (vimeo.com); they can do this in groups (high-tech version), or all the vodcasts can be uploaded on the teacher computer (low-tech version). These can then be shared with other classes, parents, or the general public, depending on the privacy settings chosen. Alternatively, ask students to share their posters by putting them up on the classroom or school walls (no-tech version).

Extension

Encourage students to upload their vodcasts to their e-portfolios, or to add hyperlinks from their e-portfolios to their vodcasts on YouTube or Vimeo (see Chapter 3: *Assessing digital work, Assessing through e-portfolios*) (high-tech version).

Activity 45: Global dancing

Students watch a video featuring a number of countries and think about travel to other cultures.

This activity encourages students to think about the world they live in, especially the advantages of travelling and learning about other cultures. This is a good activity to combine with Activity 44, *Vox pop*, and Activity 46, *Travel tips*.

Literacy: **Intercultural literacy** and **Multimedia literacy**
(overall complexity: ****)

Topic: Countries

Aim: To introduce the topic of countries, cultures and travel

Level: Beginner +

Time: 90 minutes +

Language	
Areas	*Vocabulary:* Countries, cultures, travel, languages and customs *Grammar:* Present simple tense; past simple tense
Functions	Giving opinions; discussing
Skills	Speaking

Resources	
High-tech	*Equipment:* One internet-enabled teacher computer and data projector
Low-tech	*Equipment:* One internet-enabled teacher computer and data projector
No-tech	Not available for this activity

Procedure

1. Put students into groups and give them 2 minutes to brainstorm as many names of countries as they can in English. When the 2 minutes are up, get them to count up how many they have, and announce a winner. How did they go about this task (*groups sometimes take half of the alphabet each, go in alphabetical order or do it by geographical area, e.g. Europe, the Americas, etc.*). What was the winning strategy in this case?

2. Depending on the level of your group (and the language you may want to review) there are a couple of follow-up activities you can do with these lists. For higher levels, students might choose a country they would like to visit and say why, what they would do there, etc. For lower levels, get each student to choose one of the countries on their list that they have visited and tell their group when they went, what they saw and did, etc. Conduct feedback as a group.

3. Tell students they are going to watch a video that features a wide variety of countries. Their task is to try to identify as many countries as possible. If they can, they should note down the name of each country, and how they recognised it (*e.g. France – the Eiffel Tower*).

4. Show the *Matt Dancing* video (www.youtube.com/watch?v=zlfKdbWwruY). Note that the country names are subtitled in the video, so you will need to cover the lower portion of the video display to obscure them (moving the browser window down your screen so that the bottom part is no longer visible is the easiest way). When students have watched the video once, get some general feedback on the countries they spotted – how did they recognise them?

5. Students will want to watch the video again to confirm what they have seen and to find out the names of all the countries. Depending on the composition of your class, some may be disappointed that their country is not featured. It may be in one of Matt's other videos (see www.wherethehellismatt.com/videos.shtml for more), but it is also an opportunity to discuss where he might go in a particular country, and – perhaps – to write to him to invite him.

6. Ask students what they think the advantages are of travelling and learning about other cultures. What do they think is the 'message' of Matt's video?

7. The video can be further exploited at all levels and in a variety of language areas, ranging from elementary vocabulary (e.g. colours, nationalities, languages) through intermediate grammar (e.g. present perfect versus past simple, conditionals) to advanced speaking (e.g. cultural issues, differences between countries).

Extension

Matt's website lends itself to many extension activities, including brain-storming questions for him and seeing if they are answered on the FAQ page, drafting an email to him to invite him to a specific country, and more.

Activity 46: Travel tips

Students prepare a visitor guide to their country (or the country where they study).

Cultural misunderstandings happen all the time, especially when visiting another country. This activity encourages students to think about their own country or countries, and produce a list of travel tips on a wiki for foreign visitors. It follows on well from Activity 40, *Our city guide*, and Activity 41, *Our city on Wikipedia*, which it parallels in many ways.

Literacy: **Intercultural literacy** and **Print literacy** (complexity: ****)

Topic: Travel advice

Aim: To consider cultural norms in different societies

Level: Intermediate +

Time: 90 minutes

Tech support: Quizzes/Quiz makers:

- General: e-language.wikispaces.com/quizzes

- QuizStar: quizstar.4teachers.org

Wikis:

- General: e-language.wikispaces.com/wikis

- PBworks: usermanual.pbworks.com

- Wikispaces: help.wikispaces.com

Language	
Areas	*Vocabulary:* Travel, culture, behaviour, customs and food *Grammar:* Modal verbs (for permission and obligation)
Functions	Giving advice and making suggestions; discussing rules
Skills	Speaking, reading, writing

Resources	
High-tech	*Equipment:* One internet-enabled teacher computer and data projector; internet-enabled student computers or mobile devices (one per group) *Tools:* Class wiki (e.g. PBworks or Wikispaces) *Tools (optional):* Quiz maker (e.g. QuizStar) *Documents:* Online worksheet (www.pearsoned.co.uk/hockly)
Low-tech	*Equipment:* One internet-enabled teacher computer and data projector *Tools:* Class wiki (e.g. PBworks or Wikispaces) *Documents:* Printed worksheet (follows Activity)
No-tech	*Documents:* Printed article (see below); printed worksheet (follows Activity)

Procedure

Before class

- Print copies of Sallie Brady's 2012 article, 'World's Worst Cultural Mistakes' (goo.gl/UU2LU) for each student, for use in Step 3 (no-tech version).

- Ensure that you have set up a wiki for your students in advance of this class, for use in Step 7. You could make use of the wiki set up for Activity 40, *Our city guide*, if you did this activity.

1. Start with a personal anecdote about a travel incident you have experienced – some occasion when you have inadvertently 'put your foot in it' or offended someone through lack of knowledge or understanding of local culture in a country you visited. Ask students if they have experienced similar incidents in their lives.

2. Ask students to refer to **Activity 46 Worksheet – True or false?** and give them a chance to consider the statements in small groups. They should give reasons why they think each statement is true or false. Conduct feedback as a whole group (see Appendix: Answer keys).

3. Students should check their answers in Sallie Brady's 2012 article, 'World's Worst Cultural Mistakes', for *Yahoo! Travel* (as described above), where she highlights some potential cultural mistakes for travellers. You can direct students to view the website in groups (high-tech version), show it to them on the projector screen (low-tech version), or distribute it as a printout (no-tech version). What else can they learn from the website?

4. Now is a good opportunity to evaluate the source of this information – is it reliable (*it should be, as it comes from a reputable online company*) (see Activity 27, *Tree octopus* for more on evaluating websites; you may want to review these evaluation skills).

5. Now ask students to produce a guide to their country (note that you may need to make groups if working in a multicultural context), either as a word-processed document (high-tech version) or on paper (low-tech and no-tech versions). This is another good chance to practise traditional print literacy skills by taking a process writing approach (see Chapter 3: *Choosing activities for different levels and contexts, Students' linguistic competence*).

   Begin by giving students time to brainstorm things that a foreign visitor should know. You may want to give them some hints here, but also let them add areas of their own:

What visitors should know
• eating and drinking
• driving
• doing business
• greeting people
• personal space and physical contact
• language
• . . .
• . . .

6. Divide students into groups, giving each group one of the subject areas. Give them time to draft an initial text containing advice and tips for their country. (Alternatively, in multicultural classes, groups could work on different countries.)

7. Once students have the first drafts of their texts ready, they can copy and paste them into dedicated subject area pages added to the class wiki you prepared earlier (as described under Before class; high-tech version). Encourage students to search for Creative Commons images to include with their texts on the wiki (see Activity 10, *Copycat*). Then ask each group to visit another group's wiki page. Students should edit and correct any language mistakes they see, and improve each other's texts if they can. Ensure that you continue to monitor and help with language at this stage.

If students are writing their texts on paper, they can exchange papers to edit and mark up each other's work (low-tech and no-tech versions).

8. After this first round of peer correction, students should look again at their own original texts, and focus particularly on any corrections that have been made. To do this, students can click on the 'History' tab for their individual wiki pages, and then compare their original drafts with the corrected versions, which will clearly show up any changes (high-tech version). Otherwise, students can examine the marked-up paper copies of their work and create new, improved drafts (low-tech and no-tech versions). Continue to monitor, and help students to spot any erroneous 'corrections' made by classmates. Students can ask you to confirm any corrections they are unsure about. Encourage students to make any further changes they wish to their texts. Help them with language.

9. Once students are happy with the final drafts of their texts, ask them to visit all the other wiki pages in the guide. For each page they visit, they should leave a comment under the 'Discussion' tab. Their comments can consist of additional information or tips. In the case of a world guide created by a multinational class, classmates could leave questions they would like to have answered (high-tech version). Texts created on paper can be put up on the classroom walls, with a blank piece of paper added below each for written comments (low-tech and no-tech versions). Students can walk around the class reading the texts and adding comments on the paper.

Finally, let the students return to their original texts and read the comments and/or questions that their classmates have left for them. Students should further modify their texts to incorporate some of their classmates' suggestions and ideas, or to respond to their questions.

Variation

If you're working in a group of mixed nationalities, students might prepare a quiz about their own country for their classmates to answer. This can be done online using one of the many free quiz makers (e.g. QuizStar: quizstar.4teachers.org) (high-tech version) or on paper (low-tech and no-tech versions).

Activity 46 Worksheet – True or false?

1. Always take off your shoes when visiting friends at home in the UK.
2. Never pat a child on the head in Thailand.
3. In India it is important always to eat with your left hand.
4. Always wear a swimsuit in the sauna in Sweden.
5. When doing business in Korea, always maintain eye contact.
6. Finishing your glass of vodka in one shot in Russia is polite.
7. In Japan dinner conversation is as important as the meal.
8. In France you should never serve wine to anyone else at dinner.
9. Using a handkerchief to clean your nose in China is offensive.
10. In Hawaii you should use your car horn at every corner for safety.

Activity 47: LOLcats

Students discuss the internet phenomenon of LOLcats, and create their own LOLcats photos and captions.

LOLcats are an example of an early and long-lived internet 'meme', an idea in the form of a picture, video, phrase or hashtag (#) which is spread via the internet. This activity focuses on LOLcats, which are essentially 'remixed' photos of cats with added subtitles, and encourages students to analyse the genre so as to produce their own contributions. It also examines the commenting and rating function on a LOLcats site – both key elements of many web 2.0 tools. This activity fits well with Activity 5, *Cryptic messages*, and Activity 10, *Copycat*. As a simple introduction to remix, it leads well into Activity 48, *Texting Hillary* and Activity 49, *I'mma let you finish*.

Literacy:	**Remix literacy**, **Texting literacy** and **Multimedia literacy** (overall complexity: *****)
Topic:	Cats
Aim:	To explore and respond to an internet meme, and to begin learning about remix
Level:	Elementary +
Time:	60 minutes
Tech support:	Presentation software:

- Keynote: support.apple.com/manuals/#iwork
- PowerPoint: goo.gl/vfLwD

Language	
Areas	*Vocabulary:* Cats *Grammar:* Present simple tense *Register:* Informal versus standard communication
Functions	Giving opinions; discussing
Skills	Reading, speaking, writing

Resources	
High-tech	*Equipment:* One internet-enabled teacher computer and data projector; internet-enabled student computers or mobile devices (one per pair) *Tools:* Presentation software (e.g. Keynote or PowerPoint) *Documents:* Online worksheet (www.pearsoned.co.uk/hockly)
Low-tech	*Equipment:* One internet-enabled teacher computer and data projector *Documents:* Printed LOLcats pictures; printed worksheet (follows Activity)
No-tech	*Documents:* Printed LOLcats pictures; printed worksheet (follows Activity)

Digital risks

While there is a risk of students encountering inappropriate images or comments on many websites, this is not the case with the LOLcats site, where content is moderated.

Procedure

Before class

- Put four or five LOLcats pictures (www.lolcats.com), including at least one with a rating and comments, into a PowerPoint slideshow (high-tech and low-tech versions), or print out the pictures (no-tech version), for use in Step 1. Note that some LOLcats captions deliberately use inaccurate spelling and abbreviations for effect (see Step 3 for an example). Choose pictures with intelligible captions for your students.

- Print the LOLcats pictures referred to in Task 4 of **Activity 47 Worksheet – LOLcats**, for use in Step 7 (no-tech version).

- Print out Creative Commons images of cats – at least one image for each pair of students in your class – for use in Step 8 (low-tech and no-tech versions).

1. On the projector screen, show your students a slideshow of 4–5 collated pictures from the LOLcats site (high-tech and low-tech versions). Alternatively, show printed pictures (no-tech version). Ensure that your

students understand the captions and how they relate to each picture. Explain that LOLcats are a famous example of an internet 'meme', an idea that is spread via the internet, often because it's amusing or because it provides commentary on current events, or both (see Chapter 1: *Remix literacy*). Elicit the fact that 'LOL' = 'laugh[ing] out loud', reflecting the fact that these are amusing picture of cats (see Chapter 1: *First focus: Language, Texting literacy*).

Show students a series of comments added by visitors beneath one of the LOLcats pictures. Comments are often in a mixture of standard English and textspeak, and are generally short, positive comments such as 'Cute', or 'I love this'. Draw attention also to the 1–5 star rating for each picture.

2. Ask students to work in pairs, giving them a 5-minute time limit to browse the LOLcats site and find three more pictures they like, with or without captions; then, using the internet-enabled teacher computer and projector screen, get each pair to share *one* of their chosen three pictures with the class, and explain what they like about it (high-tech version). Alternatively, choose three more pictures from the LOLcats site and display them on the projector screen as a whole class activity (low-tech version), or simply show more printed pictures, plus ratings and comments, from the site (no-tech version). Draw attention to the rating (1–5 stars) for each picture again.

3. Focus on the language in the LOLcats captions from Steps 1 and 2 above. Point out the deliberate errors that are often used for effect in LOLcats captions, e.g.

   - grammatical errors: *I is / I are / I does* . . .
   - spelling errors: *fashun* instead of *fashion*, *meking* instead of *making*
   - textspeak: *i* instead of *I*, *cnt* instead of *can't*, *u* instead of *you*, *c* instead of *see*

   These errors are often combined, e.g. 'I <u>cees</u> u on d other side' – 'I see you on the other side'. This caption has a grammatical and spelling error ('I cees' for 'I see'), and textspeak ('u' for 'you', and 'd' for 'the').

   Ask students what is the intended effect of these errors (*the idea is to convey a childlike quality in the captions – children often misspell or misuse grammar when younger, which makes the cats seem like cute young children*).

4. Tell students that contributing to a meme like LOLcats means understanding the genre and its unwritten rules. The pictures themselves are

frequently of cats in unusual places or costumes, and the humour comes from the caption, which contributes an often incongruous thought to the cat, expressed in childlike language.

Visitors often leave comments on LOLcats pictures. These are submitted via the site and monitored, so there is no danger of offensiveness or spam.

5. Ask students to refer to **Activity 47 Worksheet – LOLcats**. In pairs, students should rewrite the captions in standard English in Task 1. They should then move on to Task 2, where they identify error types as well as examples of the use of textspeak in each caption (see Appendix: Answer keys).

6. Ask students to continue to work in pairs to complete Task 3, where they make predictions about the photos accompanying the captions.

7. Ask students to complete Task 4, where they check their predictions about the pictures on the LOLcats site itself and rate each picture with a star from 1–5 (high-tech version). Alternatively, show the pictures on the projector screen as a whole class activity and get students to agree on the star rating to add (low-tech version), or simply show students the printed pictures with the captions and discuss what ratings they would like to give them (no-tech version).

8. Ask students to produce their own LOLcats images. To do this, each pair should search for a Creative Commons picture of a cat on Google Images or Flickr (see Activity 10, *Copycat* on how to conduct Creative Commons searches for images) and add a text to the chosen image using presentation software like Keynote or PowerPoint (high-tech version). Otherwise, bring in pictures of cats for students to choose from or assign one picture per pair, and have each pair add a caption beneath their image (low-tech and no-tech versions). At lower levels, you may wish to ask students to create standard English captions, but with more advanced classes, you could let students play with the grammar and spelling of their captions to reflect the conventions you outlined in Step 3.

9. Ask students to share their pictures and captions with the class. Slides can be emailed to the teacher and shared on the projector screen, possibly collated into a single slideshow (high-tech version). Otherwise, students can post their images around the walls of the classroom for others to see (low-tech and no-tech versions). Vote for which picture and caption is the best.

Extension 1

If your students have chosen Creative Commons images of cats, and written their captions in textspeak, you can encourage each pair to save their slide as an image (a jpg, gif or png of up to 650 Kb), and then submit it to the LOLcats site itself (high-tech version). As individuals or as a class, students can then monitor and respond to any comments they receive on their pictures. Feedback on this commenting stage can be conducted a week or so after the initial activity.

Extension 2

Encourage students to upload their LOLcats slides or images to their e-portfolios, or to add hyperlinks from their e-portfolios to their images on the LOLcats sites itself (see Chapter 3: *Assessing digital work*, *Assessing through e-portfolios*) (high-tech version).

Activity 47 Worksheet – LOLcats

1. Put each LOLcats caption into standard English:

   (a) U liek dat? U wunt sum mor?

   _____

   (b) I'm in ur castle eating ur peasants

   _____

   (c) I iz in ur lolcats. Ratein me 5 starz

   _____

   (d) i swallowd mah toy. im goin 2 be sik

   _____

   (e) But . . . but . . . I don't know what puzzles is

   _____

2. Identify the deliberate errors in the captions in Task 1 above. Are they errors of grammar, or spelling, or examples of textspeak? For example:

   (a) U liek dat? U wunt sum mor?

   - **grammar:** error in question formation: *U liek dat?* Correct form: *Do you like that?*
   - **grammar:** error in question formation: *U wunt sum mor?* Correct form: *Do you want some more?*
   - **spelling:** *liek, dat, wunt.* Correct forms: *like, that, want.*
   - **textspeak:** *u, sum, mor.* Standard forms: *you, some, more.*

3. What do you think each cat picture looks like? Discuss your ideas in pairs. Think about:

   - where the cat is (inside, outside, in a room, on or near an object?);
   - whether it is wearing a costume or hat (what?);
   - whether it is holding an object (what?);
   - its facial expression.

4. Now check your predictions by looking at the original picture for each of the captions. Give each picture a star rating.

   (a) http://www.lolcats.com/view/26825/

   (b) http://www.lolcats.com/view/1494-im-in-ur-castle-eating-ur-peas-ants.html

   (c) http://www.lolcats.com/view/1094-i-iz-in-ur-lolcats-ratein-me-five-starz.html

   (d) http://www.lolcats.com/view/22680/

   (e) http://www.lolcats.com/view/50/

Activity 48: Texting Hillary

Students learn about remix through a set of imaginary text messages.

This activity introduces students in a more explicit way to the concept of remix – which is seen by many cultural critics as the hallmark of contemporary popular culture – through a set of imagined text messages between Hillary Clinton and a variety of famous people. Students look first at examples from this popular meme, building on the idea of the LOLcats meme introduced in Activity 47, *LOLcats.* They then produce their own using images and imagined texts. This activity leads well into Activity 49, *I'mma let you finish.*

Literacy:	**Remix literacy, Texting literacy** and **Multimedia literacy** (complexity: *****)
Topic:	Popular culture
Aim:	To further explore internet memes and the phenomenon of remix
Level:	Intermediate +
Time:	60 minutes
Tech support:	Blogs:

- General: e-language.wikispaces.com/blogs
- Blogger: support.google.com/blogger/?hl=en
- Edublogs: help.edublogs.org

Presentation software:

- Keynote: support.apple.com/manuals/#iwork
- PowerPoint: goo.gl/vfLwD

Language	
Areas	*Vocabulary:* Mobile phones; textspeak *Grammar:* Present simple tense *Register:* Informal communication
Functions	Giving opinions; discussing
Skills	Reading, speaking, writing

Resources	
High-tech	*Equipment:* One internet-enabled teacher computer and data projector; internet-enabled student computers (one per group) *Tools:* Presentation software (e.g. Keynote or PowerPoint) *Tools (optional):* Class blog (e.g. Blogger or Edublogs); Skitch app
Low-tech	*Equipment:* One internet-enabled teacher computer and data projector *Tools:* Presentation software (e.g. Keynote or PowerPoint) *Tools (optional):* Class blog (e.g. Blogger or Edublogs); Skitch app
No-tech	Not available for this activity

Procedure

1. Start by displaying the Obama-Hillary remix from the *Texts from Hillary* blog (goo.gl/jshcE) on the projector screen. Ask students the following questions:

   - Who are the two people in the photograph? (*Barack Obama is in the top one, and Hillary Clinton in the bottom one*)

   - What are/were their jobs? (*President of the USA/Secretary of State of the USA*)

   - Where were the pictures taken? (*Obama seems to be in an office; Hillary seems to be on a plane*)

   - What are they doing? (*They're both texting, using BlackBerrys*)

   - Who are they texting? (*Each other*)

   - Who sent the first text? (*Obama*)

   - Why is this exchange of text messages humorous? (*Even though Obama has a higher position, Hillary seems to be claiming that she has a more important role – running the world, not just the USA!*)

2. Ask students whether they think these are real text messages. How do they know? (*Obama and Hillary probably wouldn't send these kinds of text messages to each other, and their texts would not be made public.*)

3. Tell students that this is a simple example of a 'remix' (which involves taking an original digital artefact and changing it so that it takes on a new significance; see Chapter 1: *Fourth focus: (Re-)design* for more details). In this case someone has created a blog which includes imaginary text message conversations between Hillary Clinton and other famous people. Remixes are often meant to be amusing (see Activity 47, *LOLcats*; remind students about this activity if they have already done it) but sometimes they can also be used to make a serious point. Could there be a more serious message in the Obama-Hillary remix?

4. Give students time to look through some more of the remixes in the blog archive (textsfromhillaryclinton.tumblr.com/archive) (high-tech version), or show them on screen (low-tech version). Help students interpret the text message conversations and decide whether each is meant to be amusing, serious or both. Explain that, like LOLcats (Activity 47, *LOLcats*), 'Texts from Hillary' is an example of an internet 'meme'.

5. Finish by directing students to the last example, a remix actually contributed by Hillary Clinton herself in response to this internet meme! You can direct students to the URL (goo.gl/NRelh) (high-tech version) or show it on the projector screen (low-tech version). Point out that the two men shown are the original creators of the internet meme, Adam and Stacy. Help students interpret the meaning of the conversation (*in more standard English, the conversation might read: 'What's up, Adam? Nice self-portrait, Stacy [smiley emoticon]' / 'Oh my God . . . busted' / 'Sorry Hillary' / 'Rolling on the floor laughing at your Tumblr [blog]. Got to go – scrunchie [a type of hair tie] time. Talk to you later? . . .'*). This could also be a good time to review students' knowledge of textspeak (see Activity 5, *Cryptic messages* and Activity 6, *Codeswitching*). Point out that the meme only lasted for a month. Ask students what happened, and why it stopped. (*The real Hillary Clinton created a remix, which completed and put an end to Adam and Stacy's remix idea*).

   Ask students whether they know of any other remixes, and whether they are meant to be amusing, serious, or both!

6. Tell students that they are going to remix a conversation between two famous people they like (or dislike). Give them time to work in groups to find a set of appropriate photos (high-tech version) or do this as a whole class activity on the projector screen (low-tech version), voting on two appropriate people that the class find interesting. Ensure that students use Creative Commons images (see Activity 10, *Copycat* for more details).

7. Students should work in small groups to compose their 'text messages'. These texts can be added to the images using presentation software like Keynote or PowerPoint. This can be done in small groups, with the final results being emailed to the teacher and shared on the projector screen, possibly collated into a single slideshow (high-tech version). Otherwise, it can be done as a whole class activity using the teacher computer and the projector screen, with a series of texts being added to copies of the chosen images (low-tech version). Students can vote on the best remix.

Variation

If students have access to mobile devices, they could experiment with one of the growing number of other apps that allow users to add captions to photos or make cartoons from them. These can be fun and motivating to use, and lead to very professional results which can then be shared.

Extension 1

There is scope for this to become a regular activity, with students adding a new mini-conversation each week. They could even create a blog (e.g. with Blogger or Edublogs) where they can post any new remixes they make, either individually or as a class (as long as they continue to use Creative Commons images).

Extension 2

Encourage students to upload their remixed photos to their e-portfolios, or to add hyperlinks from their e-portfolios to the blog where these are stored (see Chapter 3: *Assessing digital work, Assessing through e-portfolios*) (high-tech version).

Activity 49: I'mma let you finish

Students look at examples of remixed images based on a real-life incident, and create their own.

In this activity, students go further in their exploration of remix, particularly remix used to make a serious point. The activity is based on a real-life incident which took place between two singers, Kanye West and Taylor Swift, at the MTV Video Music Awards in 2009. It quickly became an internet meme. Students examine remixed images created as part of the meme, and make their own remixed images with captions. This activity follows on well from Activity 48, *Texting Hillary*.

Literacy: **Remix literacy** and **Multimedia literacy** (complexity: *****)

Topic: Celebrities and famous people

Aim: To further explore internet memes and the phenomenon of remix

Level: Intermediate +

Time: 60 minutes

Tech support: Blogs:

- General: e-language.wikispaces.com/blogs
- Blogger: support.google.com/blogger/?hl=en
- Edublogs: help.edublogs.org

Presentation software:

- Keynote: support.apple.com/manuals/#iwork
- PowerPoint: goo.gl/vfLwD

Language	
Areas	*Vocabulary:* Celebrities and famous people; music; textspeak *Grammar:* Present simple tense *Register:* Informal communication
Functions	Giving opinions; discussing
Skills	Reading, speaking, writing

Resources	
High-tech	*Equipment:* One internet-enabled teacher computer and data projector; internet-enabled student computers or mobile devices (one per pair) *Tools:* Presentation software (e.g. Keynote or PowerPoint) *Tools (optional):* Blog(s) (e.g. Blogger or Edublogs)
Low-tech	*Equipment:* One internet-enabled teacher computer and data projector *Stationery:* Poster-sized paper, coloured pens and magazines (for images)
No-tech	*Documents:* Printed images (see below) *Stationery:* Poster-sized paper, coloured pens and magazines (for images)

Digital risks

Depending on your political, cultural, religious and educational context, as well as your students' ages, you may need to carefully select which remixed images to show them in Step 3. You may also wish to provide guidelines on acceptable images, topics and language for students' own remixes in Step 4.

Procedure

Before class

- Print the first picture of Kanye West and Taylor Swift in the *Daily Mail*'s report of the MTV Video Music Awards incident (goo.gl/xe57s), along with several additional images from the report, for use in Step 1 (no-tech version).

- Print a selection of the remixed photos from Step 3 (no-tech version).

1. Show students the first picture of Kanye West and Taylor Swift from the *Daily Mail* article (as described above) on the projector screen (high-tech and low-tech versions). Alternatively, show students a printed copy of the image (no-tech version). Ask if students know who these celebrities are. Ask if they know about a famous incident that took place between these two singers at the 2009 MTV Music Video Awards (*Kanye West stormed the stage during Taylor Swift's prize acceptance speech and*

said to her: 'Yo Tay, I'm really happy for you and I'mma let you finish, but Beyoncé had one of the best videos of all time. One of the best videos of all time'). Ask students if they know who Beyoncé is (*another famous singer*). Let them read about and see photos of what happened on the projector screen (high-tech and low-tech versions), or show a few printed photos (no-tech version).

2. Put Kanye West's words on the board, and ensure that students understand them. Point out that 'I'mma' is a deliberate contraction and misspelling of 'I'm going to' that reflects fast spoken English. Ask students how they think Taylor Swift felt about Kanye's interruption. What about music fans? Explain that very shortly after this incident, remixed photos showing Kanye West began to appear on the internet, and 'I'mma let you finish' soon became a popular internet meme. Indicate that although many of these images are humorous, they also make a serious point (see Activity 48, *Texting Hillary* for a discussion of this point; remind students about this activity if they have already done it).

3. Show students some of the remixed photos online (high-tech and low-tech versions) or printed out (no-tech version) from the I'mma Let You Finish.com blog (kanyegate.tumblr.com/archive). Many of these photos show Kanye West confronting someone (or something) significant or famous, using the same phrases he used to confront Taylor Swift. The photos range from the witty, to the silly, to the potentially offensive. We suggest showing some of the following remixed photos of Kanye confronting:

   - The Beatles – kanyegate.tumblr.com/post/194212823
   - Martin Luther King – kanyegate.tumblr.com/post/188741396
   - Kublai Khan – kanyegate.tumblr.com/post/188597694
   - Hurricane Katrina – kanyegate.tumblr.com/post/188749985
   - Second Wold War marines – kanyegate.tumblr.com/post/188886625
   - dinosaurs – kanyegate.tumblr.com/post/190228199
   - vampires – kanyegate.tumblr.com/post/191189849
   - Abraham Lincoln* – kanyegate.tumblr.com/post/188269648
   - Jesus* – kanyegate.tumblr.com/post/188741692
   - Anne Frank* – kanyegate.tumblr.com/post/191201863
   - God* – kanyegate.tumblr.com/post/188756585

Note: Some of the images are deliberately designed to make viewers feel uncomfortable in order to convey their message strongly. Indeed, this is a hallmark of remix. We suggest you choose images appropriate to your students and context (see Digital risks).

Ask students whether they think each image is funny, or serious, or both. Do the images have different messages? Or do they all share a common message?

4. Ask students to work in pairs to create their own remixed image of Kanye's interruption. They can search for a Creative Commons image (see Activity 10, *Copycat* for more details), add it to a Keynote or PowerPoint slide, and then add a caption to it on their slide (high-tech version). Alternatively, students can create their remix on poster paper by using an image cut out of a magazine or their own drawing, and writing the caption across or beneath it (low-tech and no-tech versions). In both cases, students need to use the text: '*Yo XX, I'm really happy for you and I'mma let you finish, but XX had one of the best XX of all time. One of the best XX of all time.*' It's up to them to replace the 'XX' in each case! Depending on the teaching context, you may wish to provide some guidelines on acceptable images, topics and language (see Digital risks).

5. Ask students to share their pictures and captions with the class. Slides can be emailed to the teacher and shared on the projector screen, possibly collated into a single slideshow (high-tech version). Otherwise, students can post their images around the walls of the classroom for others to see (low-tech and no-tech versions). Vote on which images are the most imaginative, witty, scandalous, etc.

Extension 1

If you have a class blog, or students have their own blogs (see Activity 35, *Personal blogging*), ask students to add their remixed images to the blog(s). They can include a short text description of the incident in their own words, and add the tags 'Kanye West' and 'meme' to their post(s) (see Activity 24, *Travel tags* for more on tagging).

Extension 2

Encourage students to add hyperlinks from their e-portfolios to their blog posts (see Chapter 3: *Assessing digital work, Assessing through e-portfolios*) (high-tech version).

Activity 50: Movie mashup

Students create subtitles for a film trailer.

This activity encourages students to create a remix (or 'mashup') of a film trailer, by adding their own original subtitles. Issues of copyright, fair use, and the legality of remix culture are explored in the final round-up stage. Knowing to what extent original content can be repurposed to create new works ('remixing') is a key digital literacy.

Literacy:	**Remix literacy** and **Multimedia literacy** (overall complexity: *****)
Topic:	Cinema
Aim:	To create a remix by adding original subtitles to a film trailer
Level:	Elementary +
Time:	60 minutes
Tech support	Subtitling:

- CaptionTube: captiontube.appspot.com/help/
- Overstream: www.overstream.net/help.php
- Subtitle Horse: subtitle-horse.com

Word-processing software:

- Apple Pages: support.apple.com/manuals/#iwork
- Microsoft Word: goo.gl/KXnLe

Language	
Areas	*Vocabulary:* Cinema and films *Grammar:* Present simple tense; present continuous tense
Functions	Creating dialogues and narratives; describing scenes
Skills	Writing, speaking

Resources	
High-tech	*Equipment:* One internet-enabled teacher computer and data projector; internet-enabled student computers or mobile devices (one per pair) *Tools:* Subtitling site (e.g. CaptionTube, Overstream or Subtitle Horse); word-processing software (e.g. Apple Pages or Microsoft Word)
Low-tech	*Equipment:* One internet-enabled teacher computer and data projector *Tools:* Subtitling site (e.g. CaptionTube, Overstream or Subtitle Horse); word-processing software (e.g. Apple Pages or Microsoft Word)
No-tech	Not available for this activity

Digital risks

It is important for teachers to familiarise students with copyright law in the local jurisdiction. Subtitled films created in this activity are for educational purposes only and should not be shared publicly unless it is clear they do not contravene local copyright law (see Box 1.12).

Procedure

Before class

- Make a list of five or six films currently showing in local cinemas. Find the trailer for one of these films, in a foreign language which will *not* be familiar to students, and bookmark the page for use in Step 2.

- Use a subtitle creation site (see Step 5 for suggestions) to create fake subtitles for the trailer you have selected, to be shown in class in Step 3.

- *(Optional)* Pre-select a trailer for the whole class activity in Step 4 (low-tech version).

1. Introduce the topic of cinema by putting the titles of five or six films currently showing on the board. Ask students which ones they have seen, and what they thought of each film. Instead of titles, you could show images of film posters, e.g. from the Internet Movie Database website (www.imdb.com).

2. Prepare the film you subtitled before class to show students. Start by showing them the *un*-subtitled trailer with the sound turned off, and ask them to identify which film from Step 1 it is. Play the trailer again with the sound turned on, and ask students to identify the language (tell them if they don't know!), and what it might be about.

3. Show students the trailer with your subtitles. Afterwards, ask them if they think your subtitles were literal translations (they clearly shouldn't be!). Tell students that this is an example of what you would like them to produce in pairs.

4. Put students into pairs to work on their own subtitles for a film trailer. Pairs can each choose a foreign language film trailer by searching YouTube for a trailer film name and language e.g. 'Harry Potter trailer in French' (high-tech version). Alternatively, you can choose a trailer as a whole class activity and show it on the projector screen (low-tech version). You may need to play the whole trailer more than once. Put the following points on the board to help students plan the subtitles:

   For each scene in the trailer, think about:

   • Who are the characters (name, age, relationship between the characters)?
   • Where are they?
   • Is the situation dangerous/romantic/funny/scary/ . . . ?
   • Write down what each character says in each scene.

   Ask students to work in their pairs, stopping and starting their film trailer as necessary while they write their subtitles (high-tech version); otherwise, work with the whole class on the trailer shown on the projector screen (low-tech version). Students can write their subtitles initially as a word-processed document (high-tech version), or you can note their ideas on the board (low-tech version). Monitor and help students with language while they are producing subtitles.

5. Using the internet-enabled teacher computer and data projector, show students how to use a subtitle creation site such as CaptionTube (captiontube.appspot.com), Overstream (www.overstream.net) or Subtitle Horse (subtitle-horse.com). Note that these sites create subtitles for videos that are already online.

6. Ask students to work in their pairs and use a subtitle creation site to add their subtitles to the trailer (high-tech version). They should keep the URLs of their subtitled videos private, and share them only with other class members. Alternatively, add subtitles to one trailer as a whole class

activity (low-tech version). Once the subtitled trailer(s) is/are ready, it/they can be shown on the projector screen (high-tech and low-tech versions).

7. Ask students to view other pairs' subtitled videos and write down one thing they particularly like about each; these comments can later be shared orally with the class (high-tech version). Alternatively, ask students to comment on the overall effectiveness of the class video (low-tech version). Would students do anything differently next time if they were making a similar remix?

8. To round off this activity, hold a discussion with students about remix culture and mashups (see Chapter 1: *Fourth focus: (Re-)design, Remix literacy*). You could use some or all of the following questions as prompts:

   - Who normally creates remixes? (*It is largely, though not exclusively, a youth phenomenon.*)
   - Why do they create remixes? (*Sometimes to make people laugh, at other times to make a serious social or political point.*)
   - Where do they normally share remixes? (*Often on videosharing sites like YouTube, but also through links – frequently to YouTube – on social networking sites like Facebook or microblogging services like Twitter.*)
   - What copyright issues might be involved? (*Copyright holders might object to remixes being made, might ask services like YouTube to remove them and, in extreme cases, might sue the creators of remixes. It's important to check out copyright law, including fair use or fair dealing provisions – see Box 1.12 – before creating and sharing remixes online.*)

Future learning

By working through a selection of the activities described in this chapter, contextualised appropriately, teachers can foster the digital literacies which are central to any contemporary language classroom. As they begin to develop their literacies and build their PLNs (see Box 1.10), students may take on more responsibility for customising their own learning according to their needs and interests. By the time they leave the classroom, they should be well on their way to becoming lifelong learners who can continue to extend their language and literacy skills – both traditional and digital – throughout their future lives.

Further reading

- For further practical reading on working with digital literacies, the web and mobile technologies, see: Bonk and Zhang (2008); Brooks-Young (2010); Burniske (2008); Hobbs (2011); Kist (2010); Knobel and Lankshear (2010); Kolb (2008); Kolb (2011); Levinson (2010); Nielsen and Webb (2011); November (2010); Parker (2010).

Chapter 3
From application to implementation

Incorporating activities into the syllabus and timetable

We have seen that the affordances of particular technologies can support specific pedagogical approaches (see Box 2.1). The more static informational orientation of web 1.0 lent itself to delivering and consuming content (e.g. students reading a webpage for information), whereas the more social nature of web 2.0 is suited to collaborative and communicative activities and a more constructivist approach to teaching and learning (e.g. students creating a blog or video). Similarly, many educational apps for mobile devices are oriented towards consumption rather than production (e.g. students learning vocabulary with flashcards), though there has recently been an increase in the number of apps which offer at least some of the creativity and networking typical of web 2.0 (e.g. students producing and circulating content through multimedia sharing apps). This doesn't mean that web 2.0 and productive apps should entirely replace web 1.0 and consumption apps. There is a place for consuming content in our classrooms, as there is for the drill and practice exercises typical of web 1.0 and consumption apps. But if we don't also include activities that encourage our students to be 'prosumers' or 'produsers' (see Chapter 1: *Third focus: Connections, Participatory literacy*), we severely limit the potential of the technology to transform, rather than merely enhance, our students' learning (see Chapter 2: *The SAMR model for evaluating technology use*).

What does this mean for the practising teacher, and how can we include a range of activity types in our classrooms? How do we ensure that our students' digital literacies – and our own – are developed incrementally, and in a principled manner, within our English language teaching (or indeed our teaching of other languages, or of communications and new media more generally)?

Most teachers work within the framework of a syllabus. This may be in the form of a coursebook, an institution-wide course programme, or even a syllabus negotiated between the teacher and a specific class (Candlin, 1987; 2001). Many modern-day syllabuses reflect a communicative approach to language teaching. What actually happens in the classroom may subvert the communicative principles embodied within the syllabus (Thornbury, 1988), but there is general agreement, at least, that language should be taught for communicative purposes and that there is no one 'right' approach or method for achieving this. A cursory glance at the syllabus of any current coursebook will show an eclectic approach to teaching, with traces of a range of different methodologies contained in the activities, from grammar translation ('*Translate these sentences into your own language*') to audiolingual ('*Listen and repeat these words*') to communicative ('*Discuss these points with a partner*'). Our so-called 'postmethod condition' (Kumaravadivelu, 2006) may seem rather unfocused, but it reflects what most teachers, researchers and coursebook writers feel works best, and it provides a measure of variety and choice for both teachers and learners. However, this does not mean that the more rigid approaches of the past have simply been replaced with 'unconstrained pluralism', which may be 'arbitrary, atheoretical, incoherent, naïve, uncritical, unsystematic, and lacking in philosophical direction' (Mellow, 2002). Rather, in the postmethod era, teachers are called on to engage in 'principled eclecticism', that is, to adopt a 'coherent, pluralistic approach to language teaching' (ibid.) governed by an integrated, logical view of language, learning and teaching, but one which encourages diversity and always allows the syllabus to be challenged by practice, and vice versa (cf. Larsen-Freeman, 2000; Mellow, 2000).

When considering how to integrate digital literacies into our teaching practice, we can start by looking at the syllabus. A typical syllabus from a current intermediate level communicative coursebook will include some core components, often laid out in the form of a grid on the first few pages, something like this:

Unit & Topic	Language (vocabulary, grammar, pronunciation)	Skills (reading, writing, listening, speaking)
1		
2		
3		

Depending on the focus or aims of the coursebook, additional syllabus components might include:

- Practical English (specific examples of functional language, or English in use)

- Business communication skills (in Business English coursebooks)

- English around the world (regional variations or differences in language and culture)

- A project (a task carried out by learners to put into practice everything covered in a unit)

It is not difficult to envisage an extra column, digital literacies, being added to the basic syllabus grid:

Unit & Topic	Language (vocabulary, grammar, pronunciation)	Skills (reading, writing, listening, speaking)	Digital literacies
1			
2			
3			

There is no one correct order in which digital literacies need to be taught (but for suggestions see: *Choosing activities for different levels and contexts* in this chapter). The digital activities we decide to integrate into our syllabus will depend on several kinds of factors. We can loosely group these into three categories, though there is certainly some overlap between the categories, and some factors (such as attitude) might arguably fit into more than one category (in this case *Personal* or *Digital factors*).

Table 3.1 Factors affecting digital activity choice

Pedagogical factors (relating to our students as language learners)
- *Syllabus:* whether the literacy and activities 'fit' with the coursebook aims, units and topics.
- *Class type:* whether we are teaching General English, Business English, EAP (English for Academic Purposes) or ESP (English for Specific Purposes), etc.
- *Class context:* whether or not we are teaching in an English-speaking environment.
- *Language level:* the linguistic proficiency of our students.
- *Language needs:* the particular language needs our students may have.
- *Language wants:* the types of language our students most want to learn or practise.

Personal factors (relating to our students as private individuals)
- *Ages:* whether our students are young learners, adolescents or adults.
- *Interests:* what sorts of activities and topics motivate our students (see also *Language wants* above and *Attitudes* below).
- *Culture(s):* the cultural context as well as the cultural backgrounds of students in our class.

Table 3.1 (*cont'd*)

Digital factors (relating to our students as technology users)

- *Attitudes:* our students' attitudes towards digital technologies in general as well as specific tools.
- *Tech levels:* the technological proficiency and confidence of our students.
- *Digital literacy levels:* how digitally literate our students already are.
- *Equipment and tools:* what hardware and software we and our students have access to.

A key question is how exactly we should integrate digital literacies into the syllabus. This will depend on our own teaching context and the syllabus we may have to teach. In most cases, teachers have a syllabus imposed, frequently in the form of a coursebook, or possibly one designed by their institution or company. In some contexts, these syllabuses may be derived from a framework or curriculum created by the local Ministry of Education or an international body. However, there are occasions when teachers have at least some freedom to create their own syllabuses. Below, we look at three options for integrating digital literacies into the syllabus:

- *The coursebook-driven approach:* how to integrate digital literacies into an existing coursebook-determined syllabus.
- *The topic-driven approach:* how to integrate digital literacies into less structured classes.
- *The digital literacies-driven approach:* how to use digital literacies as a basis for the syllabus itself.

The coursebook-driven approach

A good place to start is by mapping specific digital literacies and related activities onto the syllabus. How can this be done?

Meet Carla, a teacher with an intermediate level (say, Common European Framework B1) group, using a General English communicative coursebook as her syllabus. Below (on pages 322–323) is an extract from her coursebook, in which a digital literacies component has been added to the first five units of the syllabus. Carla has chosen several options from the *Digital activities grid* (see Chapter 2, Table 2.1) for each unit of her coursebook. In some cases the digital literacy activity could *replace* coursebook activities, and in some cases it could *supplement* them. Let's look in detail at the digital literacy activity options Carla has added to her syllabus for Unit 1, and the thinking behind her decisions.

Because Carla is unsure about what digital literacy skills her students already have, and because she wants to introduce the topic of digital literacies for the first time with this intermediate group, she decides she will do both of the introductory activities from the *Digital activities grid*. Together, these activities function well as an orientation to the topic of digital literacies. Activity 1, *Technology past and present* will give her a good idea of her students' (and her own) digital competence. Activity 2, *Being digitally literate* acts as a springboard for helping students to reflect on the technology they already use. It is very unlikely that the students will all be digitally literate in the same areas or to the same degree. This will depend on previous training, past experience in personal, school and/or work contexts, and pre-existing attitudes to technology. Getting a good sense of how developed each student's digital competence is will enable Carla to judiciously group students for future activities that require different skills.

The topic of Unit 1 of the coursebook is identity and personal information. Carla starts by considering *Pedagogical factors* from the table of *Factors affecting digital activity choice* (Table 3.1). She looks at options which could replace or supplement the Unit 1 *writing* and *speaking* tasks, that is, the productive skills tasks. She looks at the *Digital activities grid*, and by considering the *Literacy 1*, *Literacy 2*, *Topic* and *Language* columns, she is able to map a choice of digital literacy activity options onto her syllabus. She identifies three activities which fit neatly with Unit 1 of the coursebook syllabus:

- Activity 13, *Showcasing hobbies* (Multimedia literacy)
- Activity 34, *Online me* (Personal literacy and Multimedia literacy)
- Activity 35, *Personal blogging* (Personal literacy, Print literacy and Multimedia literacy)

The Unit 1 coursebook writing task requires students to compose a text about themselves and their families. In a traditional classroom, students would typically produce a handwritten (or word-processed) text, which would then be given to the teacher for correction and feedback. However, Carla thinks about how students might produce a *digital* text, including images, audio and even video, which could then be shared online with classmates (or with parents, in the case of young learners). The three digital literacy activity options she has identified require students to produce online texts in different formats:

- Activity 13, *Showcasing hobbies* asks each student to produce an audio text, i.e. to record a spoken text as an audio voiceover for a digital slideshow.

CONTENTS

CONTENTS

LISTENING/DVD	SPEAKING	WRITING	DIGITAL LITERACIES
			Introductory activities Activity 1: *Technology past and present* Activity 2: *Being digitally literate*
listen to someone describing their family history	talk about family events; talk about people in your life	write an email of introduction; learn to use formal and informal styles	**Option 1** Activity 13: *Showcasing hobbies* (Multimedia literacy)
listen to a set of instructions and do a test	discuss the differences between men and women		**Option 2** Activity 34: *Online me* (Personal literacy and Multimedia literacy) **Option 3**
listen to a set of interviews; learn to understand and use two-word responses	talk about type of interviews and interview experiences; role-play an interview		Activity 35: *Personal blogging* (Personal literacy, Print literacy and Multimedia literacy)
The Money Programme: Second Life: watch and understand a documentary about life online	discuss and create a new identity	write answers to a questionnaire	
listen to a radio programme about important roles in films	talk about life experiences; talk about your life story		**Option 1** Activity 3: *Writing the news* (Print literacy)
listen to news reports	talk about an important news story/event	write a news report; learn to use time linkers: *as soon as*, *while*, *during*, *until* and *by the time*	**Option 2** Activity 8: *Building links* (Hypertext literacy, Search literacy and Information literacy)
listen to people telling anecdotes; learn to keep a story going	tell a true story or a lie		**Option 3** Activity 11: *Envisioning the facts* [see also Unit 5, Option 1]
Hustle: watch and listen to a drama about a burglar and a famous painting	discuss fictional crime dramas; tell a narrative	write a short newspaper article	(Multimedia literacy)
	discuss attitudes now in comparison to ones you had earlier in life	write messages; learn to use note form	**Option 1**
listen to predictions about the future of communication	talk about how things will change in the future		Activity 5: *Cryptic messages* (Texting literacy)
listen to telephone conversations involving misunderstandings	learn to reformulate and retell a story about a misunderstanding; role-play resolving a misunderstanding		**Option 2** Activity 17: *Choose your own adventure* (Gaming literacy)
The Virtual Revolution: watch and understand a documentary about the impact of the internet	talk about communication preferences	write a memo	
	discuss the qualities needed for different jobs; complete a survey and discuss the results		**Option 1**
listen to two people describing dream jobs gone wrong	talk about past habits	write a covering letter; learn to organise your ideas	Activity 31: *My digital life* (Filtering literacy) **Option 2**
listen to people making decisions in a meeting	learn to manage a discussion; participate in a meeting and create a business plan		Activity 42: *Flickr vocabulary book* (Participatory literacy and Multimedia literacy)
Gavin and Stacey: watch and understand a comedy programme about a man's first day in a new job	describe a day in your life	write about daily routines	
	discuss how technology has changed the world; talk about different types of transport and their uses	write an advantages versus disadvantages essay; learn to use discourse markers	**Option 1** Activity 11: *Envisioning the facts* [see also Unit 2, Option 3] (Multimedia literacy)
listen to people answering difficult general knowledge questions	do a short general knowledge questionnaire; answer questions on your area of expertise		**Option 2** Activity 19: *A picture a day* (Mobile literacy, Multimedia literacy
listen to conversations about technical problems; learn to respond to requests	role-play asking and responding to requests		and Personal literacy)
Top Gear: watch and understand a programme about a race between a car and two people	present and describe a new machine	write an advertisement for a new machine	

COMMUNICATION BANK page 158   AUDIO SCRIPTS page 164

- Activity 34, *Online me* asks each student to create an online multimedia poster with images (and possibly videos), which they can then present orally to the class.

- Activity 35, *Personal blogging* asks each student to set up a personal blog and write a first blog post (again accompanied by images and videos).

This class's speaking skills are significantly weaker than their writing skills, so Carla is keen to ensure that the digital literacies activities she chooses include speaking practice. Carla sees that the Unit 1 coursebook speaking task encourages students to talk about their families. She realises that if she asks students to produce an audio slideshow which includes images of their families – thus giving the activity a slightly more specific focus, which makes it directly relevant to the coursebook topic – she will also be including some elements of the speaking skill in the activity (Activity 13). On the other hand, if she asks her students to each create an online multimedia poster with images, the speaking skill will be included in the oral presentation at the end (Activity 34). Finally, a third option is for students to write individual blog posts, introducing themselves and their families and including images, and add them to a class or individual blog (Activity 35). Because this final activity emphasises writing rather than speaking, it is not as ideally suited to her students and their need to practise speaking.

In this case, Carla began by considering *Pedagogical factors*, particularly the syllabus and students' language needs. Having done so, and having narrowed her choice down to Activities 13 and 34, she can now focus on the remaining *Factors affecting digital activity choice* listed in Table 3.1 – *Personal factors* such as learners' ages and interests, as well as *Digital factors* such as their tech levels, digital literacy levels, and the equipment and tools available – as she looks at each activity in detail on the relevant pages in Chapter 2. All of these factors will potentially affect which option works best for Carla and her class.

Finally, Carla decides to use Activity 34, *Online me*. She has access to a computer lab in her school, so she will be able to have students work individually on computers to produce personal online posters. She thinks her students, who are young adults, will respond well to creating multimedia posters with images and videos, especially as they already carry images and videos on their mobile phones. She will include additional writing practice by having students prepare scripts and plan what they want to say about their posters, but she will put particular emphasis on speaking by allowing them to rehearse before presenting their posters orally to the class, and asking students to give feedback on their classmates' oral presentations. In the end, then, she has made her decision to use Activity 34 by taking into account a combination of *Pedagogical factors*, *Personal factors* and *Digital factors* from Table 3.1.

Carla then needs to consider whether the digital literacy activity she has chosen for Unit 1 will replace or supplement the coursebook writing and speaking activities. An activity using a number of digital technologies will generally take longer than a traditional skills-based activity, but it provides more extended skills practice as well as integrating digital literacies. However, time limitations may mean that some other activities need to be dropped. In this case Carla decides to do the coursebook speaking activity in a previous class for extra speaking practice, but to leave out the coursebook writing activity.

Units 2–5

Look again at the syllabus grid above, and decide which of the options for each unit *you* would choose, if you were using this coursebook with your own students. There are no right or wrong choices here: the digital literacy activity you select for each unit will very much depend on your context. To help you choose, refer back to Table 3.1 when making your decisions.

The topic-driven approach

In the section above, we looked at how activities that enhance digital literacies can be mapped onto an already existing syllabus, which is defined by the coursebook. This is the context in which a great many teachers find themselves. However, some teachers need, or want, to create their own syllabuses. Here is another common scenario.

Meet Rod, who has an advanced conversation class (say, Common European Framework C1) several times a week with adult learners. Rod does not have a specific coursebook or syllabus to follow. Instead, he needs to find out what his students are interested in, and ensure that plenty of speaking practice is designed around a variety of topics. He therefore starts out by considering a combination of *Personal factors* and *Pedagogical factors* from Table 3.1. In the first class Rod finds out what themes his students would like to explore, and as a group they draw up a list of topics and activities for the coming term. Rod finds that his students are interested in politics, current affairs, their jobs, and sports, that they enjoy debates and discussions, and that they would especially like to give individual oral presentations. Rod knows that students can archive any digital artefacts or presentations they produce in e-portfolios, along with feedback he and their peers have provided, and revisit them whenever they wish (see *Assessing digital work*, *Assessing through e-portfolios* later in this chapter). He explains this concept to the students. He also takes *Digital factors* into account by carrying out Activity 2, *Being digitally literate*, in order to determine what digital literacy skills his students already have. He then discusses with the group which digital literacy skills they could usefully develop alongside their English language skills.

During the term, Rod chooses digital literacy activities that loosely fit with the topics currently being discussed in class, by referring to the *Topic* column in the *Digital activities grid* (Chapter 2, Table 2.1) and keeping in mind the table of *Factors affecting digital activity choice* (Table 3.1). In some cases, he uses an activity from the grid but changes the content and focus to fit the class topic, as in these two examples:

- Instead of having students showcase their hobbies in Activity 13, *Showcasing hobbies*, Rod asks them to create slideshows about their work. The rehearsal and recording of these slideshows provide students with the preparation to present orally to the group. This is followed by questions from the class. The recorded slideshows form part of the students' e-portfolios, where they are invited to leave additional feedback on each other's recordings.

- Instead of having the group produce a city guide in Activity 40, *Our city guide*, Rod has students work in pairs to prepare different news items on the class wiki. Students' written wiki texts form the basis for oral presentations to the class, and each news item is followed by discussion. Students can include hyperlinks from their e-portfolios to the class wiki, which provides a useful record of the language (especially vocabulary) used in each of the news item presentations.

The digital literacies-driven approach

An alternative approach is to use the *Digital activities grid* as the syllabus itself. Let's look at an example of this in practice.

Meet Ivana, who is teaching an upper intermediate level (say, Common European Framework B2) group of adolescents on an intensive summer course. She needs to teach the class for one 'free' period of an hour every day. She has no syllabus or coursebook, and has been told she can 'do what she likes'. Rather than doing a series of disconnected lessons using whatever materials she can find, Ivana decides to work with these students on their digital literacies, and to give them plenty of opportunity to create digital artefacts, which she thinks will appeal greatly to this age group. Her initial focus, then, is on a combination of *Digital factors* and *Personal factors* from Table 3.1.

In Ivana's case, using the language/grammar required to complete each activity as the organising principle of the syllabus is arguably less useful than using the digital literacies themselves as the organising principle. This sits well with current notions of grammar as process rather than product. Scott Thornbury, for example, argues that 'from a psychological perspective, grammar is less a *thing* than something that we *do*: it is a process' (2005, p. 43). His argument, which is backed up by research into psycholinguistics (Larsen-Freeman, 1997; van Lier, 2000), is that our focus should be less on teaching separate items of grammar, and more on allowing language to emerge during the process of completing tasks (cf. Breen and Candlin, 1980). Thus, Ivana works through the *Digital activities grid* sequentially, referring to the complexity ratings, and using the development of digital literacies as the underpinning rationale for her syllabus with this group of learners. The digital literacies activities tend to be project- or task-oriented, so that language/grammar does in fact emerge from the tasks themselves and is of secondary importance in the overall aims of the activities. Having said that, the digital literacy activities that Ivana chooses will necessitate certain language choices.

For example, Ivana chooses to do Activity 18, *History hunt*, in which students produce location-based local history quizzes for mobile phones. She knows that subject/object question forms (*Who does the plaque in the main square commemorate?/Who first sang at the opera house?*) are likely to crop up. She lets students start by working in pairs to create their local history questions, while she monitors and helps with language. If she sees that the class as a whole is having problems with subject/object question forms, or with any other language area, she can use a few examples from the quizzes to draw the class's attention to this, and then let them review and correct their questions with her help.

Using the *Digital activities grid* as the organising principle of her syllabus means that Ivana's students will gradually develop a robust portfolio of digital skills at the same time as they are honing their traditional language and literacy skills. The activities in the grid provide a total of approximately 60 hours of class time, which is likely to be more than enough to supply the entire content of Ivana's course. For other teachers in other contexts, the activities might supply part rather than all of the content.

Choosing activities for different levels and contexts

When we talk about developing digital literacies with language learners, we inevitably come across the issue of *level*. Because we are dealing with *digital literacy*, students will have different levels of competence, not just in the

English language but also in the use of technology. In this section we consider how to choose and adapt activities for different levels – of linguistic competence, and also of technological competence. We then look at a number of teaching contexts and how this may affect working with digital literacies.

Students' linguistic competence

The majority of the activities in the *Digital activities grid* (Table 2.1) are suitable for intermediate students and higher, although some are suitable for elementary students. Of course, many of the activities can be adapted for lower and/or higher levels. Because almost all of the activities are based on production (that is, students actually create or *produce* a digital artefact as part of the activity), they are to some extent self-grading. In other words, students will create digital products that reflect the language of which they are capable. A student with a very low level of English will produce a simple text, which may need close monitoring and teacher support at the creation stage. The text may also need to go through one or two drafts in order to improve. A higher level student will produce a digital text with more complex linguistic structures and a wider vocabulary, and may need to spend less time redrafting, although some redrafting could still be valuable. Having students work through several drafts of their own (and others') written work is key to the *process approach* to writing. Research has shown that redrafting based on teacher (and peer) feedback can help students develop and improve their writing skills (Hedge, 2005; White and Arndt, 1991). As such, it is an approach encouraged in many of the writing activities in Chapter 2, particularly those which use wikis as their main platform (see Activity 40, *Our city guide*, Activity 41, *Our city on Wikipedia* and Activity 46, *Travel tips* for example).

The greatest challenge is in using activities at lower levels rather than at higher levels. There are a number of general practices we can adopt to help lower level students cope with more linguistically challenging activities. These include:

- creating a model text for students to base their own work on;

- teaching necessary language in advance;

- pairing weaker and stronger students to produce texts together;

- monitoring and providing feedback and corrections while students are producing texts;

- using a process approach to writing activities, with students redrafting and improving their texts based on feedback over a number of correction stages;

- negotiating with students the amount of correction that we, as teachers, will do on their texts, and how much inaccuracy is acceptable (or un-acceptable) to both our students and ourselves;

- encouraging students to use dictionaries and thesauruses to enhance their work;

- allowing some first language use in instructions and any preparation stages;

- allowing plenty of rehearsal time if students need to audio- or video-record themselves, or give an oral presentation.

All of these practices are aimed at supporting students linguistically. They are not unique to classes that are working with technology; rather, they are common practice when working with lower level students. Just because we are working with digital literacies does not mean we can afford to drop the pedagogical practices that underpin *all* sound language teaching in the classroom.

The *Pedagogical factors* in Table 3.1 serve as a general reminder that we must consider language elements when choosing activities to use with our students.

Students' technological competence

It is a common fallacy that students with a lower language level have less developed technological abilities. However, you may have an IT technician in an elementary class – she will be an expert technology user, but not an expert English language user. You may have an advanced student who has been studying and speaking English for decades, but is a novice with technology. So we shouldn't assume that lower level students will be less proficient with technology, or that higher level students will be more profi-cient with it.

Most classrooms are heterogeneous in terms of technological competence. Some of your learners may be extremely competent and habitual users of technology, while others will be less so. Previous experience with technology obviously plays a part. So, too, may age, but it is not always the case that younger students are more tech-savvy than older students (see Box 1.2). Not only will there be a range of technological competence among your students, but some students may be very competent in some areas, and less so in others. For example, those of your students who habitually use social networking sites may have well-developed *personal* and *network literacies.* Those who use the internet for study or research may have well-developed *search* and *information literacies.* Those who have used mobile phones for a number of years may have well-developed *mobile literacy.* Or not . . .

To obtain a clearer picture of the range of your students' technological competence in any one class, we have therefore suggested that you start by doing one or both of the introductory activities in the *Digital activities grid* (Activity 1, *Technology past and present* and Activity 2, *Being digitally literate*). As a rule of thumb, we should start by integrating activities that are less demanding in terms of technological expertise, and progress towards those that are more demanding. Of course, a teacher who happens to have a class whose members are all especially tech-savvy may be able to determine the order of activities by topic or interest value alone. However, this kind of class is still quite exceptional.

Once you have a clear idea of where your students' digital strengths (and weaknesses) lie, you can choose and/or adapt activities to suit the group. For example, if you find that in a particular class everybody already has a profile on a social networking site, you may get a good response to activities relating to personal and network literacy (e.g. Activity 33, *Faking it* and Activity 36, *Setting the scene*). Students will have plenty to contribute to a discussion on digital identity, having a lot of personal experience to draw on. On the other hand, if you have a class of students who are mostly uninter-ested in social networking, you may want to skip digital literacy activities that specifically focus on social networking sites, or at least leave them until later in the course. This is not to say that you should avoid activities in areas your students have no experience in: after all, the aim of including digital literacies in your language course is specifically to help students develop these. But in cases where students show reluctance towards certain technologies, tools or techniques (such as mobile devices or social networking sites, or indeed complex activities like coding), there is an argu-ment for introducing these much later in a course, if at all. To avoid alienating or frightening our students, we need to take not only their general *interests* into account, but their specific *attitudes* towards and *experience* with new technologies, as the digital factors in Table 3.1 remind us.

Yet, as with the teaching of language, students may not always clearly perceive their own needs and may in fact require work on a specific digital literacy. Even if they think they don't, most young learners probably *need* to learn about digital safety and online identity protection if they are regular users of social networking sites, where they may well already be using their growing English language skills to make connections with people outside their own country and culture (e.g. Activity 36, *Setting the scene* and Activity 37, *Footprints in the wires*). Students doing a university English course as part of a degree may *need* to hone their search and information literacy skills to help them write academic papers, whatever the language or languages – very likely including English – they are using for their research (e.g. Activity 26, *Search me* and Activity 27, *Tree octopus*). In other words, it's useful for us, as teachers, to distinguish between what our students may *want* (or not want) in terms of digital literacy skills, and what they may *need*. It is important, then, that we consider *Pedagogical factors* alongside *Personal factors* and *Digital factors* when deciding which activities to use. If there seems to be a clash between students' wants and their needs, it may be helpful to discuss this openly with them.

Teachers' technological competence

Finally, to be able to help students develop their digital literacies, we as teachers need to develop a certain degree of technological competence ourselves. Integrating digital technologies into our teaching practice means that we need new skills beyond the purely pedagogical (see Chapter 2: *The TPACK framework for integrating technology use*). As teachers we may have received little or no training in the use of new technologies, which can make the thought of using them with our students daunting (see Box 2.2). However, as we will see, the internet provides a wealth of opportunities for us to develop our skills (see Chapter 4: *Building and maintaining PLNs*).

In addition, working through the Chapter 2 activities with our students will help us develop our own technological competence at the same time. For example, if we decide to do a blogging activity with our students (e.g. Activity 35, *Personal blogging*), we need first to set up a blog and ensure that we ourselves are familiar with how to post comments, add images and so on. *Tech support* links are provided in the activities in Chapter 2 wherever relevant, so teachers can refer to these for extra help if needed. Indeed, the *Digital activities grid* provides a framework for us as teachers to develop our own digital literacies, as noted earlier (see Chapter 2: *The digital activities grid*). By working through the activities we will inevitably 'level up' our skills and, by extension, our teaching (see Chapter 1: *A framework of digital literacies*).

This leads us to the question of where we should start. Which literacies and activities are 'easier' for us and our students to start with? Which require less technological competence, and which require more? We address this in the next section.

Overall complexity

The overall complexity of the activities in the *Digital activities grid* (Table 2.1) depends on the complexity of both the technologies *and* the literacies involved. *Technologically* speaking, people find something they do on a daily basis less challenging than something they rarely do, of course. For example, searching the web for information, sending SMS text messages, or posting Facebook status updates are activities that our students may well do every day, depending on their ages, interests, attitudes and access to technology. Carrying out digital literacy activities in class that require any of these skills will not be challenging for these particular students. However, as we have established above, what one individual or group of students finds easy, another individual or group may find more demanding.

Although it is difficult to establish an exact hierarchy of complexity of *literacies*, there clearly are some that are conceptually and/or technologically more demanding, as reflected in the *Framework of digital literacies* (Table 1.1). *Coding literacy*, for example, requires more complex technological skills than literacies that build on practices that students already engage in, such as *search literacy* or *information literacy*. *Remix literacy*, as a macroliteracy, also requires a complex combination of technological skills, and in addition it is conceptually demanding. We have fused technological and conceptual demands together to place digital literacies into an approximate order of increasing complexity. Those that are least complex, technologically and conceptually, have one star (*), whereas those that are most complex have five stars (*****). In Chapter 2, the individual activities in the *Digital activities grid* are marked with these stars, as are the activities themselves through-out the chapter, to indicate relative levels of complexity. When selecting activities to use with our students, we can keep these levels in mind.

Contexts

English is taught in a wide range of different contexts, as we are reminded in Table 3.1. The ages and levels of the students, the class size, the amount of access to technology, the wider language environment (an ESL or EFL context, for example), the learning culture – these all vary considerably. Learners themselves will have an array of reasons and motivations for learning English (Dörnyei and Hadfield, 2013). Indeed, each individual class composed of students and a teacher forms its own very specific context or microcosm, which makes it difficult to generalise about what approach works best for any single class (Senior, 2006), though digital literacies, like other content and skills, can helpfully be embedded within a class-centred framework (Senior, 2012).

We can nevertheless identify a number of typical classroom contexts, each of which requires a different approach to the digital literacies we choose to develop with our students.

Context 1: Teaching General English to adults

This is one of the most common language teaching contexts: a group of adults following a General English course, often with the help of a prescribed syllabus. For this group of learners, the syllabus-driven approach suggested earlier in the chapter is one way to start integrating digital literacies into classroom practice.

Context 2: Teaching General English to young learners

This is another common language teaching context. Young learner classes can be roughly divided into three groups according to age: very young learners (aged approximately 3–7), young learners or 'juniors' (aged approximately 8–12), and adolescents/teenagers (aged approximately 13–16). The activities that can be used with each of these three groups are different, as in this case age is clearly a key factor. There is a significant difference between a class of 6-year-olds and a class of 10-year-olds, for example, in terms of motor and cognitive skills (Cameron, 2001). Issues of digital safety are also of paramount importance when working with young learners (see Box 1.9).

Very young learners *(3–7)*   Teachers of this age group can focus on basic technological skills, such as helping students learn to use a drawing program, or to use a mouse to drag puzzle pieces around a screen. Many children in this age group have not yet learned to read and write, so the activities in this book need a considerable amount of adaptation if they are to be used with this cohort, and only some of them will be suitable. However, if the teacher's focus is mainly on technological skills, children at the older end of this age range can certainly contribute to the production of audio and video, e.g. by being audio-recorded singing songs or chants, or being filmed performing movement songs. With the help of the teacher they can play audio-visual language learning games, or choose and manipulate images to create visual digital storybooks, perhaps with audio voiceovers. By the age of 6, children are usually starting to develop basic reading and writing skills at school, so simple textual elements can be introduced into digital activities, such as matching pictures with vocabulary.

Young learners *(8–12)*   Children in this age group have more developed motor skills, as well as the ability to read and write to various degrees of proficiency. In many curricula around the world, mainstream primary school-ing includes an introduction to critical thinking as part of traditional (print) literacy, especially in the older age range of this group, and this fits well with some of the digital literacy activities in this book. When choosing digital literacy activities to map onto the young learner syllabus, the most import-ant factors to keep in mind include age appropriacy, and identifying topics of relevance and interest.

Adolescents *(13–16)*   Students in this age range usually have a good com-mand of reading and writing skills in their own language, and may well have experience of using technology both inside and outside the classroom. In teaching contexts where adolescents have regular access to technology, they tend to be confident and comfortable with technology, or 'tech-comfy', but they are not always 'tech-savvy' (see Box 1.2). Although they may know how to send text messages or update their status on social networking sites, for example, they are not always fully aware of the registers or conventions that different online genres require (see Chapter 1: *First focus: Language, Texting literacy*), or of how to protect their identity and reputation in public commu-nication forums (see Box 1.9). Similarly, although they may be confident when it comes to sharing photos or videos, they may be less aware of the importance of curating and tagging digital products (see Chapter 1: *Second focus: Informa-tion, Tagging literacy*). In many ways, this is the ideal age group with which to work on developing digital literacy skills. As with younger learners in the 8–12 age range, important factors to keep in mind include age appropriacy, and identifying topics of relevance and interest. The bulk of the activities in the *Digital activities grid* (Table 2.1) are suitable for this age group.

Context 3: Teaching Business English, ESP and EAP

Students of Business English will typically be working professionals, perhaps taking in-company classes with an English trainer, either individually or in groups. Alternatively, they may be university-age students studying a business-related undergraduate or postgraduate degree or diploma. English for Specific Purposes (ESP) students may be studying in similar contexts, although the content of their English language courses is generally more tightly focused, e.g. English for nursing, aviation, engineering, hospitality and tourism, or information technology. English for Academic Purposes (EAP) students are typically studying in an academic environment and may need to understand lectures in English, take notes, read and synthesise research, and produce essays and reports.

Most Business English, ESP or EAP teachers start work with a new student or group of students by conducting a needs analysis to determine exactly what should be taught. The first activity from the *Digital activities grid* (Activity 1, *Technology past and present*) can be carried out as part of an initial needs analysis, to help specifically identify the *digital* literacy skills most needed by these students. Choosing activities to integrate into a Business English, ESP or EAP syllabus is a matter of keeping in mind *Pedagogical factors* such as these students' language needs and wants, *Personal factors* such as their ages and interests, and *Digital factors* such as their experience of and access to technology. Many of the activities in the *Digital activities grid* are suitable for these types of students, although in some cases the teacher may want to adapt activities by choosing different lexical sets, or different topics to focus on. For example, for Activity 33, *Faking it*, students could produce an imaginary profile for a professional networking site such as LinkedIn, rather than a more personal site like Facebook. For Activity 35, *Personal blogging*, students could be asked to design and contribute to a company blog, rather than a personal blog.

Context 4: Teacher training

While the situation is beginning to change, many teacher training courses still have a limited focus on technology (see Box 2.2). This is partly because many teacher trainers have received little or no technological training themselves, so they are often not in a position to pass on any knowledge to their trainees, or are at a loss about how to effectively integrate new technologies into their training programmes. In addition, trainers may be unaware of the importance of digital literacies, their increased role in mainstream educational curricula, and their value in language teaching.

The first step for teacher trainers is to recognise the increased importance now being placed on digital literacies and twenty-first-century skills by governments, ministries of education and educational institutions, and to explore the growing role of digital competencies in mainstream curricula (see Chapter 1: *A framework of digital literacies*). For teacher trainers who feel that their own digital skills are underdeveloped and wish to 'level up' in this area, using some of the activities from Chapter 2 with language students, or carrying out activities themselves, is one way to acquire basic digital literacies. Alternatively, teacher trainers can adapt some of the activities in Chapter 2 to use on teacher training courses, in much the same way that Business English teachers can adapt activities for their contexts (see above). For example, when working with teacher trainees on how to teach *reading* skills, the trainer can demonstrate activities that focus on *print literacy*, with a particular emphasis on reading (e.g. Activity 3, *Writing the news*, and Activity 4, *Extreme weather*). When working on how to teach *writing* skills, the trainer can demonstrate activities that focus more heavily on producing written digital artefacts such as blog posts (Activity 35, *Personal blogging*) or wiki contributions (Activity 40, *Our city guide*, and Activity 41, *Our city on Wikipedia*), or can ask trainees to work with *hypertext literacy* (Activity 7, *Sports linking*, and Activity 8, *Building links*). If the course includes hands-on teaching practice for trainees, they can be encouraged to try out some of the activities themselves with their language students.

In short, it is possible to adapt many of the digital literacy activities in Chapter 2 to a range of English language teaching situations. Indeed, it is possible, as noted at the outset of the chapter, to adapt many activities to the teaching of languages other than English, and even to more general communications and new media courses. When adapting activities, it is useful to keep in mind the *Factors affecting digital activity choice* (Table 3.1) and to work with the information provided in the *Digital activities grid* (Table 2.1).

Generating further activities

The activities in the *Digital activities grid* can help students (and teachers) build up a core skillset of digital literacies. They also introduce students to activities with lifelong benefits: students can continue to engage in many of them on current and future language courses, as well as using them in their personal, social and professional lives outside the classroom. For example, in Activity 35, *Personal blogging*, students set up and start posting to a blog as a means of developing *personal literacy* (as well as *print* and *multimedia literacy*). They can continue to write blog posts at regular intervals in order to create a portfolio of written work. They may also continue to enhance their blogging skills by learning how to insert images and videos into their posts or add widgets to their blogs. Some students may already have per-sonal blogs, and they will be able to transfer their pre-existing digital skills to their language course blogs. On the other hand, students who have never blogged before may decide to create personal blogs in their own language on topics of personal interest. In this way, developing digital literacies can not only benefit language learning but can have repercussions well beyond the language classroom walls. But most importantly, perhaps, from the language teacher's perspective, once the students have learned to blog, a range of tasks can be set up around individual or class blogs as part of longer-term writing projects.

Blogging is not the only activity which provides teachers with the potential to generate further activities in the classroom. Many of the technological skills that students acquire while developing their digital literacies can be used in other language-focused classroom tasks. The list below contains a small sample of the digital skills covered in the activities in Chapter 2:

- Writing hypertext (e.g. Activity 7, *Sports linking*)
- Creating an infographic (e.g. Activity 11, *Envisioning the facts*)
- Creating a vodcast (e.g. Activity 14, *Selling English*)
- Creating a multimedia poster (e.g. Activity 34, *Online me*)
- Writing a blog post (e.g. Activity 35, *Personal blogging*)
- Contributing to a wiki (e.g. Activity 40, *Our city guide*)
- Uploading and tagging photos (e.g. Activity 42, *Flickr vocabulary book*)
- Creating a remix (e.g. Activity 50, *Movie mashup*)

Some of these skills are used in more than one activity, so students can apply the skills they learn several times as they create a range of digital artefacts. For example, once they learn to contribute to a wiki, they can reuse this skillset in several other activities. Moreover, other wiki tasks can be set up by the teacher in future classes, going well beyond the activities outlined in Chapter 2.

In addition, language learning activities in which students use the skills listed above do not need to be restricted to the classroom. As we will see below, some of the most exciting current educational developments involve teachers and learners working in the new kinds of learning spaces which are emerging thanks to the spread of mobile technologies and wireless networks.

Building new learning spaces

Our *learning spaces* have a dramatic impact on the kind of education that takes place within them (Brown, 2005; Oblinger, 2006). The idea that these 'spaces embody the pedagogical philosophies of their designers' is referred to by Torin Monahan as 'built pedagogy' (2002). He explains:

> *Built pedagogies operate along a continuum between discipline and auto-nomy. On the disciplinary side, they can restrict learning possibilities by not allowing for certain movements or flows. For example, desks bolted to the ground make flexible interpretations of spatial use extremely*

difficult, and they impose directions for how space should be used. In the middle of the discipline/autonomy spectrum, there are built pedagogies that enable but do not require flexible behaviors: movable partitions and desks illustrate space left open to interpretative use. Finally, on the autonomy end, open classrooms invite and almost demand that individuals appropriate space to their perceived needs.

Over recent decades, we've seen a transformation of *physical learning spaces*: we've begun to move away from rigidly structured classrooms, with their immovable rows of desks facing the teacher, towards flexible spaces where everything from the furniture to the walls can be repositioned. Over little more than a decade, we've seen an accelerated version of the same transformation in *virtual learning spaces*: we've started to move from locked-down institutional VLEs towards individualised PLEs and PLNs which draw on the richness and variety of web 2.0 (see Box 1.10). These parallel movements in our physical and virtual built pedagogy reflect the growing prominence of learner-centred educational approaches based on active participation, collaboration and personalisation. Such approaches are easier to put into practice in flexible spaces, whether those spaces are physical or virtual.

In fact, today's learning contexts are a hybrid of overlapping physical and virtual spaces which flow into and out of each other, tied together by new technologies. In an ideal scenario (and growing numbers of real-world scenarios) physical and virtual learning spaces reinforce each other's plasticity. Digital technologies give us access to customisable virtual learning spaces as they untether education from the fixed classrooms, set timetables and lockstep syllabuses typical of traditional physical learning spaces. But as we shift away from desktop and laptop computers and increasingly access our virtual learning spaces through mobile devices (see Box 1.1), our physical learning spaces can also become more flexible and customisable, with classrooms being reconfigured from lesson to lesson, and learning spreading into wirelessly networked physical spaces anywhere in the world. This is part of the promise of *m-learning* or, more accurately perhaps, *u-learning* (see Chapter 1: *First focus: Language, Mobile literacy*).

Students in new learning spaces

A number of the activities in the *Digital activities grid* focus specifically on *mobile literacy* (Activity 18, *History hunt,* Activity 19, *A picture a day* and Activity 20, *Mobile rules*). These are designed to help students think about new learning spaces, learn to navigate and communicate in them effectively, and come to appreciate the value of learning seamlessly across in-class and out-of-class contexts (see Chapter 1: *First focus: Language, Mobile literacy*). Mobile apps designed especially for language learning, along with educational podcasts and vodcasts, are resources students can use to practise English or other languages outside the classroom. But mobile devices also allow students to take on more *productive* roles. For example, Activity 18, *History hunt* encourages students to leave the classroom and explore their local environment, building their own quiz in a mobile app. Students can produce a whole range of English content outside the classroom, for instance in Activity 19, *A picture a day*, where they take photos and add accompanying text. Numerous activities have optional variations or extensions, where students can extend their learning outside formal learning spaces and engage in virtual learning networks using mobile apps such as Pinterest (Activity 9, *Food boards*), VoiceThread (Activity 13, *Showcasing hobbies*), Foursquare (Activity 18, *History hunt*), Instagram (Activity 19, *A picture a day*), TED (Activity 26, *Search me*), Flipboard (Activity 29, *News in my networks*) and TEDiSUB (Activity 38, *Going viral*).

Teachers and teacher trainers in new learning spaces

Hybrid learning spaces are also emerging as the new context for the application of teachers' TPACK (see Chapter 2: *The TPACK framework for integrating technology use*). For the foreseeable future, of course, teachers in many parts of the world will experience limitations on the flexibility of both their physical and virtual environments (see below). But no matter how restricted our current teaching spaces are, there are ways in which we can make a difference, as suggested in the list below.

- *We can make the most of whatever flexibility we already have to rearrange or expand our current physical learning spaces*, e.g. grouping desks together while students work on shared devices in the classroom, or allowing students to use mobile technologies outside the classroom in libraries, common rooms or even outdoors (e.g. Activity 18, *History hunt*).

- *We can ask our institutions for more flexibly furnished classrooms*, so that as wireless networks and mobile devices become more common we can adapt our classrooms more easily to the needs of each lesson.

- *We can suggest that our institutions invest in wireless networks and mobile technologies instead of upgrading hardwired computer labs*, which will allow students to use technology collaboratively in flexible physical spaces rather than sitting in rows in computer labs.

- *We can promote a BYOD (Bring Your Own Device) or BYOT (Bring Your Own Technology) model* (see Box 1.1) *and integrate our students' own personal mobile devices into lessons*, which will allow learning to flow more seamlessly between in-class and out-of-class activities (e.g. Activity 19, *A picture a day* and Activity 20, *Mobile rules*).

- *We can use flexible web 2.0 tools instead of rigid institutional VLEs*, for instance by helping students to build blogs (e.g. Activity 35, *Personal blogging*), contribute to wikis (Activity 40, *Our city guide* and Activity 41, *Our city on Wikipedia*), share images on photosharing sites (Activity 42, *Flickr vocabulary book* and Activity 47, *LOLcats*) or share videos on video-sharing sites (Activity 14, *Selling English* and Activity 50, *Movie mashup*). All of these are platforms students can continue to use in their personal lives, both in English and in their mother tongue.

Even a small start can be enough to establish a new direction in the shaping of learning spaces. Teacher trainers, in particular, can make a large difference, not only by trying to institute some of the listed changes in their own teaching contexts, but by sensitising teacher trainees to the emergence of new spaces and how they can use some of the above strategies to capitalise on these.

Teaching in technology-limited environments

Teachers may find themselves in environments which are technology-limited in a variety of ways. In much of the developing world, and in less advantaged parts of the developed world, obtaining adequate hardware and software may be problematic, internet access may be restricted or slow, and even the electricity supply may sometimes be unreliable.

While initiatives such as OLPC show promise, some of the greatest potential currently lies in student-owned mobile phones which, under a BYOD model or an even more open BYOT model (see Box 1.1; on BYOT, see: Ferries-Rowe, 2012; Macgibbon and Tarica, 2012), could allow the integration of the internet into educational contexts where it is otherwise unavailable (Nielsen and Webb, 2011; Richardson and Mancabelli, 2011). A BYOD or, more so, a BYOT model raises certain issues to do with standards and specifications of devices, network capacity and security, and equity of access, but it appears to be the only viable and sustainable option for institutions which cannot fund regular, ongoing rollouts of hardware (Pegrum, Oakley and Faulkner, 2012). Yet many educational institutions and many teachers, especially in the developed world, continue to require students to turn off their mobile devices at the classroom door, often confining students in physical learning spaces with little or no computing power or net access. It may instead be far more productive to negotiate the ways in which students can use their mobile devices to support and enhance their language learning during class time, with clear guidelines about acceptable behaviour (see Activity 20, *Mobile rules*).

Where internet access is available, it may be limited by governmental and institutional initiatives to keep students safe as well as focused on their work by blocking access to large sections of the web, typically including social networking and social sharing sites. While well-meaning, such initiatives are ultimately futile (since students find ways to circumvent them) and educationally punishing, because they limit access to valuable media content on YouTube, informative conversations on Facebook, or up-to-the-minute commentary on Twitter. We saw in Activity 4, *Extreme weather*, for example, how a specific focus on tools such as Twitter and Facebook can help develop students' *print* and *information literacy*. As the 2008 Australia–New Zealand *Horizon Report* puts it in a discussion of higher education:

> *Security concerns too often go too far. Both policies and firewalls are severely limiting access to – and hampering the utility of – the Internet, the use of digital materials, and many benefits of social networking. (Johnson, Levine and Smith, 2008, p. 3)*

These limitations are compounded still further by the national internet filtering schemes employed in some countries, which may well prevent access to services like YouTube, Facebook and Twitter, along with a great deal of other educationally useful material, on a much wider scale (see Box 1.11).

Teachers working in technology-limited environments may be able to employ some of the low-tech or no-tech versions outlined for the activities in the *Digital activities grid* (Table 2.1). Where such versions are possible, the absence of technology does not undermine the learning aims. In the low-tech and no-tech versions of Activity 16, *Avatars*, for example, students can create online characters (avatars) in drawings, and this does not detract from the discussion about projective identity which follows. The low-tech and no-tech versions of Activity 34, *Online me* work on a similar premise: if students produce posters on paper instead of online, this does not detract from the important follow-up discussion about what elements of our identities we should share on the internet. Even in the absence of technology, then, it is possible to teach students about digital literacies. It is also worthwhile: students may well have internet access outside of class, and many will spend a lot of time online in their future personal and professional lives.

Assessing digital work

Assessment should be aligned with both the learning objectives and the context (Palloff and Pratt, 2009). If digital technologies allow greater customisation of learning, they also allow – even require – greater customisation of assessment. Traditional assessments, which are normally standardised and individually focused, are ill-matched with the assessment of collaborative digital literacies (Gillen and Barton, 2009; Mills, 2010). More creative and collaborative approaches to assessment not only permit students to display a greater range of learning in a greater variety of ways, but can help avoid traditional bugbears like plagiarism (see Box 1.12).

Given the importance of collaboration in contemporary workplaces, as noted in the 2012 Higher Education *Horizon Report*, it is appropriate that students are increasingly evaluated not just on overall outcomes but on group dynamics (Johnson, Adams and Cummins, 2012). Moreover, Rena Palloff and Keith Pratt (2009, p. 36) remind us that 'collaborative activities are best assessed collaboratively': this might include students' *self-assessment* of their own contributions alongside *peer assessment* of other participants' contributions. Of course, such assessment can be *formative* as well as *summative*, with students being invited to add to teacher feedback on classmates' online work during a course. Writing for a broader audience is not only motivating for students (see Chapter 1: *First focus: Language, Print literacy*) but helps them develop good feedback techniques when responding to others, while ensuring that they themselves receive more extensive feedback than they would otherwise.

More specifically, from a language learning point of view, activities that require students to comment on each other's writing in progress, and then to redraft their own work in light of comments received, fit with a *process approach* which, as noted earlier, can help students improve their writing (see *Choosing activities for different levels and contexts, Students' linguistic competence* earlier in this chapter). This approach to writing can be seen in Activity 40, *Our city guide* and Activity 41, *Our city on Wikipedia*, for example, and can potentially be applied to any writing activity in which students provide feedback on each other's drafts. Wikis are an ideal platform for such activities.

Students can even be asked for input on the design and execution of assessments, giving them greater ownership of the assessment process (Palloff and Pratt, 2009). For example, if students are producing blog posts as part of their coursework (e.g. Activity 35, *Personal blogging*), they can be asked to contribute to the assessment criteria for the posts. Criteria might include not just language-related areas, but use of supporting images and videos in posts, appropriate hyperlinking, design elements, and so on. This is a particularly valuable technique when used by teacher trainers with their trainees.

A digital assessment matrix

When there is digital work to be assessed, teachers like Carla, Rod and Ivana, whom we met earlier (see *Incorporating activities into the syllabus and time-table*), might begin with a matrix such as that in Table 3.2.

Let's take Carla as an example. Given that her use of digital activities is closely tied to her students' completion of a coursebook syllabus, she will need to fuse elements of traditional language and literacy assessment with digital elements she considers to be important. For each piece of work she sets, Carla will need to decide whether to emphasise:

- *process*, i.e. elements such as *organisation, interaction* and *communication*, which are demonstrated through students' individual and group work (which in high-tech contexts will occur in their PLEs), and which can be tracked through discussion board comments, blog feedback, wiki history logs, or reflective journals in various formats;

- *product*, i.e. elements such as *language, (digital) literacies* and *task achievement*, which are demonstrated through students' final individual or group products; of course, these elements have many possible components, with *language* potentially covering areas as diverse as vocabulary, grammar, discourse conventions and style, and *digital literacies* covering any of the many literacies discussed in this book (see Chapter 1).

She will also need to decide on the most appropriate combination of *self-assessment, peer assessment* and *teacher assessment. Self-assessment* can be very valuable when students are required to reflect on and compose a narrative of their learning journey, for example in a final macrotask (see below). *Peer assessment* is valuable when group work has been carried out and collaborative skills are important. *Teacher assessment*, the most traditional approach, is valuable when it comes to authoritative evaluation of products – such as the lexical appropriacy of an individual blog post (see e.g. Activity 35, *Personal blogging*) or the level of multimedia literacy displayed in a group-produced video advertisement (see e.g. Activity 12, *Sales techniques*) – and in order to ensure standardisation of marking.

In the matrix, which might be applied to a collaborative wiki-based group exercise (see e.g. Activity 40, *Our city guide*), Carla has chosen to allow *self-assessment* of individual *organisation* and *peer assessment* of key group work elements, namely *interaction* and *communication*. She has chosen authoritative *teacher assessment* of *language* and *digital literacies*, but has decided to balance *self-* and *peer assessment* with her own *teacher assessment* of overall *task achievement*. Having made these decisions,

Table 3.2 Digital assessment matrix

		Self-assessment	Peer assessment	Teacher assessment
Process	Organisation	X		
	Interaction		X	
	Communication		X	
Product	Language			X
	(Digital) literacies			X
	Task achievement	X	X	X

Carla might then go on to produce detailed descriptions of each of the above categories, indicating exactly which aspects of each will be assessed (e.g. *language*: grammar, cohesion and register; *digital literacies*: multimedia literacy and information literacy) and giving examples of the kinds of evidence of each she expects to see. In some contexts, it might be appropriate to develop detailed rubrics, giving typical indicators of student performance at different levels of the grading system. With more advanced students, or teacher trainees, it might be possible to invite student contributions to the choice of criteria as well as the development of descriptions and rubrics.

Assessing through e-portfolios

E-portfolios are collections of documents, often in multiple media, demonstrating the achievements of an individual. Dedicated e-portfolio software exists, such as the open source Mahara (mahara.org) or the commercial PebblePad (www.pebblepad.co.uk), but in fact e-portfolios – like PLEs or PLNs – can be built on any platform where it's possible to collect together documents or links to documents: the possibilities include blogs, wikis and websites. Naturally, e-portfolios are typically associated with high-tech environments, as indicated in many Chapter 2 activities.

In such high-tech contexts, students can be encouraged to set up PLEs during their courses (see Box 1.10), and to export key examples of their best work from their PLEs to e-portfolios during or at the end of their studies. E-portfolios ensure that the flexibility of PLEs carries through into flexibility of assessment: they are an ideal way of capturing personalised learning and turning it into a narrative of a student's learning journey, which can be commented on by both the student and their peers, as well as discussed with (and ultimately assessed by) teachers. Even in contexts where students do not have well-developed PLEs, any completed digital work can still be stored in an e-portfolio.

If we return to the list of digital literacy activities Carla chose to integrate into her coursebook syllabus (see *Incorporating activities into the syllabus and timetable*, *The coursebook-driven approach* earlier in the chapter), we see that many of the products of the high-tech versions of these activities could be included in students' e-portfolios. For Unit 1 of her coursebook, Carla chose Activity 34, *Online me*, in which students produce multimedia posters, which could easily be added to, or hyperlinked to from, their e-portfolios. Equally, most of the activities Carla identified for Units 2–5 require students to produce appropriate digital artefacts which could be included in their e-portfolios:

- Unit 2:
  - Option 1 (Activity 3, *Writing the news*): students produce news articles.
  - Option 2 (Activity 8, *Building links*): students produce lists of links.
  - Option 3 (Activity 11, *Envisioning the facts*): students produce infographics.

- Unit 3:
  - Option 2 (Activity 17, *Choose your own adventure*): students produce group games.

- Unit 4:
  - Option 1 (Activity 31, *My digital life*): students produce a list of advice.
  - Option 2 (Activity 42, *Flickr vocabulary book*): students produce an image-based vocabulary book.

- Unit 5:
  - Option 1 (Activity 11, *Envisioning the facts*): students produce infographics.
  - Option 2 (Activity 19, *A picture a day*): students produce daily photographic records.

Thus, after completing the first five units of the coursebook, Carla's students will already have several digital artefacts, created either individually or in small groups, that can be added to, or linked to from, their e-portfolios. The Extension sections at the end of these activities and many others (see Chapter 2) remind teachers of this possibility.

However, it is likely that if they are given the choice, each student will wish to include a different selection of digital artefacts in their e-portfolio. There is inevitably some tension between the individualised nature of e-portfolios, which allow students freedom to express and represent themselves in varying ways, and the need for authoritative feedback and standardised grading.

One possibility is that the pieces of work included in students' e-portfolios have already been assessed individually, making the e-portfolios a record of assessed achievements. In this case, Carla might require students to include a certain number and range of work samples and might then set a final macrotask, for example asking students to reflect on their learning journeys, perhaps with a focus on key areas of language or literacy. Even when using a matrix like the one in Table 3.2, such reflective macrotasks may be challenging to assess, but they can contribute substantially to students' understanding of their own learning while also nicely rounding out their e-portfolios.

A second possibility is that not all of the work, or none of it, has already been assessed, in which case Carla will need to apply flexible assessment criteria in order to make the most of the individualised nature of the e-portfolios, while still communicating her expectations to students and standardising her marking. In order to do this, she could draw on the matrix outlined in Table 3.2 for each task she intends to assess, as well as giving students some choice in which tasks they undertake (for example, requiring them to complete four out of five possible assessments). Thus, within the e-portfolios, she will need to assess a series of tasks and to combine the resulting assessments to produce an overall grade for each student. She might also include a compulsory final macrotask, such as that outlined in the paragraph above.

A third possibility, which could be combined with either of the first two, is to evaluate the completed e-portfolios as digital 'showcases', that is, treating them as though students were using them to support college admissions procedures or job applications. As is always the case with e-portfolios, students still require detailed instructions about what to include, how to present it, how much flexibility they have to customise their work, and how they will be assessed. Carla might even bring in an 'expert panel' of professionals – say, college admissions officers or employers – to give feedback as part of the assessment process. Of course, the development of digital showcases doesn't have to be merely a classroom assessment task. Well-conceptualised e-portfolios, with some additional polishing up in the light of self-, peer and teacher assessment, can be used by students as actual digital CVs. In presenting these to future admissions officers or potential employers, students can demonstrate their standard language and literacy skills at the same time as they demonstrate their digital literacies and technological competence – a winning combination!

Chapter 4
From implementation to research

In this final chapter we suggest ways in which you can continue learning about digital literacies and new technologies, improve your understanding of theory and practice, and work through issues and challenges. In particular, we suggest ways to share and enhance your learning through professional networks. As such, this chapter closes the loop of teacher activity, which leads from research to (reflective) practice and back to (action) research, including dissemination of new understandings.

Conducting and sharing action research

Given the speed of technological development, it's hard to future-proof guidelines on using new tools. For that reason, it's useful for all of us to engage in action research to investigate and report on the value of new technologies in our classrooms. According to Tom O'Donoghue and Simon Clarke (2010, p. 9), action research:

> involves thinking systematically about what happens in the classroom (or in the wider school environment), implementing action where improvements are thought possible, and monitoring and evaluating the effects of the action with a view to continuing the improvement.

An old and broad tradition that has gained popularity internationally as a means of professional development, action research has found particular resonance in education, notably in teacher development (McNiff and Whitehead, 2011; Mertler, 2009). Although it has many variations, all are based on an action-reflection cycle like the one shown in the figure. Action research allows us, as teachers, to move beyond our intuitions about best practice in local contexts, and engage in more systematic inquiry to develop explicit understandings that can be shared across contexts (Baumfield, Hall and Wall, 2008). Typically, we might formulate a question or problem related to our teaching or our students' learning; review literature and gather ideas relevant to the question or problem; take action designed to improve our

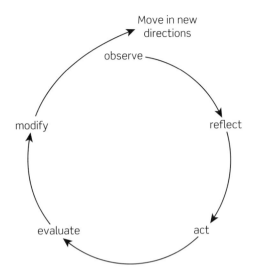

An action-reflection cycle
Source: McNiff and Whitehead, 2011

teaching or our students' learning; evaluate the effectiveness of the action by collecting data (through observations, surveys, interviews or assessments); develop a plan which could involve extension or modification of the initial action (and which could also lead to a new research cycle); and disseminate the results.

There are few limitations to the areas that can be investigated, or indeed that need to be investigated. Here are a handful of ideas about broad areas to consider:

- ways of developing or extending any of the literacies discussed in Chapter 1;

- ways of modifying or supplementing any of the activities discussed in Chapter 2;

- ways of tailoring the teaching of digital literacies to any of the contexts discussed in Chapter 3;

- ways of extending the teaching of digital literacies beyond the contexts discussed in Chapter 3;

- ways of making the most of web 2.0 tools in language teaching and learning;

- ways of making the most of mobile apps in language teaching and learning;

- ways of developing intercultural literacy across widely differing cultures.

When we disseminate the results of our action research, we crystallise our own learning, contribute to the development of the field, and help enrich our own and others' classroom practice. Dissemination options include *talks*, ranging from staffroom presentations to conference papers, and *publications*, ranging from newsletter reports to refereed journal articles. But there are digital options, too. If we share our findings through our PLNs (see below), we not only enhance our own learning networks, but may also benefit from feedback and commentary that could feed into new action research cycles.

Building and maintaining PLNs

In a world of ever-changing information and knowledge, we have no choice but to become lifelong learners. While PD courses and seminars have a role to play, it's equally important for us as teachers – just like our students – to foster our PLNs (see Box 1.10 for more on PLNs, including the distinction between more tightly focused PLEs, which are typically attached to time-limited courses of study, and more extensive PLNs, which can be cultivated over a lifetime). These are the trusted networks of people and resources we can rely on for support (when we have a question or problem and would like help from experts or more experienced colleagues) and information (whether for regular updates or specific details we need at a given moment). Of course, PLNs are not just about receiving information, but sharing it; they're not just about asking questions, but answering them; and they're not just about learning from others' experiences, but reporting on our own action research (see above).

As a result, in addition to helping us to keep *learning*, PLNs can help us to cultivate a positive online *reputation* (see Box 1.9) as we collaborate with others and disseminate knowledge. Cristina Costa (2011, pp. 92–3) writes:

> *Learning how to develop and manage a professional online presence is of prime importance in today's world. . . . In a nutshell, a digital identity resembles an enhanced business card to which an extensive list of examples of the person's practice and professional activities [is] attached. In the case of knowledge workers it can comprise their publications and academic memberships, but it will also include the networks and communities they belong to (PLN), as well as their PLEs. In this sense, one's professional digital identity is a dynamic representation of one's learning process and professional development.*

PLNs also provide a basis for demonstrating to students the practice of lifelong learning. Like our students, we can start small on just one platform before expanding our networks to take in other options. Any of the platforms outlined below – nearly all of which are free to use, at least in their basic versions – offer a good starting point.

Keeping a blog

One way to kick off a PLN is to set up a blog with one of the popular blogging services referred to in Chapter 2. Blogs provide a good anchor for a PLN, because they allow you to set up a blogroll which links to other blogs you choose to follow; to disseminate questions and comments to your own followers; and to converse with your followers around your postings. In comparison to microblogging services such as Twitter and even social networking sites such as Facebook (see below), blogs typically encourage more sustained conversation and may offer greater opportunities for deep reflection.

Finding relevant blogs

There are numerous informative blogs dedicated to English language teaching, such as *Jeremy Harmer's Blog* (jeremyharmer.wordpress.com) and Scott Thornbury's *An A–Z of ELT* (scottthornbury.wordpress.com). *Larry Ferlazzo's Websites of the Day* (larryferlazzo.edublogs.org) and *Nik* [Peachey]*'s Learning Technology Blog* (nikpeachey.blogspot.com) are situated at the intersection of English teaching and new technologies. You'll find many other relevant English language teaching blogs listed in Macmillan's *One Stop Blogs* list (blogs.onestopenglish.com). Blogs with a broader focus on digital literacies include Julia Davies's *Digital Literacies* (www.digital-literacies.com), while there's a still broader focus on new technologies in education in Lisa Nielsen's *The Innovative Educator* (theinnovativeeducator.blogspot.com), Shelly Terrell's *Teacher Reboot Camp* (teacherbootcamp.edublogs.org) and Steve Wheeler's *Learning with 'e's* (steve-wheeler.blogspot.com).

All three authors of the current book maintain blogs, reflecting our commitment to this kind of interaction with our PLNs. Gavin Dudeney's blog, *That'SLife* (slife.dudeney.com), contains reflections on current issues in English language teaching, with a particular focus on learning technologies. Nicky Hockly's *E-moderation Station* (www.emoderationskills.com) is aimed primarily at moderators of online and technology-mediated learning. Mark Pegrum's blog, *E-language* (elanguage.edublogs.org), consists of commentary on e-learning, mobile learning and language learning conferences and courses. You can feel free to visit us on our blogs, join in our conversations, and build our blogs into your own networks. Note that you can keep track of blogs you're interested in either by setting up a blogroll (see above) or using an aggregator service like Google Reader (see below).

Getting started with your blog

Setting up a blog is relatively straightforward. Commonly used blogging services include Blogger (www.blogger.com) and Edublogs (edublogs.org); for help with either of these, take a look at the *Tech support* sections attached to the relevant activities (see e.g. Chapter 2: Activity 3, *Writing the news*). In this way, the activities covered in this book can serve to develop your own technological competence as a teacher, as indicated previously (see Chapter 2: *The digital activities grid* and Chapter 3: *Choosing activities for different levels and contexts, Teachers' technological competence*). Note that both Blogger and Edublogs have mobile apps for Apple iOS devices, while Blogger also has apps for Android and BlackBerry devices. This makes it easy to access and post to blogs wherever you may be, allowing you to carry your PLN with you into a variety of formal and informal learning spaces.

As can be seen from the example blogs listed above, it's a good idea to decide on an overarching theme for your blog, so that it has a well-defined target audience and an obvious developmental strand for you and your readers. Keeping a blog involves some commitment, and it helps to write regularly and to respond fully to comments when a conversation does develop. Scott Thornbury's *An A–Z of ELT*, as one example, features a weekly post, and each new post signals the end of the previous conversation. This kind of structure helps keep both the writer and the readers focused and makes the content stimulating as well as manageable. On the other hand, some blogs, like Mark Pegrum's *E-language*, contain more irregular posts made in response to specific events, in this case conferences and courses. Naturally, as stressed throughout Chapter 2, blogs can include a great deal of multimedia content alongside traditional text (see e.g. Activity 35, *Personal blogging*). Communicating multimodally is a good way of developing your own digital literacies as well as engaging differing audiences!

When writing your blog entries, try to focus on topics that are currently relevant to your work, such as the theory or practical application of digital literacies, or useful tools you have found. Sharing your questions, reflections and research with a network of professional educators will provide you with feedback on topics of relevance to you and your students, while enriching the understandings and practices of those you interact with. You may well find yourself taking ideas and suggestions from blog discussions back into your classroom and putting them into practice, before sharing your revised thoughts with your blog audience. In this way, your blogging platform can be an important complement to your action research (see above).

Finding an audience will undoubtedly be your biggest challenge. You might start by inviting colleagues and peers to visit and subscribe to your blog, but as it grows you could also leverage the power of Twitter, Facebook and similar channels to advertise your blog and announce new posts.

Tweeting and Facebooking

Establishing an account on a microblogging service like Twitter (twitter.com) or a social networking site like Facebook (www.facebook.com) is quick and easy. Both have apps for Android, Apple iOS, BlackBerry and Windows devices, meaning once again that it's possible to access your PLN wherever you have a 3G/4G or wifi connection.

Twitter doesn't require mutual acceptance of friendship links, so once you have your own account, you can sign up to follow any public account. Use the search box to locate some experts and/or colleagues to follow. Many English language educators *tweet* regularly, and there's even a forum known as *ELTchat* (eltchat.com), where an ever-changing group of professionals meets twice weekly to discuss issues in English language teaching. Subjects are proposed – and voted on – by members of the network and there is a lively support site featuring transcripts alongside

E-learning experts on Twitter
URL: goo.gl/lB0We

additional resources such as articles and documents. Many professionals working in the broader area of e-learning are also very active on Twitter; for a regularly updated list, scan the QR code (shown above) or type the URL into your web browser. Once again, all three authors of the current book can be found on Twitter, with Gavin Dudeney and Nicky Hockly being contactable under the Twitter handle @TheConsultantsE (see also: twitter.com/TheConsultantsE) and Mark Pegrum being contactable under the Twitter handle @OzMark17 (see also: twitter.com/OzMark17).

Once you have identified a few key individuals, you should check out the lists of people they follow in order to find further people you might like to follow. It will take some time to 'curate' your list, as you add new names and perhaps remove others, depending on the relevance of their tweets to your own interests. You'll need to decide whether to take a *maximalist approach* (where you follow hundreds, even thousands, of people, and dip into your Twitter stream from time to time, not worrying about reading everything but assuming that important information will be retweeted often enough that you're likely to eventually see most of it), or a *minimalist approach* (where you follow a smaller network of key people who are likely, between them, to tweet or retweet most of the information that's of interest to you, and where you try to read most, if not all, of their tweets). As you start to post material yourself, your own network of followers will begin to build up so that, in time, you can invite their responses to questions or problems you might be facing in your teaching.

There are numerous educators' groups that liaise through Facebook and other social networking sites. On Facebook, there are *pages* you can 'like' as well as *groups* (some public and some private) you can join; use the search box to find those which are relevant to you. Many international or regional English language teaching organisations (like IATEFL, TESOL Arabia and TESOL Asia) as well as national organisations (in countries including Argentina, Brazil, Chile, France, Italy, Peru, Spain and Vietnam) already have pages or groups on Facebook. Of course, if there's no local English language teaching organisation for your country represented on Facebook, you could always set one up! Once you have liked a page or joined a group, you can receive status updates in your news feed, as well as being able to communicate with others on the page timeline or group wall.

Alternatively, you can build up mutual friendship links with colleagues and peers, communicating with them on educational matters either publicly or in closed lists. You could also consider joining educators' groups that have set up their own miniature social networks through services like Grou.ps (grou.ps) and Ning (www.ning.com) (see Box 1.3 for more on these services). You can find these through a Google search or by searching within each service.

Working with aggregators

A PLN can in fact be built on any platform which allows you to link to other people and places on the web (see Box 1.10). Beyond blogging services like Blogger and Edublogs, microblogging services like Twitter, and social networking sites like Facebook, Grou.ps and Ning, other options include website services like Google Sites (sites.google.com) and wiki services like PBworks (pbworks.com) and Wikispaces (www.wikispaces.com) (see e.g. Activity 7, *Sports linking* for *Tech support* links on using these wiki services). While websites and wikis lack the chronological structure of blogs, micro-blogs and social networking sites, they are good platforms for embedding feeds from Twitter, Facebook and other services. Although they are rarely used for diary-style thinking, they do allow room for a more complex organisational structure, divorced from time considerations, which may be appropriate for developing sophisticated reflections. Wikis, in particular, can support conversation around each page, with their inbuilt discussion boards being used for extended debate and interaction. They also make collaborative authorship of pages very easy, which may be appropriate in some contexts. For an example of a wiki used as part of a PLN, see Mark Pegrum's *E-language wiki* (e-language.wikispaces.com).

We're now seeing the emergence of aggregator services like Flavors (flavors.me) and Symbaloo (www.symbaloo.com, with apps available for Android and Apple iOS devices), and dedicated mobile apps like Flipboard (for Android and Apple iOS devices), which automate the process of collecting updates from multiple sites and services. Social bookmarking services like Delicious (delicious.com, with apps available for Android, Apple iOS, BlackBerry and Windows devices) and Diigo (www.diigo.com, also with apps available for Android, Apple iOS, BlackBerry and Windows devices) have long been used by teachers and students to build collections of useful online references, with their publicly available indexes being searchable. Delicious now offers the capability to collect bookmarks in a magazine-style format called Stacks, which is paralleled by other services such as the recently popular Scoop.it (www.scoop.it, with apps available for Android and Apple iOS devices). Scoop.it topics worth exploring include Nik Peachey's *Tools for Learners* (www.scoop.it/t/tools-for-learners), Mark Pegrum's *Ubiquitous Learning* (www.scoop.it/t/ubiquitous-learning) and Vance Stevens's *Multiliteracies* (www.scoop.it/t/multiliteracies/).

Perhaps the best-known aggregator service used to underpin PLNs is Google Reader (www.google.com/reader/, with apps available for Android, Apple iOS, BlackBerry and Windows devices), which allows you to subscribe to blogs, magazines, journals and any other websites which offer regular updates through RSS feeds. As with all PLN tools, in order to avoid information overload (see Box 1.7) you have to make judicious choices about just how many sources of information to sign up for. Nevertheless, with some ongoing adjustment, regular pruning and occasional additions, a Google Reader account can be a great way of keeping track of content and conversations you're interested in – and you should always be ready to jump into these conversations with your own thoughts!

Working across platforms

PLNs don't have to be confined to a single platform – and, in reality, they almost never are. While it may be a good idea to start small, as with new technologies in general (see Chapter 1: *A framework of digital literacies*), and build a presence and a network on one platform before branching out onto others, the fact is that many web 2.0 and mobile tools work in very complementary ways. Nik Peachey's *Learning Technology Blog*, mentioned above, links to his Twitter feed and several Scoop.it topics. Mark Pegrum's *E-language* wiki links to his blog, his Twitter feed and his Scoop.it topic.

One of the best examples of a cross-platform network situated at the crossover point between language learning and new technologies is Webheads (webheadsinaction.org). It makes use of blogs (like Blogger and Wordpress), wikis (like PBworks and Wikispaces), Edmodo, Moodle, Ning, Posterous Spaces and Yahoo Groups – to mention just a few of the platforms employed by its members! Webheads describes itself as a 'community of practice', which has been defined by Etienne Wenger (2006) as a 'group[ ] of people who share a concern or a passion for something they do and learn how to do it better as they interact regularly'. Apart from a lively Yahoo Groups site with daily discussions, Webheads offers opportunities for deeper research and development, with free online courses running every year. Both the discussions and the courses are wide-ranging in scope and content, and the mutually developmental ethos of the network makes it a welcoming place to come for support in your reflective practice and for inspiration in your action research. It's also a great space in which to explore a host of new technologies which can be used not only for our professional development as teachers, but can be taken into our classrooms. The Webheads network, then, is certainly worth tapping into as you go about setting up your own PLN.

If you're just beginning to use digital technologies in education, a PLN is a good place to start your explorations of the possibilities. You can join a pre-existing community, like *ELTchat* on Twitter, a national page on Facebook, or a cross-platform organisation like Webheads, and/or you can start your own PLN on any of the platforms described above. If you're already using digital technologies in education, you may already have a PLN, which is a good place to continue your explorations and to share your action research, thereby contributing to others' lifelong learning. Because a PLN can keep growing and changing for as long as you wish to keep learning and discovering, it's the ideal support structure to help you keep pace with the dynamic world of new technologies and new literacies.

Further reading

- For more on how educators can build PLNs, see: Ferriter, Ramsden and Sheninger (2011); Nielsen (2010); Nussbaum-Beach and Ritter Hall (2012); Richardson and Mancabelli (2011).

Appendix
Answer keys

Activity 1 Worksheet – Internet skills

Each of the statements below maps onto specific activities in this text.

I can . . .

☐ use digital technologies in my daily life (e.g. a mobile phone, a computer . . .)
Introduction to digital literacies – Activity 2, *Being digitally literate*

☐ create different types of online texts (e.g. blog posts, status updates, tweets . . .)
Print literacy – Activity 3, *Writing the news* and Activity 4, *Extreme weather*

☐ write mobile phone text messages in my own language and in English
Texting literacy – Activity 5, *Cryptic messages*

☐ recognise when I should and shouldn't use *textspeak* (abbreviated SMS language)
Texting literacy – Activity 6, *Codeswitching*

☐ create an online text with an appropriate number of hyperlinks
Hypertext literacy – Activity 7, *Sports linking*

☐ understand how the use of hyperlinks can influence a reader's opinion
Hypertext literacy – Activity 8, *Building links*

☐ create a multimedia noticeboard
Multimedia literacy – Activity 9, *Food boards*

☐ find online images that I am free to use
Multimedia literacy – Activity 10, *Copycat*

☐ produce an *infographic* (a display of facts and figures on a given topic)
Multimedia literacy – Activity 11, *Envisioning the facts*

☐ understand how online images can be used to create or manipulate opinions
Multimedia literacy – Activity 12, *Sales techniques*

☐ combine media (e.g. images, audio and video) into a digital product
Multimedia literacy – Activity 13, *Showcasing hobbies*, Activity 14, *Selling English* and Activity 15, *Transmedia stories*

☐ create an online *avatar* (character)
Gaming literacy – Activity 16, *Avatars*

☐ create a simple online game
Gaming literacy – Activity 17, *Choose your own adventure*

☐ use multiple media (images, audio and video) on a mobile phone
Mobile literacy – Activity 18, *History hunt* and Activity 19, *A picture a day*

☐ share multimedia artefacts (images, audio and video) with others online
Mobile literacy – Activity 18, *History hunt* and Activity 19, *A picture a day*

☐ use my own mobile devices for learning
Mobile literacy – Activity 20, *Mobile rules*

☐ recognise when it's appropriate or inappropriate to use mobile devices in class
Mobile literacy – Activity 20, *Mobile rules*

☐ understand HTML code
Code literacy – Activity 21, *HTML basics* and Activity 22, *HTML advanced*

☐ interpret word clouds
Tagging literacy – Activity 23, *Travel clouds*

☐ navigate tag clouds
Tagging literacy – Activity 24, *Travel tags*

☐ use a variety of search engines for different types of online searches
Search literacy – Activity 25, *Search race*

☐ understand personalised search
Search literacy – Activity 26, *Search me*

☐ evaluate information I find online
Information literacy – Activity 27, *Tree octopus* and Activity 28, *Fun facts*

☐ filter online information to find what is useful and relevant to me
Filtering literacy – Activity 29, *News in my networks* and Activity 30, *Connecting people*

☐ cope with digital distractions
Filtering literacy – Activity 31, *My digital life* and Activity 32, *Turn off, tune out*

☐ manage my own online identity or identities
Personal literacy – Activity 33, *Faking it* and Activity 34, *Online me*

☐ set up a personal blog
Personal literacy – Activity 35, *Personal blogging*

☐ deal with difficult people or situations online
Personal literacy – Activity 36, *Setting the scene*

☐ manage my digital footprint
Personal literacy – Activity 37, *Footprints in the wires*

☐ understand and follow a 'viral' image or video
Network literacy – Activity 38, *Going viral*

☐ set up and use a PLN (Personal Learning Network)
Network literacy – Activity 39, *A class PLN*

☐ contribute to collaborative online projects (e.g. wikis, photosharing sites . . .)
Participatory literacy – Activity 40, *Our city guide*, Activity 41, *Our city on Wikipedia*, Activity 42, *Flickr vocabulary book* and Activity 43, *A good cause*

☐ interpret media artefacts produced in different cultural contexts
Intercultural literacy – Activity 44, *Vox pop*, Activity 45, *Global dancing* and Activity 46, *Travel tips*

☐ understand and contribute to an internet *meme* (an idea or concept spread virally online, e.g. LOLcats)
Remix literacy – Activity 47, *LOLcats*, Activity 48, *Texting Hillary* and Activity 49, *I'mma let you finish*

☐ create a *mashup* or *remix* (a media artefact created by combining and/or altering pre-existing artefacts)
Remix literacy – Activity 47, *LOLcats*, Activity 48, *Texting Hillary*, Activity 49, *I'mma let you finish* and Activity 50, *Movie mashup*

Activity 4 Worksheet – Extreme weather

Task 1

1. Drought – blog
2. Rising sea levels – Twitter
3. Hurricane/flood – news website
4. Bush (forest) fires – Facebook

Activity 5 Worksheet – Cryptic messages

Task 2

Happy face

Cheeky face (with tongue sticking out)

Surprised face

Sad face

Worried or irritated face

Annoyed face

Angry face (or shouting, yelling)

Very happy face

Kiss

Activity 6 Worksheet – Summer holidays

My summer holidays were a complete waste of time. Before, we used to go to New York to see my brother, his girlfriend and their three screaming kids face-to-face. I love New York; it's great. But my parents were so worried because of 9/11 that they decided to stay in Scotland and spend two weeks up north. Up north, what you see is what you get – nothing. I was very, very, very bored in the middle of nowhere. Nothing but sheep and mountains. At any rate, my parents were happy – they said it could be worse, and that they were happy for the peace and quiet . . . I don't think so! I wanted to go home as soon as possible, to see my mates again. Today, I came back to school. I feel very angelic because I have done all my homework. Now it's business as usual . . .

Activity 7 Worksheet – Sports linking

1. g
2. h
3. a
4. e
5. d
6. c
7. b
8. f
9. j
10. i

Activity 11 Worksheet – Sixty seconds online

60+   new blogs are created
6,600+   images are uploaded to Flickr
1,700+   downloads of Firefox are made
600+   videos are added to YouTube
694,445   searches are done on Google
13,000+   iPhone apps are downloaded
168,000,000   emails are sent
98,000+   tweets are written
70+   domains are registered
79,364   wall posts are made on Facebook

Activity 26 Worksheet – Search them

Rena may be interested in travel or in finding a holiday. She may be particularly interested in Indonesia or South-East Asia, or she may be looking for news about the island of Java.

Ahmed is obviously a coffee fan. He probably likes expensive speciality coffees and is happy to spend money on them! He is looking for a particular type of coffee, perhaps to buy it online.

Olga works in computing, possibly in web design or in programming web applications – or she may be interested in finding out a little bit about the Java programming language as a beginner.

Ramón is a music lover and possibly a fan of a group called 'Java', 'East of Java' or 'The Hot Java Band'. He may not know exactly what he is looking for, but it's obviously something connected to music and has the word 'Java' in the title. He may be looking to buy some music by one of these groups, or for a video of a performance.

The search results are different because these individuals have different interests, jobs, hobbies and so on, which are reflected in their past searches and other online activities. Google has access to this information and tailors the results to each person's profile.

For more details, see Google's own pages entitled 'Manage your data: Search personalisation' (goo.gl/lYfkj) and 'Basics: Search history personalization' (goo.gl/MsBb0).

This means that no two people get the same search results, generally, but also that you are usually shown things you are interested in, rather than general results. On the one hand, this is very convenient, but on the other hand, it can mean that you are less likely to learn new things as a result of your web searches.

Activity 36 Worksheet – Setting the scene

Card 1

It's a bad idea to give out personal information to people you don't know. You don't know what the person's intentions are. This may even be the first step in identity theft, where a person finds out enough information about you to be able to use your identity in other contexts. If you do decide to meet some-body you don't know in real life, you must tell friends and family first, so they know where you are. Consider taking a friend with you on the first meeting.

Card 2

If you send photos of yourself to a stranger, they may use them in contexts you are not happy with. It's also important to realise that any photos you post on a social networking site belong to the site, not to you. This means the photo could be used by the social networking site for advertising or any other purpose without your explicit permission.

Card 3

Although you may like the idea of having more friends, some of them may not be the kind of people you would want as friends in real life. First, check out the profile of each new 'friend' individually to see whether you have common interests. If you do accept a new 'friend' and, later on, you are unhappy in any way with the interaction that occurs, you can always delete or block the person.

Card 4

Never click on a link which doesn't clearly show what website it is linking to. Be aware that a message like this is irresistible to most people, and the link is almost certainly to a webpage containing a virus. If you are ever in doubt about a link, or an email attachment from a friend, contact that person online or offline to check that they really meant to send it to you. If it seems that it may be a malicious link, tell your friend to change their username and password so that these messages won't continue to be sent out.

Card 5

When you set up a profile on a social networking site, or any online account, think carefully about the username you choose, and what sort of impression it will give. In this case, you need to change your username to something less suggestive – although it's not a good idea to use your full name as your username either.

Card 6

Remember that any photos or videos taken of you can quickly and easily be shared on the internet, without your permission. In some real cases teenagers have been put in this sort of situation, and have been blackmailed. Never allow anyone to take photos or videos of you that you are not comfortable about sharing with the rest of the world.

Card 7

Most social networking sites allow you to untag (remove your own name from) a photo. This is the first step. Then contact your friend and ask them to remove the photo. If they refuse, you may be within your legal rights to demand this, depending on the law in your country. If you are under 18, tell your parents or teachers at school. They will contact the friend's parents, or the social networking site itself, to ask for this to be done. In extreme cases it may be possible to take legal action, although usually an agreement is reached before this stage.

Card 8

Never enter your personal details into a website without being aware of the privacy policy, and what the site can do with your information. There have been several internet scams in which users enter their mobile phone number, then agree to the terms and conditions on the site, only to receive expensive daily mobile phone text messages – which they have agreed to pay for by agreeing to the terms and conditions. Although it can be time-consuming, you should always read through any terms and conditions before agreeing to them.

Card 9

The first step is to speak to the person concerned if you feel comfortable doing so. If not, or if nothing changes, then this sort of activity should be reported to the school, and this can be done anonymously. Making unpleasant or untrue comments about somebody else on a social networking site is similar to making comments in public. In other words, it's similar to publishing comments in a newspaper, and in many countries this can be considered libel. Think about whether the comment would be shouted out in a crowded room. If not, it's not acceptable, and should not appear online.

Card 10

Take screen captures of the messages. Then report this situation to your parents and teachers. The messages are evidence of bullying, and the girl will have to deal with the consequences. Your teachers will fully support you in this.

Card 11

Tell your friend not to do it and warn him about the possible consequences. Although this is meant as a joke, any threat made publicly (e.g. via a social networking site, or via a microblogging site like Twitter) will be taken seriously by the police. There have been several examples of individuals posting joke threats, only to be arrested and sentenced. Although things may not come to this point for your friend, the school may take the threat seriously and he could face disciplinary action.

Card 12

Immediately change your profile and create a new username and password. Then post publicly with your new username disclaiming the unpleasant message. If the message is threatening or libellous enough, the police may get involved and can track down the computer from which the original message was sent.

Activity 38 Worksheet – Viral videos

Task 1

(a) tastemakers;

(b) communities of participation;

(c) unexpectedness.

Task 2

(a) Double Rainbow;

(b) Friday;

(c) Nyan Cat (aka Neon Cat);

(d) Bicycle Fines.

Activity 46 Worksheet – True or false?

1. F
2. T
3. F
4. F
5. F
6. T
7. F
8. F
9. T
10. F

Activity 47 Worksheet – LOLcats

(b) I'm in ur castle eating ur peasants
I'm in your castle eating your peasants

- **textspeak:** *ur.* Standard form: *your.*

(c) I iz in ur lolcats. Ratein me 5 starz
I am in your LOLcats. Rating myself with 5 stars.

- **grammar:** error in verb agreement: *I iz (is).* Correct form: *I am.*
- **grammar:** error with reflexive pronoun: *me.* Correct form: *myself.*
- **spelling:** *iz, ratein, starz.* Correct forms: *is, rating, stars.*
- **textspeak:** *ur.* Standard form: *your.*

(d) i swallowd mah toy. im goin 2 be sik
I swallowed my toy. I'm going to be sick.

- **spelling**: *mah, sik.* Correct forms: *my, sick.*
- **textspeak:** *i, swallowd, im, goin, 2.* Standard forms: *I, swallowed, I'm, going, to.*

(e) But . . . but . . . I don't know what puzzles is
But . . . but . . . I don't know what puzzles are.

- **grammar:** error in verb agreement: *puzzles is.* Correct form: *puzzles are.*

References

Abelson, H. (2011) 'Mobile ramblings', *EDUCAUSE Quarterly*, 34(1), http://www.educause.edu/EDUCAUSE+Quarterly/EDUCAUSEQuarterlyMagazine Volum/MobileRamblings/225869.

Aboujaoude, E. (2011) *Virtually You: The dangerous powers of the e-personality*, New York: W.W. Norton.

Abram, C. (2012) *Facebook for Dummies* (4th edn), Hoboken, NJ: John Wiley & Sons.

Alexander, B. (2006) 'Web 2.0: A new wave of innovation for teaching and learning?', *EDUCAUSE Review*, 41(2), 32–44. http://net.educause.edu/ir/library/pdf/ERM0621.pdf.

Alexander, B. (2011) *The New Digital Storytelling: Creating narratives with new media*, Santa Barbara, CA: Praeger.

Ally, M. (ed.) (2009) *Mobile Learning: Transforming the delivery of education and training*, Edmonton: University of Alberta Press.

Alvermann, D.E. (2008) 'Why bother theorizing adolescents' online literacies for classroom practice and research?', *Journal of Adolescent and Adult Literacy*, 52(1), http://uga.academia.edu/DonnaAlvermann/Papers/129947/Why_Bother_Theorizing_Adolescents_Online_Literacies_for_Classroom_Practice_and_Research.

Anderson, S. (2009, 17 May) 'In defense of distraction', *New York*. http://nymag.com/news/features/56793/.

Anderson, T. and Dron, J. (2011) 'Three generations of distance education pedagogy', *International Review of Research in Open and Distance Learning*, 12(3), 80–97.

Aufderheide, P. and Jaszi, P. (2011) *Reclaiming Fair Use: How to put balance back in copyright*, Chicago: University of Chicago Press.

Ayers, P., Matthews, C. and Yates, B. (2008) *How Wikipedia Works: And how you can be a part of it*, San Francisco: No Starch Press.

Baron, N.S. (2008) *Always On: Language in an online and mobile world*, New York: Oxford University Press.

Baron, N.S. (2011) Assessing the internet's impact on language. In M. Consalvo and C. Ess (eds), *The Handbook of Internet Studies* (pp. 117–36), Malden, MA: Wiley-Blackwell.

Barton, D. (1994) *Literacy: An introduction to the ecology of written language*, Oxford: Blackwell.

Barton, D. and Hamilton, M. (2000) Literacy practices. In D. Barton, M. Hamilton and R. Ivanič (eds), *Situated Literacies: Reading and writing in context* (pp. 7–15), London: Routledge.

Baumfield, V., Hall, E. and Wall, K. (2008) *Action Research in the Classroom*, London: Sage.

Bawden, D. (2008) Origins and concepts of digital literacy. In C. Lankshear and M. Knobel (eds), *Digital Literacies: Concepts, policies and practices* (pp. 17–32), New York: Peter Lang.

Baym, N.K. (2010) *Personal Connections in the Digital Age*, Cambridge: Polity.

Baynham, M. and Prinsloo, M. (eds) (2009) *The Future of Literacy Studies*, Basingstoke: Palgrave Macmillan.

Beins, B.C. (2011) A brief stroll down Random Access Memory lane: Implications for teaching with technology. In D.S. Dunn, J.H. Wilson, J.E. Freeman and J.R. Stowell (eds), *Best Practices for Technology-enhanced Teaching and Learning: Connecting to psychology and the social sciences* (pp. 35–51), New York: Oxford University Press.

Belicove, M.E. and Kraynak, J. (2011) *The Complete Idiot's Guide to Facebook* (2nd edn), New York: Penguin.

Belshaw, D.A.J. (2011) *What is 'digital literacy'? A pragmatic investigation*, Ed.D. thesis, http://neverendingthesis.com/doug-belshaw-edd-thesis-final.pdf.

Benkler, Y. (2006) *The Wealth of Networks: How social production transforms markets and freedom*, New Haven: Yale University Press.

Benkler, Y. (2011) *The Penguin and the Leviathan: The triumph of cooperation over self-interest*, New York: Crown Business.

Bennett, S., Maton, K. and Kervin, L. (2008) 'The "digital natives" debate: A critical review of the evidence', *British Journal of Educational Technology*, 39(5), 775–86.

Bilton, N. (2010) *I Live in the Future and Here's How it Works: Why your world, work, and brain are being creatively disrupted*, New York: Crown Business.

Bily, C.A. (ed.) (2009) *What is the Impact of E-waste?*, Farmington Hills, MI: Greenhaven Press.

Blair, A.M. (2010) *Too Much to Know: Managing scholarly information before the modern age*, New Haven: Yale University Press.

Blum, S.D. (2009) *My Word! Plagiarism and college culture*, Ithaca, NY: Cornell University Press.

Bonk, C.J. (2009) *The World is Open: How web technology is revolutionizing education*, San Francisco: Jossey-Bass.

Bonk. C.J. and Zhang, K. (2008) *Empowering Online Learning: 100+ activities for reading, reflecting, displaying, and doing*, San Francisco: Jossey-Bass.

boyd, d. (2009, 11 Jun.) 'Jeff Hancock: What you put up online is . . .' *Twitter*, https://twitter.com/#!/zephoria/status/2117105322.

boyd, d. (2010a, 23 Aug.) 'Social steganography: Learning to hide in plain sight', *DMLcentral*, http://dmlcentral.net/blog/danah-boyd/social-steganography-learning-hide-plain-sight.

boyd, d. (2010b) 'Streams of content, limited attention: The flow of information through social media', *EDUCAUSE Review*, 45(5), 26–36, http://net.educause.edu/ir/library/pdf/ERM1051.pdf.

boyd, d. (2011) Social network sites as networked publics: Affordances, dynamics, and implications. In Z. Papacharissi (ed.), *A Networked Self: Identity, community, and culture on social network sites* (pp. 39–58), New York: Routledge.

Brabazon, T. (2009, 31 Jul.) 'The hare or the tortoise?', *Times Higher Education*, http://www.timeshighereducation.co.uk/story.asp?sectioncode=26&storycode=407615&c=1.

Breen, M.P. and Candlin, C.N. (1980) 'The essentials of a communicative curriculum in language teaching', *Applied Linguistics*, 1(2), 89–112.

Bridle, J. (2010, 6 Sep.) 'On Wikipedia, cultural patrimony, and historiography', *booktwo.org*, http://booktwo.org/notebook/wikipedia-historiography/.

Brooks-Young, S. (2010) *Teaching with the Tools Kids Really Use: Learning with web and mobile technologies*, Thousand Oaks, CA: Corwin.

Broughton, J. (2008) *Wikipedia: The missing manual*. Sebastopol, CA: O'Reilly Media.

Brown, M. (2005) Learning spaces. In D.G. Oblinger and J.L. Oblinger (eds), *Educating the Net Generation* (pp. 12.1–12.22), Washington: EDUCAUSE, http://net.educause.edu/ir/library/pdf/pub7101l.pdf.

Bruckman, A. (2011, 18 May) 'Should you believe Wikipedia?', *The Next Bison: Social computing and culture*, http://nextbison.wordpress.com/2011/05/18/should-you-believe-wikipedia/.

Bruns, A. (2008) *Blogs, Wikipedia, Second Life, and Beyond: From production to produsage*, New York: Peter Lang.

Buckingham, D. (2008) Defining digital literacy: What do young people need to know about digital media? In C. Lankshear and M. Knobel (eds), *Digital Literacies: Concepts, policies and practices* (pp. 73–89), New York: Peter Lang.

Burbules, N.C. (2009) Meanings of 'ubiquitous learning'. In B. Cope and M. Kalantzis (eds), *Ubiquitous Learning* (pp. 15–20), Urbana: University of Illinois Press.

Burniske, R.W. (2008) *Literacy in the Digital Age* (2nd edn), Thousand Oaks, CA: Corwin.

Byron, T. (2008) *Safer Children in a Digital World: The report of the Byron review*. Nottingham: DCSF Publications, http://media.education.gov.uk/assets/files/pdf/s/safer%20children%20in%20a%20digital%20world%20the%202008%20byron%20review.pdf.

Cameron, L. (2001) *Teaching Languages to Young Learners*, Cambridge: Cambridge University Press.

Candlin, C.N. (1987) Towards task-based language learning. In C.N. Candlin and D.F. Murphy (eds), *Language Learning Tasks* (pp. 5–22), Englewood Cliffs, NJ: Prentice Hall.

Candlin, C. N. (2001) Afterword: Taking the curriculum to task. In M. Bygate, P. Skehan and M. Swain (eds), *Researching Pedagogic Tasks: Second language learning, teaching and testing* (pp. 229-43), London: Pearson.

Carr, N. (2009, 22 Jan.) 'All hail the information triumvirate!', *Rough Type*. http://www.roughtype.com/archives/2009/01/all_hail_the_in.php.

Carr, N. (2010) *The Shallows: What the internet is doing to our brains*, New York: W.W. Norton.

Carrington, V. and Robinson, M. (eds) (2009) *Digital Literacies: Social learning and classroom practices*, London: Sage.

Castells, M. (2009) *Communication Power*, Oxford: Oxford University Press.

Chen, B.X. (2011) *Always On: How the iPhone unlocked the anything-anytime-anywhere future – and locked us in*, Cambridge, MA: Da Capo Press.

Coiro, J., Knobel, M., Lankshear, C. and Leu, D.J. (eds) (2008) *Handbook of Research on New Literacies*, New York: Lawrence Erlbaum.

Collin, P., Rahilly, K., Richardson, I. and Third, A. (2011, Apr.) *The Benefits of Social Networking Services*, Melbourne: YAW-CRC. http://www.fya.org.au/wp-content/uploads/2010/07/The-Benefits-of-Social-Networking-Services.pdf.

Cope, B. and Kalantzis, M. (eds) (2009) *Ubiquitous Learning*, Urbana: University of Illinois Press.

Costa, C. (2011) Educational networking in the digital age. In M. Thomas (ed.), *Digital Education: Opportunities for social collaboration* (pp. 81–99), New York: Palgrave Macmillan.

Couros, A. (2010) Developing personal learning networks for open and social learning. In G. Veletsianos (ed.), *Emerging technologies in distance education* (pp. 109–28), Edmonton: University of Alberta Press, http://www.aupress.ca/books/120177/ebook/06_Veletsianos_2010-Emerging_Technologies_in_Distance_Education.pdf.

Creative Commons (2011) *The Power of Open*, http://thepowerofopen.org/.

Crystal, D. (2008) *Txtng: The gr8 db8*, Oxford: Oxford University Press.

Crystal, D. (2011) *Internet Linguistics: A student guide*, London: Routledge.

Cummings, R.E. (2009) *Lazy Virtues: Teaching writing in the age of Wikipedia*, Nashville, TN: Vanderbilt University Press.

Dalby, A. (2009) *The World and Wikipedia: How we are editing reality*, Draycott: Siduri Books.

Danielson, D.R. (2006) Web credibility. In C. Ghaoui (ed.), *Encyclopedia of Human Computer Interaction* (pp. 713–21), Hershey, PA: Idea Group Reference.

Davidson, C.N. (2011) *Now You See It: How the brain science of attention will transform the way we live, work, and learn*, New York: Viking.

Deibert, R., Palfrey, J., Rohozinski, R. and Zittrain, J. (eds) (2010) *Access Controlled: The shaping of power, rights, and rule in cyberspace*, Cambridge, MA: MIT Press.

Dezuanni, M. (2010) Digital media literacy: Connecting young people's identities, creative production and learning about video games. In D.E. Alvermann (ed.), *Adolescents' Online Literacies: Connecting classrooms, digital media, and popular culture* (pp. 125–43), New York: Peter Lang.

Dignan, A. (2011) *Game Frame: Using games as a strategy for success*, New York: Free Press.

Doctorow, C. (2006) 'On "Digital Maoism: The Hazards of the New Online Collectivism" by Jaron Lanier', *Edge: The Reality Club*, http://www.edge.org/discourse/digital_maoism.html.

Doctorow, C. (2008) *Content: Selected essays on technology, creativity, copyright, and the future of the future*, San Francisco: Tachyon.

Dörnyei, Z. and Hadfield, J. (2013) *Motivation*, Harlow: Pearson.

Drexler, W. (2010) 'The networked student model for construction of personal learning environments: Balancing teacher control and student autonomy', *Australasian Journal of Educational Technology*, 26(3), 369–85, http://www.ascilite.org.au/ajet/ajet26/drexler.pdf.

Dudeney, G. (2009, 26 May) 'The Luddite codex', *That'SLife*, http://slife.dudeney.com/?p=238.

Dunn, H.S. (2010) The carbon footprint of ICTs. In A. Finlay (ed.), *Global Information Society Watch 2010: Focus on ICTs and environmental sustainability* (pp. 15–16), APC/Hivos, http://www.giswatch.org/sites/default/files/gisw2010thematicthecarbonfootprint_en.pdf.

Eagleman, D. (2010) *Why the Net Matters: How the internet will save civilization*, Edinburgh: Canongate.

Egbert, J., Akasha, O., Huff, L. and Lee, H. (2011) 'Moving forward: Anecdotes and evidence guiding the next generation of CALL', *International Journal of Computer-Assisted Language Learning and Teaching*, 1(1), 1–15.

Ensslin, A. (2012) *The Language of Gaming*, Basingstoke: Palgrave Macmillan.

Erasmus, D. (1964) *The 'Adages' of Erasmus: A study with translations* (trans. M. Mann Phillips), Cambridge: Cambridge University Press.

Ess, C. (2009) *Digital Media Ethics*, Cambridge: Polity.

Ferries-Rowe, J.D. (2012, 29 Mar.) 'Choosing between BYOT and BYOD: Why one letter might make a difference', *Confessions of a Jesuit School CIO*. http://geekreflection.blogspot.com.au/2012/03/choosing-between-byot-and-byod-why-one.html.

Ferriter, W.M., Ramsden, J.T. and Sheninger, E.C. (2011) *Communicating and Connecting with Social Media*, Bloomington, IN: Solution Tree Press/NAESP.

Fogg Phillips, L. (2011) *Facebook for Educators*, http://facebookforeducators.org/.

Frazel, M. (2010) *Digital Storytelling Guide for Educators*, Eugene, OR: ISTE.

Fuchs, C., Boersma, K., Albrechtslund, A. and Sandoval, M. (eds) (2011) *Internet and Surveillance: The challenges of web 2.0 and social media*, New York: Routledge.

Gagnon, D.J. (2010) 'Mobile learning environments', *EDUCAUSE Quarterly*, 33(3), http://www.educause.edu/EDUCAUSE+Quarterly/EDUCAUSEQuarterly MagazineVolum/MobileLearningEnvironments/213690.

Gasser, U. and Palfrey, J. (2009) 'Mastering multitasking', *Educational Leadership*, 66(6), 14–19.

Gee, J.P. (2007a) *Good Video Games and Good Learning: Collected essays on video games, learning and literacy*, New York: Peter Lang.

Gee, J.P. (2007b) *What Video Games Have to Teach us About Learning and Literacy* (new ed.), New York: Palgrave Macmillan.

Gee, J.P. and Hayes, E.R. (2011) *Language and Learning in the Digital Age*, London: Routledge.

Giles, J. (2005) 'Internet encyclopaedias go head to head', *Nature*, 438, 900–1.

Gillen, J. and Barton, D. (2009, 12–13 Mar.) *Digital Literacies: A discussion document for the TLRP-TEL (Teaching and Learning Research Programme – Technology Enhanced Learning) workshop on digital literacies*, Lancaster University.

Gillmor, D. (2010) *Mediactive*, Lulu.com.

Gleick, J. (2011) *The Information: A history, a theory, a flood*, London: HarperCollins.

Godwin-Jones, R. (2003) 'Emerging technologies. Blogs and wikis: Environments for on-line collaboration', *Language Learning and Technology*, 7(2), 12–16. http://llt.msu.edu/vol7num2/pdf/emerging.pdf.

Grant, L. (2010, 18 Nov.) 'New media literacy: Critique vs re-design', *DMLcentral*, http://dmlcentral.net/blog/lyndsay-grant/new-media-literacy-critique-vs-re-design.

Greenfield, S. (2008) *ID: The quest for identity in the 21st century*, London: Sceptre.

Gregory, C. (2010, 10 Mar.) 'The SAMR model', *One thing I've learned*, http://cherionethingivelearned.blogspot.com.au/2010/03/samr-model.html.

Grossman, E. (2006) *High Tech Trash: Digital devices, hidden toxics, and human health*, Washington: Island Press.

Hagel III, J., Seely Brown, J. and Davison, L. (2010) *The Power of Pull: How small moves, smartly made, can set big things in motion*, New York: Basic Books.

Hague, C. and Williamson, B. (2009, Aug.) *Digital Participation, Digital Literacy and School Subjects: A review of the policies, literature and evidence*, Bristol: Futurelab, http://www.futurelab.org.uk/resources/documents/lit_reviews/DigitalParticipation.pdf.

Hallowell, E.M. (2007) *Crazybusy: Overstretched, overbooked, and about to snap! Strategies for handling your fast-paced life*, New York: Ballantine Books.

Hargittai, E. (2010) 'Digital na(t)ives? Variation in internet skills and uses among members of the "net generation"', *Sociological Inquiry*, 80(1), 92–113.

Hargittai, E. and Walejko, G. (2008) 'The participation divide: Content creation and sharing in the digital age', *Information, Communication and Society*, 11(2), 239–56.

Hartley, J. (2009) *The Uses of Digital Literacy*, St Lucia: University of Queensland Press.

Haythornthwaite, C. (2007) Digital divide and e-learning. In R. Andrews and C. Haythornthwaite (eds) *The Sage Handbook of E-learning Research* (pp. 97–118), London: Sage.

Hedge, T. (2005) *Writing* (2nd edn), Oxford: Oxford University Press.

Helm, F., Guth, S. and Farrah, M. (2012) 'Promoting dialogue or hegemonic practice? Power issues in telecollaboration', *Language Learning and Technology*, 16(2), 103–27.

Helsper, E.J. (2008) *Digital Inclusion: An analysis of social disadvantage and the information society*, London: Department for Communities and Local Government, http://www.communities.gov.uk/documents/communities/pdf/digitalinclusionanalysis.

Hobbs, R. (2010) *Copyright Clarity: How fair use supports digital learning*, Thousand Oaks, CA: Corwin/NCTE.

Hobbs, R. (2011) *Digital and Media Literacy: Connecting culture and classroom*, Thousand Oaks, CA: Corwin.

Hos-McGrane, M. (2011, 9 Feb.) 'The SAMR model', *Tech transformation*, http://www.maggiehosmcgrane.com/2010/03/samr-model.html.

Hyde, L. (2011) *Common as Air: Revolution, art, and ownership* (with a new afterword), New York: Farrar, Straus & Giroux.

Internet Safety Technical Task Force (2008, 31 Dec.) *Enhancing Child Safety and Online Technologies*. Final report of the Internet Safety Technical Task Force to the Multi-State Working Group on Social Networking of State Attorneys General of the United States. Cambridge, MA: The Berkman Center for Internet and Society at Harvard University, http://cyber.law.harvard.edu/pubrelease/isttf/.

'Internet world users by language: Top 10 languages' (2012, 18 Mar.) *Internet World Stats: Usage and population statistics*, http://www.internetworldstats.com/stats7.htm.

Jackson, M. (2009) *Distracted: The erosion of attention and the coming dark age*, Amherst, NY: Prometheus Books.

Jarvis, J. (2009a, 8 May) 'Openness and the internet', *Bloomberg Businessweek*, http://www.businessweek.com/managing/content/may2009/ca2009058_754247.htm.

Jarvis, J. (2009b, 7 Jun.) 'Product v. process journalism: The myth of perfection v. beta culture', *BuzzMachine*, http://www.buzzmachine.com/2009/06/07/processjournalism/.

Jenkins, H. (2008) *Convergence Culture: Where old and new media collide* (new edn), New York: New York University Press.

Jenkins, H. (2009, 4 May) '"Geeking out" for democracy (Part two)', *Confessions of an Aca-Fan*, http://www.henryjenkins.org/2009/05/geeking_out_for_democracy_part_1.html.

Jenkins, H. (2010, 21 Jun.) 'Transmedia education: The 7 principles revisited', *Confessions of an Aca-Fan*, http://henryjenkins.org/2010/06/transmedia_education_the_7_pri.html.

Jenkins, H., Purushotma, R., Weigel, M., Clinton, K. and Robison, A.J. (2009) *Confronting the Challenges of Participatory Culture: Media education for the 21st century*, Cambridge, MA: MIT Press, http://mitpress.mit.edu/books/full_pdfs/Confronting_the_Challenges.pdf.

Johnson, L., Adams, S. and Cummins, M. (2012) *The NMC Horizon Report: 2012 Higher Education Edition*, Austin, TX: The New Media Consortium. http://net.educause.edu/ir/library/pdf/HR2012.pdf.

Johnson, L., Levine, A. and Smith, R. (2008) *The Horizon Report: 2008 Australia–New Zealand Edition*, Austin, TX: The New Media Consortium. http://www.nmc.org/pdf/2008-Horizon-Report-ANZ.pdf.

Johnson, L., Smith, R., Willis, H., Levine, A. and Haywood, K. (2011) *The 2011 Horizon Report*, Austin, TX: The New Media Consortium. http://www.nmc.org/pdf/2011-Horizon-Report.pdf.

Kalantzis, M. and Cope, B. (2012) *Literacies*, New York: Cambridge University Press.

Kelly, K. (2010, 16 Sep.) 'Achieving techno-literacy', *The New York Times*. http://www.nytimes.com/2010/09/19/magazine/19FOB-WWLN-Kelly-t.html.

Kemp, N. (2011) 'Mobile technology and literacy: Effects across cultures, abilities and the lifespan', *Journal of Computer Assisted Learning*, 27(1), 1–3.

Kirkpatrick, D. (2010) *The Facebook Effect: The inside story of the company that is connecting the world*, New York: Simon & Schuster.

Kirn, W. (2007, Nov.) 'The autumn of the multitaskers', *The Atlantic*, http://www.theatlantic.com/doc/200711/multitasking.

Kist, W. (2010) *The Socially Networked Classroom: Teaching in the new media age*, Thousand Oaks, CA: Corwin.

Knobel, M. and Lankshear, C. (2008) 'Remix: The art and craft of endless hybridization', *Journal of Adolescent and Adult Literacy*, 52(1), 22–33.

Knobel, M. and Lankshear, C. (eds) (2010) *DIY Media: Creating, sharing and learning with new technologies*, New York: Peter Lang.

Koehler, M.J. (n.d.) *TPACK: Technological pedagogical and content knowledge*, http://www.tpck.org/.

Koehler, M.J. and Mishra, P. (2008) Introducing TPCK. In AACTE Committee on Innovation and Technology (ed.), *Handbook of Technological Pedagogical Content Knowledge (TPCK) for Educators* (pp. 3–29), New York: Routledge.

Kolb, L. (2008) *Toys to Tools: Connecting student cell phones to education*, Eugene, OR: ISTE.

Kolb, L. (2010) 'Facebook and learning . . . ?' *SlideShare*, http://www.slideshare.net/elizkeren/macul-socialnetwork.

Kolb, L. (2011) *Cell Phones in the Classroom: A practical guide for educators*, Eugene, OR: ISTE.

Kress, G. (2003) *Literacy in the New Media Age*, London: Routledge.

Kress, G. (2010) *Multimodality: A social semiotic approach to contemporary communication*, London: Routledge.

Kumaravadivelu, B. (2006) *Understanding Language Teaching: From method to postmethod*, Mahwah, NJ: Lawrence Erlbaum.

Lamy, M.-N. and Goodfellow, R. (2010) Telecollaboration and learning 2.0. In S. Guth and F. Helm (eds), *Telecollaboration 2.0: Language, literacies and intercultural learning in the 21st century* (pp. 107–38), Bern: Peter Lang.

Lange, P.G. (2010) Learning about civic engagement. In J.K. Parker, *Teaching Tech-savvy Kids: Bringing digital media into the classroom, grades 5–12* (pp. 45–8), Thousand Oaks, CA: Corwin.

Lange, P.G. and Ito, M. (2010) Creative production. In M. Ito *et al.*, *Hanging Out, Messing Around, and Geeking Out: Kids living and learning with new media* (pp. 243–93), Cambridge, MA: MIT Press, http://mitpress.mit.edu/books/full_pdfs/Hanging_Out.pdf.

Lanier, J. (2010) *You Are Not a Gadget: A manifesto*, London: Penguin.

Lankshear, C. and Knobel, M. (2006) *New Literacies: Everyday practices and classroom learning* (2nd edn), Maidenhead: Open University Press/McGraw-Hill.

Lankshear, C. and Knobel, M. (2008a) Introduction: Digital literacies – Concepts, policies and practices. In C. Lankshear and M. Knobel (eds), *Digital Literacies: Concepts, policies and practices* (pp. 1–16), New York: Peter Lang.

Lankshear, C. and Knobel, M. (eds) (2008b) *Digital Literacies: Concepts, policies and practices*, New York: Peter Lang.

Lankshear, C. and Knobel, M. (2011) *Literacies: Social, cultural and historical perspectives*, New York: Peter Lang.

Larsen-Freeman, D. (1997) 'Chaos/complexity science and second language acquisition', *Applied Linguistics*, 18(2), 141–65.

Larsen-Freeman, D. (2000) *Techniques and Principles in Language Teaching* (2nd edn), Oxford: Oxford University Press.

Lenhart, A., Arafeh, S., Smith, A. and Rankin Macgill, A. (2008, 24 Apr.) *Writing, technology and teens*, Washington: Pew Internet and American Life Project, http://www.pewinternet.org/Reports/2008/Writing-Technology-and-Teens.aspx.

Lenhart, A., Madden, M., Rankin Macgill, A. and Smith, A. (2007, 19 Dec.) *Teens and social media*, Washington: Pew Internet and American Life Project, http://www.pewinternet.org/Reports/2007/Teens-and-Social-Media.aspx.

Lessig, L. (2007, Mar.) *Larry Lessig on laws that choke creativity*. TED Talks [posted Nov.], http://www.ted.com/index.php/talks/larry_lessig_says_the_law_is_strangling_creativity.html.

Lessig, L. (2008) *Remix: Making art and commerce thrive in the hybrid economy*, London: Bloomsbury, http://www.bloomsburyacademic.com/view/Remix_9781849662505/book-ba-9781849662505.xml.

Levinson, M. (2010) *From Fear to Facebook: One school's journey*, Eugene, OR: ISTE.

Levmore, S. and Nussbaum, M.C. (eds) (2010) *The Offensive Internet: Speech, privacy, and reputation*, Cambridge, MA: Harvard University Press.

Lih, A. (2009) *The Wikipedia Revolution: How a bunch of nobodies created the world's greatest encyclopedia*, London: Aurum.

Liu, M., Kalk, D., Kinney, L. and Orr, G. (2012) 'Web 2.0 and its use in higher education from 2007–2009: A review of literature', *International Journal on E-learning*, 11(2), 153–79.

Livingstone, S. (2009) *Children and the Internet: Great expectations, challenging realities*, Cambridge: Polity.

Looi, C.-K., Seow, P., Zhang, B., So, H.-J., Chen, W. and Wong, L.-H. (2010) 'Leveraging mobile technology for sustainable seamless learning: A research agenda', *British Journal of Educational Technology*, 41(2), 154–69.

Luther, M. (1857) *The Table Talk of Martin Luther* (trans. and ed. W. Hazlitt, new edn), London: H.G. Bohn, http://hdl.handle.net/2027/nyp.33433082263850.

Macgibbon, A. and Tarica, E. (2012, 28 May) 'BYO: Next wave in the eRevolution', *The Age*, http://www.theage.com.au/national/education/byo--next-wave-in-the-erevolution-20120526-1zayg.html.

MacKinnon, R. (2012) *Consent of the Networked: The worldwide struggle for internet freedom*, New York: Basic Books.

Madden, M. and Smith, A. (2010, 26 May) *Reputation Management and Social Media*, Washington: Pew Internet and American Life Project. http://www.pewinternet.org/Reports/2010/Reputation-Management.aspx.

Mangen, A. and Velay, J.-L. (2010) Digitizing literacy: Reflections on the haptics of writing. In M.H. Zadeh (ed.), *Advances in Haptics* (pp. 385–401), Vukovar, Croatia: In-Tech.

Manjoo, F. (2008) *True Enough: Learning to live in a post-fact society*, Hoboken, NJ: John Wiley & Sons.

Mayer-Schönberger, V. (2009) *Delete: The virtue of forgetting in the digital age*, Princeton: Princeton University Press.

McBride, M. (2011, 5 Mar.) 'Praxis 2.0: Escaping the edu-travelogue'. *melanie mcbride.net*, http://melaniemcbride.net/2011/03/05/praxis-2-0/.

McElvaney, J. and Berge, Z. (2009) 'Weaving a personal web: Using online technologies to create customized, connected, and dynamic learning envir-onments', *Canadian Journal of Learning and Technology*, 35(2), http://www.cjlt.ca/index.php/cjlt/article/viewArticle/524/257.

McGonigal, J. (2011) *Reality is Broken: Why games make us better and how they can change the world*, London: Jonathan Cape.

McLeod, S. (2012, 11 Mar.) 'Economically-disadvantaged students learn to do what the computer tells them', *Dangerously irrelevant!* http://dangerouslyirrelevant.org/2012/03/economically-disadvantaged-students-learn-to-do-what-the-computer-tells-them.html.

McNiff, J. and Whitehead, J. (2011) *All You Need to Know about Action Research* (2nd edn), London: Sage.

Mellow, J.D. (2000) Western influences on indigenous language teaching. In J. Reyhner, J. Martin, L. Lockard and W. Sakiestewa Gilbert (eds), *Learn in Beauty: Indigenous education for a new century* (pp. 102–13), Flagstaff, AZ: Northern Arizona University, http://jan.ucc.nau.edu/~jar/LIB/LIB9.html.

Mellow, J.D. (2002) 'Toward principled eclecticism in language teaching: The two-dimensional model and the centring principle', *TESL-EJ*, 5(4), http://tesl-ej.org/ej20/a1.html.

Merchant, G. (2010a) View my profile(s). In D.E. Alvermann (ed.), *Adolescents' Online Literacies: Connecting classrooms, digital media, and popular culture* (pp. 51–69), New York: Peter Lang.

Merchant, G. (2010b) Visual networks: Learning and photosharing. In M. Knobel and C. Lankshear (eds), *DIY Media: Creating, sharing and learning with new technologies* (pp. 79–102), New York: Peter Lang.

Mertler, C.A. (2009) *Action Research: Teachers as researchers in the class-room* (2nd edn), Thousand Oaks, CA: Sage.

Miedema, J. (2009) *Slow Reading*, Duluth, MN: Litwin Books.

Mills, K.A. (2010) 'A review of the "digital turn" in the New Literacy Studies', *Review of Educational Research*, 80(2): 246–71.

Mishra, P. and Koehler, M.J. (2006) 'Technological pedagogical content knowledge: A framework for teacher knowledge', *Teachers College Record*, 108(6), 1017–54.

Monahan, T. (2002) 'Flexible space and built pedagogy: Emerging IT embodiments', *Inventio*, 4(1), 1–19, http://www.torinmonahan.com/papers/Inventio.html.

Morozov, E. (2011) *The Net Delusion: The dark side of internet freedom*, New York: Public Affairs.

Naish, J. (2008) *Enough: Breaking free from the world of more*, London: Hodder & Stoughton.

The New London Group (2000) A pedagogy of multiliteracies: Designing social futures. In B. Cope and M. Kalantzis (eds), *Multiliteracies: Literacy learning and the design of social futures* (pp. 9–37), London: Routledge.

Newton, M. (2009, 20 Sep.) 'People clever enough to bypass censorware . . .' *Twitter*, https://twitter.com/NewtonMark/status/4120005536.

Nielsen, L. (2010, 1 Aug.) 'Five ways to build your 1.0 and 2.0 personal learning network', *The Innovative Educator*, http://theinnovativeeducator.blogspot.com/2010/08/5-ways-to-build-your-10-and-20-personal.html.

Nielsen, L. and Webb, W. (2011) *Teaching Generation Text: Using cell phones to enhance learning*, San Francisco: Jossey-Bass.

Norman, D. (2011, 14 Feb.) 'I have seen the future and I am opposed', *Core 77*, http://core77.com/blog/columns/i_have_seen_the_future_and_i_am_opposed_18532.asp.

November, A. (2010) *Empowering Students with Technology* (2nd edn), Thousand Oaks, CA: Corwin.

Nussbaum-Beach, S. and Ritter Hall, L. (2012) *The Connected Educator: Learning and leading in a digital age*, Bloomington, IN: Solution Tree Press.

Oakley, G., Pegrum, M. and Faulkner, R. (2012) 'Changing everything? iPads in education', *Professional Educator*, http://austcolled.com.au/publication/professional-educator.

Oblinger, D.G. (ed.) (2006) *Learning Spaces*, Washington: EDUCAUSE, http://www.educause.edu/learningspaces.

O'Donoghue, T. and Clarke, S. (2010) *Leading Learning: Process, themes and issues in international contexts*, London: Routledge.

Online College (2012, 21 May) 'One hundred ways you should be using Facebook in your classroom [updated]', *Online College*, http://www.onlinecollege.org/2012/05/21/100-ways-you-should-be-using-facebook-in-your-classroom-updated/.

OpenNet Initiative (n.d.) The Citizen Lab, Munk School of Global Affairs, University of Toronto; the Berkman Center for Internet and Society, Harvard University; the SecDev Group, Ottawa, http://opennet.net/.

O'Reilly, T. and Battelle, J. (2009) *Web Squared: Web 2.0 five years on*, Sebastopol, CA: O'Reilly Media, http://assets.en.oreilly.com/1/event/28/web2009_websquared-whitepaper.pdf.

O'Sullivan, D. (2009) *Wikipedia: A new community of practice?* Farnham: Ashgate.

Pachler, N., Bachmair, B. and Cook, J. (2010) *Mobile Learning: Structures, agency, practices*, New York: Springer.

Palfrey, J. and Gasser, U. (2008) *Born Digital: Understanding the first generation of digital natives*, New York: Basic Books.

Palloff, R.M. and Pratt, K. (2009) *Assessing the Online Learner: Resources and strategies for faculty*, San Francisco: Jossey-Bass.

Papacharissi, Z. (2011) Conclusion: A networked self. In Z. Papacharissi (ed.), *A Networked Self: Identity, community, and culture on social network sites* (pp. 304–18), New York: Routledge.

Pariser, E. (2011) *The Filter Bubble: What the internet is hiding from you*, London: Viking.

Parker, J.K. (2010) *Teaching Tech-savvy Kids: Bringing digital media into the classroom, grades 5–12*, Thousand Oaks, CA: Corwin.

Parry, D. (2011) 'Mobile perspectives on teaching: Mobile literacy', *EDUCAUSE Review*, 46(2), 14–18, http://net.educause.edu/ir/library/pdf/ERM1120.pdf.

Patry, W. (2009) *Moral Panics and the Copyright Wars*, New York: Oxford University Press.

Patry, W. (2011) *How to Fix Copyright*, New York: Oxford University Press.

Pegrum, M. (2009) *From Blogs to Bombs: The future of digital technologies in education*, Crawley, WA: UWA Publishing.

Pegrum, M. (2010) '"I link, therefore I am": Network literacy as a core digital literacy', *E-learning and Digital Media*, 7(4), 346–54.

Pegrum, M. (2011) Modified, multiplied, and (re-)mixed: Social media and digital literacies. In M. Thomas (ed.), *Digital Education: Opportunities for social collaboration* (pp. 9–35), New York: Palgrave Macmillan.

Pegrum, M., Oakley, G. and Faulkner, R. (2012) Schools going mobile: A study of the adoption of mobile handheld technologies in Western Australian independent schools. Manuscript submitted for publication.

Plester, B., Wood, C. and Bowyer, S. (2009) Children's text messaging and traditional literacy. In L. Tan Wee Hin and R. Subramaniam (eds), *Handbook of Research on New Media Literacy at the K-12 Level: Issues and challenges* (pp. 492–504), Hershey, PA: Information Science Reference.

Pope, A. (1729) *The Dunciad, Variorum. With the prolegomena of Scriblerus.* London: [printed and re-printed, for the booksellers in Dublin], http://books.google.com.au/books?id=GAwUAAAAQAAJ.

Powers, W. (2010) *Hamlet's BlackBerry: A practical philosophy for building a good life in the digital age*, New York: Harper.

Prensky, M. (2007) *Digital Game-based Learning*, St Paul, MN: Paragon House.

Prensky, M. (2010) *Teaching Digital Natives: Partnering for real learning*, Thousand Oaks, CA: Corwin.

Prensky, M. (2012a, Jan.–Feb.) 'Eliminating the "app gap"', *Educational Technology*, http://marcprensky.com/writing/Prensky-EDTECH-EliminatingtheAppGap-Jan-Feb-2012.pdf.

Prensky, M. (2012b) *From Digital Natives to Digital Wisdom: Hopeful essays for 21st century learning*, Thousand Oaks, CA: Corwin.

Puentedura, R.R. (2011, 8 Dec.) A brief introduction to TPCK and SAMR. *Ruben R. Puentedura's weblog*, http://www.hippasus.com/rrpweblog/archives/2011/12/08/BriefIntroTPCKSAMR.pdf.

Quitney Anderson, J. and Rainie, L. (2010, 9 Jul.) *Millennials Will Make Online Sharing in Networks a Lifelong Habit*, Washington: Pew Internet and American Life Project, http://www.pewinternet.org/~/media//Files/Reports/2010/PIP_Future_Of_Millennials.pdf.

Reagle, Jr., J.M. (2010) *Good Faith Collaboration: The culture of Wikipedia*, Cambridge, MA: MIT Press.

Reeves, B. and Leighton Read, J. (2009) *Total Engagement: Using games and virtual worlds to change the way people work and businesses compete*, Boston: Harvard Business Press.

Reporters Without Borders (n.d.) Internet, *Reporters Without Borders for freedom of information*, http://en.rsf.org/internet.html.

Rheingold, H. (2009a, 22 Feb.) 'Network literacy part one: The internet's architecture of freedom', *Blip TV*, http://blip.tv/file/1803355/.

Rheingold, H. (2009b, 20 Apr.) 'Attention literacy', *SFGate*, http://www.sfgate.com/cgi-bin/blogs/rheingold/detail?entry_id= 38828.

Rheingold, H. (2010, 25 Nov.) 'If I didn't follow online distractions . . .' *Twitter*, http://twitter.com/hrheingold/status/7580895607259137.

Rheingold, H. (2012) *Net Smart: How to thrive online*, Cambridge, MA: MIT Press.

Richardson, W. and Mancabelli, R. (2011) *Personal Learning Networks: Using the power of connections to transform education*, Bloomington, IN: Solution Tree Press.

Ritzer, G. and Jurgenson, N. (2010) 'Production, consumption, prosumption: The nature of capitalism in the age of the digital "prosumer"', *Journal of Consumer Culture*, 10(1), 13–36.

Rock, D. (2009) *Your Brain at Work: Strategies for overcoming distraction, regaining focus, and working smarter all day long*, New York: Harper Business.

Rose, F. (2011) *The Art of Immersion: How the digital generation is remaking Hollywood, Madison Avenue, and the way we tell stories*, New York: W.W. Norton.

Rushkoff, D. (2010) *Program or Be Programmed: Ten commands for a digital age*, New York: OR Books.

Russell, T.L. (2010) *No Significant Difference*, WCET, http://www.nosignificant difference.org/.

Saveri, A. (2009, 15 Sep.) In search of flow: An emerging culture of attention, *Andrea Saveri*, http://andreasaveri.com/?p=103.

Schneier, B. (2010, 10 Aug.) A revised taxonomy of social networking data, *Schneier on Security*. http://www.schneier.com/blog/archives/2010/08/a_taxonomy_of_s_1.html.

Selwyn, N. (2011) *Education and Technology: Key issues and debates*, London: Continuum.

Selwyn, N. and Facer, K. (2007) *Beyond the Digital Divide: Rethinking digital inclusion for the 21st century*, Bristol: Futurelab, http://archive.futurelab.org.uk/resources/documents/opening_education/Digital_Divide.pdf.

Seneca (1917) *IV: Ad lucilium epistulae morales* (trans. R.M. Gummere, vol.1), Cambridge, MA: Harvard University Press, http://ia700407.us.archive.org/9/items/adluciliumepistu01sene/adluciliumepistu01sene.pdf.

Senior, R.M. (2006) *The Experience of Language Teaching*, Cambridge: Cambridge University Press.

Senior, R.M. (2012) Class-centred teaching: A framework for classroom decision-making. In A. Burns and J.C. Richards (eds), *The Cambridge Guide to Pedagogy and Practice in Second Language Teaching* (pp. 38–45), Cambridge: Cambridge University Press.

Sheridan, M.P. and Rowsell, J. (2010) *Design Literacies: Learning and innovation in the digital age*, London: Routledge.

Shirky, C. (2008) *Here Comes Everybody: The power of organizing without organizations*, New York: Allen Lane.

Shirky, C. (2010a) *Cognitive Surplus: Creativity and generosity in a connected age*, New York: Penguin.

Shirky, C. (2010b, 4 Jun.) 'Does the internet make you smarter?', *Wall Street Journal*, http://online.wsj.com/article/SB10001424052748704025304575284973472694334.html.

Siemens, G. and Tittenberger, P. (2009, Mar.) *Handbook of Emerging Technologies for Learning*. Winnipeg: University of Manitoba, http://elearnspace.org/Articles/HETL.pdf.

Small, G. and Vorgan, G. (2008) *iBrain: Surviving the technological alteration of the modern mind*, New York: Collins.

Solomon, G. and Schrum, L. (2007) *Web 2.0: New tools, new schools*, Eugene, OR: ISTE.

Solove, D.J. (2007) *The Future of Reputation: Gossip, rumor, and privacy on the internet*, New Haven: Yale University Press.

Steele, J. and Iliinsky, N. (eds) (2010) *Beautiful Visualization: Looking at data through the eyes of experts*, Sebastopol, CA: O'Reilly.

Stone, L. (2008, 9 Jan.) 'Fine dining with mobile devices', *The Huffington Post*, http://www.huffingtonpost.com/linda-stone/fine-dining-with-mobile-d_b_80819.html.

Street, B. (2009) The future of 'social literacies'. In M. Baynham and M. Prinsloo (eds), *The Future of Literacy Studies* (pp. 21–37), Basingstoke: Palgrave Macmillan.

Sunstein, C.R. (2007) *Republic.com 2.0*, Princeton: Princeton University Press.

Tapscott, D. (2009) *Grown up Digital: How the net generation is changing your world*, New York: McGraw-Hill.

Thomas, D. and Seely Brown, J. (2011) *A New Culture of Learning: Cultivating the imagination for a world of constant change*, CreateSpace.com.

Thomas, M. (ed.) (2011) *Deconstructing Digital Natives: Young people, technology and the new literacies*, London: Routledge.

Thompson, C. (2011) 'How Khan Academy is changing the rules of education', *Wired*, 19(8), http://www.wired.com/magazine/2011/07/ff_khan/.

Thornbury, S. (1988) 'Comments on Marianne Celce-Murcia, Zoltán Dörnyei, and Sarah Thurrell's "Direct approaches in L2 instruction: A turning point in communicative language teaching?". A reader reacts . . .', *TESOL Quarterly*, 32(1), 109–16.

Thornbury, S. (2005) *Uncovering Grammar* (2nd edn), Oxford: Macmillan.

Transmedia Storytelling (2012, 5 May) *Wikipedia*, en.wikipedia.org/wiki/Transmedia_storytelling.

Tucker, B. (2012) 'The flipped classroom', *Education Next*, 12(1), 82–3, http://educationnext.org/the-flipped-classroom/.

Turkle, S. (2011) *Alone Together: Why we expect more from technology and less from each other*, New York: Basic Books.

University of Houston (2011) *The Educational Uses of Digital Storytelling*, http://digitalstorytelling.coe.uh.edu/.

Vaidhyanathan, S. (2011). *The Googlization of everything (and why we should worry)*, Berkeley: University of California Press.

Vander Veer, E.A. (2011) *Facebook: The missing manual* (3rd edn), Sebastopol, CA: O'Reilly Media.

van Lier, L. (2000) From input to affordance: Social-interactive learning from an ecological perspective. In J.P. Lantolf (ed.), *Sociocultural Theory and Second Language Learning* (pp. 245–59), Oxford: Oxford University Press.

Varnelis, K. (2008) Conclusion: The meaning of network culture. In K. Varnelis (ed.), *Networked Publics* (pp. 145–63), Cambridge, MA: MIT Press.

Weigel, M., James, C. and Gardner, H. (2009) 'Learning: Peering backward and looking forward in the digital era', *International Journal of Learning and Media*, 1(1), http://www.mitpressjournals.org/doi/pdf/10.1162/ijlm.2009.0005.

Weinberger, D. (2007) *Everything is Miscellaneous: The power of the new digital disorder*, New York: Times Books.

Weinberger, D. (2009a, 29 Jun.) *Truth and Transparency*. New York: Personal Democracy Forum, http://www.youtube.com/watch?v=o3qSDLF6lU4.

Weinberger, D. (2009b, 19 Jul.). Transparency is the new objectivity, *Joho the blog*, http://www.hyperorg.com/blogger/2009/07/19/transparency-is-the-new-objectivity/.

Weinberger, D. (2011) *Too Big to Know: Rethinking knowledge now that the facts aren't the facts, experts are everywhere, and the smartest person in the room is the room*, New York: Basic Books.

Weinberger, D. (2012, 23 Jan.) 'Thirteen ways the internet is making us smarter', *The Huffington Post*, http://www.huffingtonpost.com/david-weinberger/internet-makes-us-smarter_b_1225187.html.

Wenger, E. (2006) 'Communities of practice: A brief introduction', *Wenger-Trayner*, http://wenger-trayner.com/wp-content/uploads/2012/01/06-Brief-introduction-to-communities-of-practice.pdf.

White, D.S. (2008, 23 Jul.) 'Not "natives" and "immigrants" but "visitors" and "residents"', *TALL blog*, http://tallblog.conted.ox.ac.uk/index.php/2008/07/23/not-natives-immigrants-but-visitors-residents/.

White, D.S. and Le Cornu, A. (2011) 'Visitors and residents: A new typology for online engagement', *First Monday*, 16(9), http://www.uic.edu/htbin/cgiwrap/bin/ojs/index.php/fm/article/view/3171/3049.

White, R.V. and Arndt, V. (1991) *Process Writing*, London: Longman.

Whitworth, A. (2009) *Information Obesity*, Oxford: Chandos.

Winter, M. (2011) *Scan Me: Everybody's guide to the magical world of QR codes*, Napa, CA: Westsong.

Wright, R. (2010, 6 Jul.) 'Building one big brain', *The New York Times*. http://opinionator.blogs.nytimes.com/2010/07/06/the-web-we-weave/.

Wu, T. (2010) *The Master Switch: The rise and fall of information empires*, New York: Alfred A. Knopf.

Zimmerman, E. (2009) Gaming literacy: Game design as a model for literacy in the twenty-first century. In B. Perron and M.J.P. Wolf (eds), *The Video Game Theory Reader 2* (pp. 23–31), New York: Routledge.

Zittrain, J. (2008) *The Future of the Internet and How to Stop It*, London: Allen Lane.

Zuckerman, E. (2008, 25 Apr.) 'Homophily, serendipity, xenophilia', *My heart's in Accra*, http://www.ethanzuckerman.com/blog/2008/04/25/homophily-serendipity-xenophilia/.